TIME

70th

ANNIVERSARY

Celebration

1923 - 1993

TIME 70th Anniversary Celebration
Editor: Kelly Knauer; Associate Editor: Mark Gauthier; Research: George Fisher; Picture Research: Kathy Nelson; Design: Hoashi Communications, Inc.

Time Inc. New Business Development
Director: David Gitow; Assistant Director: Stuart Hotchkiss; Fulfillment Manager: Mary Warner McGrade; Senior Manager: Pete Shapiro;
Assistant Manager: Rebecca Bradshaw; Production Director: John Calvano; Operations Director: David Rivchin; Project Originator: Robin Cherry

ISBN #0-8487-1187-4

Copyright 1994, Time Inc. Home Entertainment

Published by TIME Books
Time Inc. Home Entertainment
1271 Ave. of the Americas
New York, NY 10020

TIME

70th

ANNIVERSARY
Celebration

1923 - 1993

Magazines drink from a fountain of youth. Reinvented with each issue, they may attain venerable age and never show it. So it may surprise some current readers to hear that TIME Magazine — which always looks as up-to-date as this week's headlines — is celebrating its 70th Anniversary in 1993.

Men, women and magazines that have lived through seven decades should be allowed to sit back and reminisce now and then, no matter how young they may appear to be. And that is just what TIME has done in this volume, which is offered to readers as a portrait of our times that is intended, without apology, to be nostalgic and entertaining as well as informative.

The book is a sort of TIME family album, one that allows the pages of the magazine to speak today just as they spoke to readers when first published. A single story has been chosen to represent each year of TIME's publication and the text has been printed as it originally appeared, though some stories have been edited for length. The design and typefaces of the original magazines have been retained, so that in traveling through the book the reader may trace the evolution of TIME's look as well as its prose.

To paint a broader picture of our times, each decade is introduced with a selection of shorter excerpts from TIME stories. Finally, a series of thematic cover galleries reminds us that TIME has met some fascinating people (and run some wonderful cover art) in its day.

This volume is not offered as a celebration of our times; for, as it amply records, those times include periods of great chaos, great wars and great suffering. Rather, it is intended as a celebration of 70 years of a wonderful collaboration: between the writers and editors at TIME who first published these stories and the countless readers who first appreciated them.

1924 A few weeks ago you called me a Bolshevik, which I am not. Now I notice that you call the *Searchlight on Congress* a Ku Klux Klan organ, which it is not. The *Searchlight on Congress* has nothing to do with the Klan. You have, since it appears that you are supporting the Klan Kandidate Koolidge.

UPTON SINCLAIR
Pasadena, Calif.

1925 Is the glorification of the Negro now an accepted policy of your magazine? I had hoped that after the protest of one Southerner you might show some consideration for the sensibilities of our people by the discontinuance of your practice of referring to the colored man as "mister." I was deeply grieved, therefore, to find two new instances in your Sept. 7 issue.

This practice, in the face of previous protest, impresses me as a flagrant affront to the feelings of our people. If it be your desire to alienate and force from your ranks such readers of TIME as hail from the South, you are pursuing a most effectual course.

BARLOW HENDERSON
Aiken, S.C.

It was not TIME's desire to lose the good will of its Southern friends. TIME will, however, continue to employ the "Mr." in referring to men who lack other titles. — ED.

1927 Personally, there is only one item I object to and that is where I advocate the players should not eat bananas. This should read "unripe bananas" as I have no objection to the fruit when it is ripe.

I have some very good friends in the banana business and I would not care to say something about their business which is not true.

K.K. ROCKNE
Notre Dame, Ind.

1930 You mention an alley cat being fed with milk by President Hoover from the White House. Is this at the expense of the American people or does the President furnish his own milk?

W.W. JONES
Batesville, Ark.

The U.S. people furnish their President with the sum of $25,000 per annum for "official entertainment." — ED.

1932 I was in the class of '86 at Harvard. I was not expelled in '87 or any other year. I never did anything very bad at Harvard nor anything very good either. I was rusticated in '86 for an excess of political enthusiasm and a certain deficiency in intellectual attainments. I did not return to be graduated. There did not seem to be either reason or hope. I think the less said about my college career the better. Perhaps that is so with the rest of my career. However, exercise your own judgement, only please print the facts, or perhaps I should say, please don't.

WILLIAM RANDOLPH HEARST
Los Angeles, Calif.

Rustication: An old-fashioned academic penalty whereby delinquent undergraduates are sent away, generally to their homes, to continue their studies under a supervisor designated by the college. — ED.

1933 Yes, very nice. Thanks for the wreathes. What about your doing a little constructive work????

1) My *How to Read* is intended for a textbook and ought to be in use. It wd. debunk 80% of the idiocy in teaching literature in high-schools and colleges and 81 and one-fourth percent of literary journalists. Literary teaching and criticism ought to get the best stuff to the reader with the least interposition of secondhand yawp.

2) You don't mention my having written two operas, i.e. the music. That is more important than my written criticism. I mean to say I have "set to music" a great deal of the best poetry of Villon and Cavalcanti with the intention of getting it out of books and to the consumer or recipient.

Whether anybody likes the tunes or not, there is at least the dimension or technical success of intelligibility. The music does not hide the words.

Naturally, if I didn't think my melodic line was stronger, "better," had more guts than the general ruck of music I wd. have burnt the mss. instead of instigating its performance.

E. POUND
Rapallo, Italy

1934 I do not know when I ever saw such a conglomeration of lies. The 638 was not the engine my husband was killed on and was never a passenger engine, and as to my son being a highway laborer, that was a base lie, he was never on a highway in his life unless he drove over it. Whoever gave you the information did not get it from me. I just want to tell you that I do not like one thing you said and please never attempt it again without my permission.

MRS. CASEY JONES
Jackson, Tenn.

1935 What's this you've been publishing about the Dook of York that our distributors have been fools enough to censor and tear out over here? Please post me (letterpost) the censored article and send me a bill

for a year's subscription to TIME. I don't know TIME. I ought to do so.

H. G. WELLS
London

1936 I can talk but I hate to interrupt Groucho. I spoke in public last year in Portland when I asked for a raise in salary but I don't think anyone heard me. I make a practice of speaking everytime Chico makes a grand slam. So you can look for another speech in 1937.

HARPO MARX
Culver City, Calif.

1937 The records on "spittin' image" should certainly be kept straight. I don't think that the expression has anything to do with saliva. It originated, I believe, among the darkies of the South and the correct phrasing — without dialect — is "spirit and image." It was originally used in speaking of someone whose father had passed on — and the colored folks would say — "the very spi't an' image of his daddy."

JOEL CHANDLER HARRIS JR.
Atlanta

1938 Pioneer and innovator in many ways of presenting the news, TIME through its first 15 years has shown a degree of originality that has been refreshing and oftentimes delightful. I wish the magazine a long life in serving the public by disseminating accurate information written in a manner to keep the reader from drowsing...

FRANKLIN D. ROOSEVELT
Washington, D.C.

1941 Many thanks for the flattering reference to my gaudily crowned head but may I file a gentle demurrer to your repeated use of the adjective "dwarfish" in describing my person. Although I actually stand five feet four inches in socks, I have never objected to being ribbed about my size. Your pet word, however, strikes me as inappropriate as it carries a connotation of the monstrous and stunted. Let me suggest that such phrases as "smallish," "minute," "miniature," and even "pocket-size" Billy Rose would be considerably more appetizing.

BILLY ROSE
New York City

1942 TIME used the words "yellow bastards" and "Hitler's little yellow friends" in speaking of the Japanese. I suggest that none of us use the word "yellow" in speaking of the Japanese, because our Allies, the Chinese, are yellow.

In this war we must, I think, take care not to divide ourselves into color groups. The tide of feeling about color runs very high over in the Orient. Indians, Chinese, Filipinos, and others are sensitive to the danger point about their relation as colored peoples to white peoples. Many Americans do not realize this, but it is true, and we must recognize it or we may suffer for it severely. The Japanese are using our well-known race prejudice as one of their chief propaganda arguments against us. Everything must be done to educate Americans not to provide further fuel for such Japanese propaganda.

PEARL S. BUCK
Perkasie, Pa.

TIME emphatically agrees with Novelist Pearl Buck that raising a race issue is as unwise as it is ignoble. However, "yellow bastards" was not TIME's phrase but the factual report of typical angry U.S. reactions. As for actual skin-color, U.S. white, pink or pale faces may well be proud to be fighting on the side of Chinese, Filipinos and other yellow or brown faces. — ED.

1943   I appreciate greatly that not once was the word obscene mentioned in your article. Epithet too easily used which assailed unanimously the appearance of "Interpretation of Dreams" by Freud, psychologic document which is and will always remain in spite of all the most important and sensational of our epoch.

SALVADOR DALI
Carmel, Calif.

1944   TIME's story on the Hollywood Free World Association *v*. the Motion Picture Alliance for the Preservation of American Ideals indicates no editorial preference for either organization but reveals in comic style an anti-Hollywood bias. We film-makers realize our community is a gorgeous subject for satire. We grant, or anyway most of us do, that we are the world's funniest people, that you can write more jokes about us than you can about plumbers, undertakers or Fuller Brush salesmen.

Hollywood is guilty of deliberate withdrawal from the living world. It seeks to entertain, and we suspect that the success of the withdrawal is what makes Hollywood funny. But let TIME Magazine view with alarm or point with pride, but not laugh off Hollywood's growing recognition of the fact that every movie expresses, or at least reflects, political opinion. Moviegoers live all over the world, come from all classes and add up to the biggest section of human beings ever addressed by any medium of communication. The politics of moviemakers therefore is just exactly what

isn't funny about Hollywood. TIME mentions "room-temperature burgundy and chopped chicken liver" as though these luxuries invalidate political opinion. TIME, whose editors eat chopped chicken liver and whose publishers drink room-temperature burgundy, knows better.

ORSON WELLES
Hollywood, Calif.

Well-fed TIME feels that the public should be kept informed about Hollywood politics, from soup to nuts. — ED.

1948   It has come to my attention that in your Current & Choice section, Lauren Bacall has consistently been left out of the cast of *Key Largo*.

Inasmuch as there are those of us in Hollywood, Miss Bacall among them, who would rather make Current & Choice than win an Academy Award or make Men of Distinction, won't you please include her in the cast of *Key Largo* in Current & Choice just once, as she is my wife and I have to live with her. Miss Bacall is extremely tired of being labeled *et al*.

HUMPHREY BOGART
Beverly Hills

1949   I didn't know I had been hired and fired by Theatre Arts until I read about it in TIME. What else has been happening to me lately that I ought to know about?

WILLIAM SAROYAN
New York City

TIME regrets that it is fresh out of Saroyan news. All that the present editor (Charles MacArthur) of Theatre Arts has to say about this crisis in American letters is that it has occurred while he was in Europe and he remains Mr. Saroyan's most faithful fan. — ED.

1950   Shouldn't *Ausserordentlichhochgesch windigkeitelectronenentwickelndesschwer abeitsbeigollitron* (TIME, March 13) read *Ausserordentlichhochgeschwindigkeit electronenentwickelndesschwerarbeits beigollitron?*

(REV.) T.M. HESBURGH, C.S.C.
Notre Dame, Ind.

Yes, as TIME's Los Angeles and Philadelphia (but not Chicago) printers had it. — ED.

1951   It gives me great pleasure again to find myself in your pages. Segment by segment I discover myself, as it were, variously listed in the index. I get myself into Letters; I've been in Books and also Radio & TV. Now I have achieved Press. I'd love to make Cinema, but despair of Art or Science. Milestones

will one day catch up with me.

Thanks. But I am saddened by the adjective ("Old Standby"); I've earned it, of course, but hate to be reminded.

FAITH BALDWIN
New Canaan, Conn.

1952   In your June 9 Letters Column, Randolph S. Churchill says TIME was wrong in referring to Czechoslovakia as "Britain's ally" and denounces the "holier than thou" attitude adopted by some Americans towards the English in regard to Munich, and states that England had no more moral or legal obligation to defend Czechoslovakia than the U.S.

Britain's military alliance with France under the Locarno pact of 1925...although it did not guarantee Czechoslovakia against aggression as it did Belgium, made it inevitable that if France went to war to fulfill its own direct obligation under the Franco-Czech Treaty of 1924, England would be drawn in...England was deeply committed, by her treaty with France and by her official actions...The illustrious father of Mr. Churchill has admitted that Great Britain was deeply involved and that "it must be recorded with regret that the British Government not only acquiesced but encouraged the French Government in a fatal course" (Churchill, *The Gathering Storm*).

The U.S. had no political involvement in Europe in 1938...

JOHN F. KENNEDY
House of Representatives
Washington, D.C.

1954   You inform your readers that in my last book (*The Doors of Perception*), I "prescribe mescaline, a derivative of peyote, for all mankind as an alternative to cocktails." Snappiness, alas, is apt to be in inverse ration to accuracy. I merely suggested that it might be a good thing if psychologists, sociologists and pharmacologists were to get together and discuss a satisfactory drug for general consumption. Mescaline, I said, would not do. But a chemical possessing the merits of mescaline without its drawbacks would be preferable to alcohol.

ALDOUS HUXLEY
Hampstead, London

1955   Many copies of the article you have published about myself have been sent to me. Your reporter has made a good job of it, and I want to express my gratitude for the successful representation.

C.G. JUNG
Küsnacht, Switzerland

1958   With your permission, I'd like to give my opinion of the Kokoschka picture of my sister. I think it's a hideous mess. As great an artist as this man may be today, he certainly goofed in 1926. My sister is a very pretty girl.

FRED ASTAIRE
Beverly Hills

1961   I am glad to see you are still batting 1,000 regarding any information concerning me. As usual your information stinks. I need a house and a night-club in Palm Beach like you need a tumor.

FRANK SINATRA
Beverly Hills

1962   Poem to the Book Review at TIME:

> You will keep hiring
> picadors
> from the back row
> and pic the bull back
> far along his spine
> you will slam sandbags
> to the kidneys
> and pass a wine
> poisoned on the vine
> you will saw the horns off
> and murmur
> the bulls are
> ah
> the bulls are not
> what once they were
> The corrida will end
> with Russians in the plaza
> Swine, some of you will say
> what did we wrong?
> And go forth to kiss
> the conquerors

NORMAN MAILER
New York City

1965   As an anti-American, I thank you for your rotten article devoted to my person. Your insult to a head of state and your odious lies dishonor not only your magazine but also your nation…You symbolize the worst in humanity.

NORODOM SIHANOUK
Chief of State
Pnompenh, Cambodia

1966   On the current cover of TIME magazine my name appears, along with the titles of many of the shows I have produced. There is, however, a very strange drawing of some person or other also on the cover, which is very puzzling to me. I consider this figure you have attached to my name monstrous in appearance, bearing no resemblance to my likeness. Therefore, this is to notify you that I am suing you for $1,000,000 for defamation of caricature.

DAVID MERRICK
New York City

1967   TIME owes it to its readers to name the anonymous Governor whom I allegedly told that "Dick Nixon is a loser." It will be especially interesting since I have never said it or thought it.

RONALD REAGAN
Governor
Sacramento, Calif.

    TIME's source is not at all "nameless," but we are bound to honor his request that he not be identified. — ED.

1969   Re your comment in the Buckley-Vidal story: George Sanders didn't divorce me, I divorced him.

ZSA ZSA GABOR
Washington, D.C.

1970   Since you mentioned nudity in your review of the movie *John and Mary,* I thought you might be interested in the following example of current studio thinking.
    Before filming began, I informed the producers that I would not consent to any nude scenes, and was reassured that there would be none. As soon as my work was completed, a double was hired without my consent, and several nude scenes were inserted. I argued and pleaded with the producers for a period of five months, but since I had no legal recourse, I lost the argument.

MIA FARROW
Manhattan

1971   I would have preferred personally to ignore J. Edgar Hoover's ungentlemanly attacks on my husband, but my husband is dead and cannot reply for himself. Mr. Hoover, in alleging that he called my husband a liar during their meeting in 1964, has exposed himself. There were witnesses present, three distinguished clergymen, who explicitly denied that Mr. Hoover made such a statement or any other attack on my husband's veracity to his face.
    It is unfortunate for our country that a person of such moral and mental capacity holds a position of such importance. It is equally unfortunate for race relations in these troubled times that a person revealed in this interview to be so arrogantly prejudiced against Puerto Ricans, Mexicans and blacks is a high Government official.

MRS. MARTIN LUTHER KING JR.
Atlanta

1972   TIME in its issue on American women made me sound like Shirley Temple! I am not really against exploring depravity. I understand it's terrific both on- and off-screen and can be done by either sex.

ELEANOR PERRY
New York City

1973   Whose voice gave Tarzan's call? I ought to know: I was there.
    Johnny Weissmuller can — and did — do his own Tarzan call. End of discussion?

MAUREEN O'SULLIVAN ("JANE")
New York City

1975   Although I appreciate your unequivocal "No" answer to the question of my alleged presence in Dallas at the time of J.F.K.'s murder, I would like to point out that my noninvolvement rests not only on "drastic differences" between the specimen photographs, but more conclusively upon the sworn testimony of several witnesses who confirm that I was in Washington, D.C. on Nov. 22, 1963. It is a physical law that an object can occupy only one space at one time.
    Correction: I am not a Watergate "burglar," but a conspirator.

HOWARD HUNT
Federal Prison Camp
Eglin A.F.B., Fla.

1976   You quoted me and identified me as a "black leader." I consider this journalistic racism. No one refers to George Wallace as a "white Governor" or Gerald Ford as a "white President." If a label must be attached to my leadership, as a minister of the gospel I prefer "moral leader." Moral leadership, which essentially deals with ideas and values, is a universal category. Black is not.

(THE REV.) JESSE L. JACKSON
Chicago

1980   Just to keep the record straight: I do not buy $5,000 dresses; I do not have an extensive jewelry collection, or paintings, or antiques; and I do not have a hairdresser and interior decorator in tow. I get my hair done once a week, and I'm at a loss as to what an interior decorator would do. Perhaps rearrange the furniture in all the Holiday Inns I've been staying in.

NANCY REAGAN
Pacific Palisades, Calif.

MAN OF THE YEAR

CHARLES A. LINDGERGH
1927

FRANKLIN D. ROOSEVELT
1932

HUGH S. JOHNSON
1933

FRANKLIN D. ROOSEVELT
1934

HAILE SELASSIE
1935

WALLIS WARFIELD SIMPSON
1936

JOSEPH STALIN
1942

GEORGE C. MARSHALL
1943

DWIGHT D. EISENHOWER
1944

HARRY S. TRUMAN
1945

JAMES F. BYRNES
1946

QUEEN ELIZABETH II
1952

KONRAD ADENAUER
1953

JOHN FOSTER DULLES
1954

HARLOW CURTICE
1955

WALTER P. CHRYSLER
1928

OWEN D. YOUNG
1929

MOHANDAS K. GANDHI
1930

PIERRE LAVAL
1931

GENERALISSIMO &
MME CHIANG KAI-SHEK
1937

ADOLF HITLER
1938

JOSEPH STALIN
1939

WINSTON CHURCHILL
1940

FRANKLIN D. ROOSEVELT
1941

GEORGE C. MARSHALL
1947

HARRY S. TRUMAN
1948

WINSTON CHURCHILL
1949

AMERICAN FIGHTING-MAN
1950

MOHAMMED MOSSADEGH
1951

HUNGARIAN FREEDOM
FIGHTER
1956

NIKITA KHRUSHCHEV
1957

CHARLES DE GAULLE
1958

DWIGHT D. EISENHOWER
1959

U.S. SCIENTISTS
1960

JOHN F. KENNEDY
1961

POPE JOHN XXIII
1962

MARTIN LUTHER KING JR.
1963

WILLIAM C. WESTMORELAND
1965

YOUNG GENERATION
1966

LYNDON B. JOHNSON
1967

ASTRONAUTS ANDERS,
BORMAN AND LOVELL
1968

THE MIDDLE AMERICANS
1969

AMERICAN WOMEN
1975

JIMMY CARTER
1976

ANWAR SADAT
1977

TENG HSIAO-P'ING
1978

AYATULLAH KHOMEINI
1979

DENG XIAOPING
1985

CORAZON AQUINO
1986

MIKHAIL GORBACHEV
1987

ENDANGERED EARTH
1988

MAN OF THE YEAR

LYNDON B. JOHNSON
1964

WILLY BRANDT
1970

RICHARD M. NIXON
1971

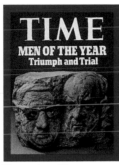

NIXON AND KISSINGER
1972

JOHN J. SIRICA
1973

KING FAISAL
1974

RONALD REAGAN
1980

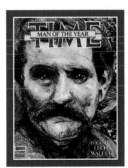

LECH WALESA
1981

THE COMPUTER
1982

RONALD REAGAN AND
YURI ANDROPOV
1983

PETER UEBERROTH
1984

MIKHAIL GORBACHEV
1989

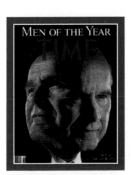

THE TWO GEORGE BUSHES
1990

TED TURNER
1991

BILL CLINTON
1992

RABIN, MANDELA,
DE KLERK, ARAFAT
1993

Execution

Guilty or not, justly or not, Nicola Sacco, clean-shaven factory worker and Bartolomeo Vanzetti, mustachioed fish-peddler, were informed last Monday evening that they must die that midnight for the murders — which to the end they denied committing — of a paymaster and guard at South Braintree, Mass., in 1920. Prisoners Sacco and Vanzetti refused last rites from the prison priest. They would die as they had lived, they said. Faith in a communistic order of mankind was enough for them.

Five guards took their posts in the death house, two to adjust electrodes, one at the blue lethal door, two to call at the cells. One newsgatherer, W.E. Playfair of the Associated Press, was included among the seven official witnesses of man killing man.

Prisoners Sacco and Vanzetti died in the order that their names had long been coupled, seven minutes apart.
August 29, 1927

Barely a Scratch

At present the bombs of Mussolini's youth find their counterpart in dangers which he deliberately courts, as though to keep his nerves steeled against Fate. When a group of admirers presented him with a lioness cub they supposed he would scarcely venture to play with her after a few months. To the despair of his guards Signor Mussolini has become so attached to the now full-grown lioness that he insists on entering her cage for an occasional frolic.

When he calls: "Italia! Italia Bella!" the lithe, tawny beast bounds up to him, is said to purr with alarming loudness. To date Il Duce has suffered barely a scratch from the claws of *Italia Bella*. Like her namesake, "Fair Italy," she appears to adore him.
July 12, 1926

Battle of the Atlantic

One million people, by the coldest reckoning, and in all probability many more, saw or tried to see Nominee Al Smith in New England last week. Some of those who tried were carried away in ambulances.

There were crowds and there was noise when the Brown Derby's train, coming from Albany, stopped at Springfield. At Worcester, the people and the noise were again one flesh. But at Boston, the people and the noise were such a People and such a Noise as no ecstasy had ever before sublimated.

It was after 9 o'clock when the Brown Derby reached the Arena, stuffy and emotionally boiling with 19,000 persons, where no more than 15,000 persons had ever been able to get in together before. After nominee Smith had finished his speech, the crowds stayed to hear *"The Sidewalks of New York"* and *"Sweet Adeline."* It was a big evening. Mrs. Smith cried softly that night in the Hotel Statler.
November 5, 1928

Chicago's Record

It was 10:20 o'clock on St. Valentine's morning. Chicago brimmed with sentiment and sunshine. Peaceful was even the George ("Bugs") Moran booze-peddling depot on North Clark Street, masked as a garage where lolled six underworldlings, waiting for their breakfast coffee to cook. A seventh, in overalls, tinkered with a beer vat on a truck. Two of the gang drifted aimlessly into the front office where ink wells stood dusty dry.

Ten minutes later they glanced at each other, startled. Was that a police gong? Into the curb eased a car, blue and fast, like the Detective Bureau's. Through the office door strode four men. Two, in police uniforms, swung sub-machine guns. Two, in plain clothes, carried stubby shotguns.

The gangsters in the office raised their hands. Their visitors marched them back into the garage, prodding their spines with gun muzzles. Tin coffee cups clattered to the stone floor. Snarled orders lined the six gangsters up against the north wall, their eyes close to the white-washed brick. The visitors booted the overalled mechanic into the line and "frisked" away hidden guns.

One of the men at the wall said: "What is this, a ..." "Give it to 'em!" was the answer. The garage became a thunder-box of explosions. From the four guns streamed a hundred bullets. Only eight of them ever reached the brick wall behind the seven targets.
February 25, 1929

Toscanini Meets Haydn

In a Carnegie Hall gay with Italian and U.S. flags, 3,000 people sat and awaited the greatest event in Manhattan's music season. Three thousand people sat, hundreds more stood, jammed tightly in back of a red plush rail, and hundreds more turned reluctant feet down 57th Street — disappointed that they could not get in to see Arturo Toscanini, famed Italian conductor, make his first appearance as guest leader at the New York Philharmonic's 2036th concert.

At 8:37 a short, thickset little man scooted out on the stage and started for the conductor's dais — as if he would at once take up the business of the meeting without any preliminary fuss. But someone spied him, then they all did — and his hopes were blasted. They cheered, beat their palms together, rose finally to their feet to pay honor to the greatest living conductor. Finally he turned his back on them, lifted his baton and Toscanini was no longer Toscanini but the voice of Haydn, the figure of Haydn, showing a band of able musicians how his "Clock" Symphony should be played.
January 25, 1926

He Rhapsodizes Blues

George Gershwin, 27, was born in Brooklyn. When he was 13, his mother purchased a piano. When he was 15, he tried to write a song. It began decently in F, but ran off into G, where it hid behind the black keys, twiddling its fingers at Gershwin. Discouraged, he went to work as a song-plugger for a music publisher.

He plugged songs on tin-pan pianos — those renegade instruments that stay up late, every night, in the back rooms of cafes, in the smoky corners of third-string night clubs, ti their keys are yellow and their tone i as hard as peroxided hair. Gershwin's fingers found a curious music in them. He made it hump along with a twang and a shuffle, hunch its shoulders and lick its lips. Diners applauded.
July 20, 1925

"Good Old Jack"

The world is about to sit in on the solution of the ancient problem of what happens when an irresistible force meets an immovable barrier. Luis Angel Firpo, Argentine heavyweight boxer, has demonstrated his irresistibility on several notable occasions. William Harrison Dempsey, American heavyweight, has sat immovable on the stool reserved for world's champions since July 4, 1919.

America's attitude toward Dempsey has changed. Dempsey is defending honor, the sporting honor of the American flag. That his defense is based solely on the fortune involved does not affect the public fancy. Never before has he felt the spotlight glow of popularity. If he should fail to win, his goose, with all its golden eggs, is finally cooked.
September 10, 1923

Enter Football

Last week the 1925 football season began. Of the many geared and wadded juggernauts whose prowess warranted attention, there was one whom the young idea, and indeed the adult, the conservative idea, lifted into eminence — Harold ("Red") Grange, halfback at the University of Illinois.

Eel-hipped runagade, no man could hold him; he writhed through seas of grasping moleskin-flints with a twiddle of his buttocks and a flirt of his shin-bone. His knee-bolt pumped like an engine piston; his straight arm fell like a Big-Wood tree. Even juvenile imaginations must strain if they are to exaggerate the glory of Grange.
October 5, 1925

THE
FOUNDING OF
TIME

"TIME is interested — not in how much it includes between its covers — but in how much it gets off its pages into the minds of its readers."

Prospectus for TIME Magazine, 1922
Briton Hadden and Henry Luce

TIME Magazine first appeared on newsstands in the spring of 1923, at a time when America was briskly reinventing itself in the wake of "The Great War." The magazine was the brainchild of two ambitious young men who had grown up with the century: Briton Hadden had just turned 25, Henry Luce was 24.

Hadden was born in Brooklyn; Luce was the son of Presbyterian missionaries and was born and raised in China. They met at Hotchkiss, a boarding school in Connecticut, where they worked together on the school newspaper. When they matriculated at Yale, Hadden became chairman and Luce the managing editor of the campus newspaper, the *Daily News*. Later they recalled concocting their scheme for a weekly news digest during a summer officers' training stint in the army at Camp Jackson, South Carolina.

The founders: Henry Luce in the 1930s, Briton Hadden in 1929

Destiny kept drawing the young journalists together. Following graduation and their first newspaper jobs, they found themselves reunited in the newsroom of the *Baltimore Sun* in late 1921. After work hours they resurrected their notion of a news digest, then quit their reporting jobs and moved to New York, determined to raise the money to bring their idea for a new magazine to life.

That idea seems ironically familiar from a vantage point 70 years further into our century. Hadden and Luce believed the public suffered from an information overload — and a knowledge deficit. Newspapers were thriving, but as the prospectus for TIME declared: "Americans are, for the most part, poorly informed…because no publication has adapted itself to the time which busy men are able to spend on simply keeping informed."

Their answer: a new kind of magazine that would assemble brief reports of all the week's news into a fixed system of classifications. Simplicity, brevity and clear organization were to be its guiding principles. Initially this "news-magazine" was to be called *Facts*. (*Hours*, *Briefs*, *The Synthetic Review*, and *The Weekly News Budget* were other early titles soon abandoned.) Henry Luce claimed he found the magazine's eventual name in an advertisement on the subway that included the phrase "time for a change."

Luce and Hadden spent 1922 raising the money to launch their magazine, refining the prospectus, and overseeing a mailing effort to sign up subscribers. Living on miniscule salaries, they hired a small staff and labored with "newspapers and scissors and paste-pots" to turn their idea into a magazine. Finally, after two dummy issues were printed, the first issue of TIME appeared in March of 1923.

It was a scrawny excuse for a magazine, 32 pages, with pictures looking, according to one wit, as if they had been engraved on pieces of bread. Charles Eliot, president of Harvard, called the idea of condensing the news "disgusting and disgraceful." But Franklin D. Roosevelt, Thomas Edison and Henry Ford were among those who praised the new weekly.

Slowly, TIME caught on. Determined to give the magazine a voice of its own, Managing Editor Hadden cultivated a brisk, staccato style and curiously inverted sentences. The result was instantly recognizable and easily parodied, most famously in Wolcott Gibbs's *New Yorker* piece that began, "Backward ran sentences until reeled the mind." The *New Yorker* also skewered TIME's adjective-crammed characterizations with a cartoon of a secretary reading to her boss: "According to TIME, sir, you are fiftyish, unpressed, bag-jowled, squat."

Despite its flair, TIME's early years were lean. In 1924, following "an exhaustive audit," the magazine reported a profit of $674.15. But its circulation had doubled, from 35,000 to 70,000, and the magazine was beginning to attract prominent advertisers. In 1927 the famous red cover border first appeared, circulation swelled to 135,000, and the editors named the first Man of the Year, Charles Lindbergh.

In the years to come, TIME would prosper and Henry Luce would launch *Fortune*, *Life*, and *Sports Illustrated*. But Briton Hadden did not live to see the magazine flourish. In 1928 he was stricken with an infection of the blood; he died on February 27, 1929, six years to the day after he put the first issue of TIME to press.

"SILENT CAL" COOLIDGE BECAME PRESIDENT AFTER THE SUDDEN DEATH OF HARDING ■ BRIGHT YOUNG THINGS DRANK BATHTUB GIN ■ THE FIRST BIRTH CONTROL CLINIC OPENED IN NEW YORK ■ AN EGYPTIAN CRAZE SWEPT EUROPE AND AMERICA AFTER THE DISCOVERY OF KING TUT'S TOMB ■ AND THE LONG-DEPRECIATING GERMAN MARK WAS, APPARENTLY, DEAD . . .

1923

The influence of the Ku Klux Klan was reaching its peak — 200,000 people attended a Klan rally in Indiana.

FOREIGN NEWS

GERMANY

Exit the Mark

The exact moment of death is as difficult to establish with currencies as it is with persons. The German mark has long since been pronounced incurably sick, and its fever has risen beyond the ability of existing thermometers to measure it. The events of the week tend to the conclusion that its definite decease can be dated at mid-September, 1923. In a single week, the amazing output of 389,000,000,000,000 of marks, or more than all outstanding marks put together, was seen. The discount rate of the Reichsbank stood at the unparalleled rate of 90%. Individual German States like Dantzig are seeking to establish new currencies of their own, and the Berlin government is frantically at work trying to invent some new gold-convertible currency for the nation. Germany's rate of currency depreciation and her State deficits now far exceed those of Soviet Russia. In foreign exchange, rates for the mark are so vastly depreciated that they can be expressed only in incalculably large figures. In both London and New York prominent banks have refused to quote, buy or sell the vanishing German currency any longer. It is likewise being stricken off the prominent European stock exchanges, where ordinarily foreign exchange is traded in actively. The mark has been an extraordinary long time dying. Now, at last, it is apparently dead.

Notes

Berlin police began a search for foreign currency, principally dollars and pounds. On the Friedrichstrasse and the Kurfürstendamm, 27 raids took place and vast quantities of real money were confiscated. All persons received the privilege of calling at the police station after two days to receive the value of their money in marks. The postage stamp was abolished in Germany, owing to the cost of printing being greater than the face value of the stamps. Hereafter German letters will bear a cancellation indicating that postage has been paid. The lightest letter from Germany costs, at the present rate of exchange, 200,000 marks to deliver in the U. S.

PUTSCHIST HITLER
A few shots in the ceiling

Grave disorders occurred at Berlin and in the Rhineland, caused by a serious food shortage. Riots and pillaging of shops occurred at many points and there were some clashes with police forces. Many people were killed and injured.

The animals in the Berlin Zoo were stated to be so hungry that they keep Berlin awake at night. The roaring of lions and tigers admixed with the "laughs" of hyenas and the howling of the wolves was reputed to have turned residential Berlin into a veritable jungle.

"Beer Hall Revolt"

Under cover of darkness General Erich van Ludendorff, flagitious, inscrutable, unrelenting, sallied forth into the streets of Munich, capital of Bavaria, accompanied by his faithful Austrian, Herr Adolf Hitler, to make a coup for the Hohenzollerns by way of celebrating Nov. 9, the fifth anniversary of the abdication of the then Kaiser.

With unerring instinct they led their men to a beer-house, called the *Bürger brau Keller*, famed Bavarian cellar. Within was Bavarian Dictator von Kahr and some others. Dr. von Kahr was in the middle of outlining his state policy in which he denounced Marxism, when the door opened and in walked Herr Hitler and General von Ludendorff with some of their followers, who fired a few shots into the ceiling by way of effect.

Herr Hitler declared the Bavarian Government had been superseded and elected himself not only head of Bavaria but Chancellor of all Germany. General Ludendorff was given command of the Army, which he accepted, and said: "We have reached the turning point in the history of Germany and the world. God bless our work!"

After this distribution of gifts by fairy godfather Hitler, there was wild talk of a march on Berlin, the destruction of the Treaty of Versailles, the deposition of President Ebert and the Berlin Government.

Everything seemed to be "going" well enough. The people cheered Ludendorff when he swaggered in or out of anywhere. The Hitler storm troops were in possession of the city and the sun was shining brightly on the following day. "Chancellor" Hitler and "Commander-in-Chief" von Ludendorff were within the War Office when the loyal Bavarian Reichswehr stormed the building, and after a short battle the "beer hall revolt" was crushed.

WARREN G. HARDING

JACK DEMPSEY

GEORGE BERNARD SHAW

1924

Fascist political ideas began to receive widespread support; in Germany, Hitler was released after serving a partial prison sentence.

LENIN'S DEATH UNLEASHED A POWER STRUGGLE IN THE SOVIET STATE ■ THE TEN MILLIONTH CAR ROLLED OFF THE FORD ASSEMBLY LINE ■ J. EDGAR HOOVER WAS APPOINTED DIRECTOR OF THE FBI ■ U.S. LEGISLATION EXCLUDED JAPANESE FROM IMMIGRATION ■ AND THE VOLSTEAD ACT PROHIBITED THE MAKING OF "INTOXICATING BEVERAGES" . . .

BERNARD BARUCH

HENRY CABOT LODGE

ETHEL BARRYMORE

NATIONAL AFFAIRS

PROHIBITION

"Not Guilty"

John Philip Hill of Baltimore, Republican Congressman from the third District of Maryland, recently indicted for violating the Volstead Act, was tried last week. And John Philip Hill was acquitted.

John Philip is a character. Hear about him in the sparkling words of Correspondent Clinton W. Gilbert:

"He lives by headlines. If newspapers were abolished, he would curl up and die. I know he will read this with delight and paste it away in his scrapbook. That's why I am writing it.

"A man who devotes all his energies to being a good story should receive some encouragement. And he is a lusty, vigorous fellow, full of animal spirits, and where one of this sort sometimes loves food, sometimes loves women, sometimes loves adventure, John Philip loves publicity . . .

"He has imagination as well as energy. Farmers could make cider and no one went around to find out how much alcohol it contained. Well, why not have a farm in a Baltimore backyard? He had two windows painted on his front fence with painted cows' heads looking out of them. Then he had apple trees with apples carefully tied on them moved into his backyard. Then he set up a cider press . . ."

Yes. He set up a cider press and allowed his cider to ferment a bit, just as he had done previously with some grapes, and he gave his neighbors to drink.

He was indicted on six counts for illegal manufacture and possession of the forbidden, and for constituting a public nuisance. But it is notorious that six counts does not constitute a knockout. John Philip took his six counts, then he took a reelection and then he took his trial.

The decision does not greatly alter the force of the Volstead Act. That Act forbids the manufacture, etc., for sale, of intoxicating beverages and defines such beverages as those containing more than $1/2\%$ of alcohol. But tucked away in the Act is a sentence which says:

"The penalties provided in this act against the manufacture of liquor without permit shall not apply to a person for manufacturing non-intoxicating cider and fruit juices exclusively for use in his home . . ."

Federal Judge Morris A. Soper interpreted this to mean that the home juice-maker was exempt from the arbitrary definition that $1/2\%$ alcoholic content makes a beverage "intoxicating." For beverages on sale, he held that the $1/2\%$ criterion was legal and unassailable, but within the walls of a man's home what he made exclusively for his own use was not to be so strictly governed.

Judge Soper therefore charged the jury that, for the purposes of this case, "the question for you to determine is whether these articles were intoxicating *in fact* . . . Intoxicating liquor is liquor which contains such a proportion of alcohol that it will produce intoxication when imbibed in such quantities as it is practically possible for a man to drink. . . Perhaps I might interpolate here that the intoxication in this law means what you and I ordinarily understand as average human beings by the word 'drunkenness' . . ."

As far as regards the two counts charging John Philip with maintaining a public nuisance, the Judge instructed the jury to return a verdict of not guilty, since none of the questionable beverages was sold.

Then the jury went out to determine whether wine containing from 3.34% to 11.65% of alcohol and cider containing 2.7% alcohol was intoxicating in the ordinary meaning of the word. For 17 hours the jurymen were closeted. Two of them held out for a verdict of guilty. At last they gave in. "Not Guilty."

John Philip, shaking hands vigorously, exclaimed: "Well, boys, you can make all the cider and wine you want now."

Then he added more formally:

"Independent of the verdict, the opinion of Judge Soper to the effect that fruit juices and cider made in the home for use there must be intoxicating in fact and are not limited to 1/2% alcoholic content, fixed by other sections of the act to regulate other beverages, is of the utmost importance.

"It strengthens us tremendously in our position in asking Congress to give us light wines and beer. It proves what I have always maintained—that the Volstead Act is hypocritical, crooked and marked by two standards . . ."

NELLIE T. ROSS OF WYOMING BECAME THE NATION'S FIRST WOMAN GOVERNOR ■ VON HINDENBURG WAS ELECTED PRESIDENT OF WEIMAR GERMANY ■ F. SCOTT FITZGERALD DESCRIBED THE JAZZ AGE IN *THE GREAT GATSBY* ■ THE GAME OF CONTRACT BRIDGE WAS INVENTED ■ AND THE SCOPES TRIAL PUT LAWYER CLARENCE DARROW IN THE LIMELIGHT . . .

1925

The modern communications era was taking shape. While millions of radio sets were now in use, Scottish inventor John L. Baird transmitted the first human image over "television."

NATION

THE GREAT TRIAL

Scene: In the fastnesses of Tennessee, the quiet of dawn is split asunder by wailing screams from a steam siren. It is the Dayton sawmill, waking up villagers and farmers for miles around. From 5 until 6:30 the blasts continue. The hamlet and the fantastic cross between a circus and a holy war that is in progress there come slowly to life.

Along the main street of the village, where everyone in town sees everyone else within five minutes, peddlers, hucksters, hot-sausage men (they call their wares "hot monkeys" now), pamphleteers, itinerant evangelists, prepare themselves and their goods for another day's trafficking.

The holder of the barbecue concession on the court-house lawn builds up his fire and heaves half an ox on the coals. The field secretary of an anti-Evolution society picks his teeth and adds a note or two of his stock harangue, delivered thrice daily: "Shall we be taxed to damn our children?"

A preacher from Georgia in a bungalow on wheels drowsily draws on his outlandish costume — alpaca coat, shabby policeman's trousers and an opera hat — and hopes that the new day may bring him an audience for his weird sermon proving that Negroes are not human beings. The barker for a tent show called *The She-Devil* clears his throat.

In a forest clearing outside the town, exhausted Holy Rollers snore under the shrubbery after a night's orgy of insane gesticulation and acrobatics incited by a mouthing, syncopating professional ecstatic. Sid Strunk, the village policeman, ruminates over his breakfast coffee that it is a good thing they have brought reserves from Chattanooga.

About 8 o'clock, dusty wagons, gigs, buggies, and small automobiles come jogging in along the country roads. In them are gaunt farmers, their wives in gingham and children in overalls, who crowd toward the court-house to get seats for the day's proceedings in the trial of Teacher John Thomas Scopes, alleged violator of the state's anti-evolution law, bewildered instrument of Science and Faith which have accidentally chosen Dayton as their battleground and in whose wake has come the usual camp-following of freaks, fakes, mountebanks and parasites of publicity.

Events: Such was the scene. Two days before the trial, Lawyer William Jennings Bryan, chief of the prosecution, lumbered off a train from Florida. The populace, Bryan's to a moron, yowled a welcome. Going to the house he had rented, Bryan took off his coat, wandered the streets in his shirt sleeves, a panoramic smile of blessing upon his perspiring countenance, an impressive pith helmet covering the bald, pink dome of his head.

He wandered to Robinson's drug store for a strawberry sundae. There sat freckle-faced young Teacher Scopes, in his blue shirt and hand-painted bow tie, grinning with bashful curiosity at passers-by ("like the Prince of Wales," said one fanciful reporter) and listening to his proud father, Thomas Scopes of Paducah, Ky., exclaim: "John was always an extraordinary boy." Father Scopes was proceeding to uncomplimentary remarks about Lawyer Bryan when the son interrupted:

"Mr. Bryan, meet my father."

The two shook hands; Bryan consumed his sundae and departed, exuding benevolence.

Lawyer Bryan addressed the Dayton Progressive Club at dinner, shrewdly comparing Dayton to Nazareth and Bethlehem, calling the trial a "duel to death," exhorting men to campaign with him to "put the Bible into the U.S. Constitution."

Trial: Lawyer Bryan, palm leaf fan in hand, collarless, led the prosecution forces into Court shortly before 9 o'clock. A few of the more courageous clung to their coats, but the heat soon overcame their vanity, with the exception of foppish double-breasted-coated Dudley Field Malone.

A long fight then began concerning the differences between the caption of the act under which Scopes was indicted and the act itself. Attorney General Stewart led off for the State. He claimed that the Constitution in no way discriminated against religious beliefs. Lawyer Clarence Darrow dominated the proceedings and aggravated in doing so a small rent in his his left shirt sleeve into a gigantic tear.

Lawyer Darrow then began his long argument for the defense, basing it on the diversion of the caption of the act from the act itself and on the ambiguity of the indictment. "I am going to argue it [the case] as if it was serious. . . . The Book of Genesis, written when everybody thought the world was flat . . . religious ignorance and bigotry as any that justified the Spanish Inquisition or the hanging of witches in New England . . . The State of Tennessee has no more right to teach the Bible as the Divine Book than it has the Koran, the Book of Mormon, the Book of Confucius, the Buddha or the Essays of Emerson. This is as brazen and bold an attempt to destroy liberty as was ever seen in the Middle Ages. . . ."

Ramifications of the Scopes trial ran all the way from a proposal by residents of Dayton that a Fundamentalist college be founded there with William Jennings Bryan as president, to expressions of astonishment in the Muslam newspapers of Constantinople at "such antiquated ideas."

English newspapers made much of the reports from Dayton, generally referring to Mr. Bryan as having "taken personal charge of God." Even the staid Paris *Temps* ran a few editorals: "It is the hot season and vacation time, and the interest of the newspapers languishes. It is necessary to find something to talk about."

HENRY FORD

HERBERT HOOVER

THOMAS EDISON

1926

The world got an intimation of the coming era of space travel as American researcher Robert Goddard fired the first liquid fuel rocket in Auburn, Mass.

Sigmund romberg charmed broadway audiences with "the desert song" ■ The "hitler youth" was founded in germany ■ Hirohito became emperor of japan ■ 19-year-old gertrude ederle swam the english channel, breaking the men's record by two hours ■ And humorist will rogers toured the country— then the world . . .

Jimmy Walker

James J. Tunney

Oliver Wendell Holmes

THE PRESS

Prairie Pantaloon

When Will Rogers, the funny man, departed on a great liner to tour Europe, the press took note of his sailing. His arrival, also, was duly recorded. Then a series of excited despatches informed the public whom he met and where he dined; a witticism dropped in a taxicab to an Associated Press reporter was cabled to all the English-speaking world; last week the wires crepitated with the announcement that he had started for Poland to be rude to Marshal Pilsudski. And suddenly a full page advertisement in the leading papers throughout the U. S. heralded the LETTERS OF A SELF MADE DIPLOMAT TO HIS PRESIDENT, A Collection of the Intimate Papers and Letters That is Changing Hands during these Perilous Times of Peace between Our President and his Ambassador — Without Portfolio — Will Rogers.

It was an advertisement, of course, for the *Saturday Evening Post.* Readers ascertained on closer scrutiny that Mr. Rogers was permitting this journal to publish a series of open epistles indited by him to Calvin Coolidge.

Careless readers, puzzled by the misleading spread, thought for an incredulous moment that this prairie pantaloon had actually wriggled into government service — then they saw their mistake, and laughed, and showed the spread to their friends just as the Curtis Publishing Co. had hoped they would. But, in actual fact, the blurb was not so silly as it seemed. Ambassador! Mr. Rogers is just that.

"Ambassador of the United States to Europe — without Portfolio" — a curious title for a joke-smith. The braided butler of the consular drawing-room chants it through his thorax, scorching the sibilants, booming the o's. The company stares at the newcomer. Famous women turn, over ivory shoulders, a glance cool with appraisal; gentlemen in dinner shirts striped with impossible decorations raise their monocles or feel for their small arms while he shambles into the room —"Viva, l'Ambassadeur." He wears an old grey suit. A jazbo necktie adorns, but fails to hide, the golden collar-stud. His shoes, surely, have never been defiled by polish. See how he bows right and left, this gangling fellow, as lean as a lariat, in the old suit and the cracked shoes. His under lip protrudes like the point of a vulgar joke. His jaws move perpetually, up and down, chewing insult, chewing fancy, chewing humor, chewing gum. It is William Penn Adair Rogers, the diplomatist.

His mother was a Cherokee Indian. His father was the Living Jingo. He was born on a reservation in Oklahoma in 1881 and grew to manhood on the back of a pinto. His early scavengings in border towns and on the property of neighboring ranchers came to the attention of an officer of the law who hinted that he might be able to advance himself more quickly in some other state. Mr. Rogers went to South America, then by cattle boat to South Africa, returning to the West in time to join the rodeo of Colonel Muhlbach which was about to start on a tour of the U. S. In May, 1905, Colonel Muhlbach's show came to New York and Rogers got into the news for the first time.

He owed this first snip of fame to a berserk steer which, pestered by circling ropes, went mad and jumped the paling that divided the ring from the spectators. In an instant a young cowboy dashed to the spot, swung his rope and, with a deft flick of the wrist, saved the life of a little girl. That young cowboy was not William Penn Adair Rogers. But a reporter liked the name. Rogers found himself a hero. The incident gave him confidence. A little later he kept a boisterous audience quiet by talking to them. Soon he was talking to audiences from the back of a wooden bronco in Keith's theatres. Then came money and fame and the Ziegfeld Follies.

Not quite all of the celebrities whom Rogers, with unerring eye, has picked from darkened boxes at the Follies and hailed onto the stage have enjoyed the fun he had at their expense. But they have all laughed. His humor is fearless, nonchalant, and aggressively Western. *The New York Times* has called him America's Aristophanes, the *Herald* has hailed him as successor of the famed Mr. Dooley (Finley Peter Dunne). Woodrow Wilson admitted that he found Will Rogers' political roulades not only funny but "illuminating."

Often he entertains at debutante parties. It is supper time. On little gilt chairs thrown up by the glazed tile of the ballroom floor, the guests settle themselves to watch Will Rogers unwrap a stick of gum and put it in his mouth. When he first began to go about in society, he tells them, he had a lot of trouble finding out which were the servants and which the gentleman. Then he found a clue — butlers had no braid on their trousers. After that he was able to distinguish the butlers. Now his only trouble is to distinguish the gentlemen . . .

He has become rich. He owns a huge house in Beverly Hills, near the Hollywood studios where he worked in the early Western movies, *Honest Hutch, Jes' Call Me Jim, Doubling for Romeo, Fruits of Faith.* He has a reputation of being one of the most close-fisted members of the joyous soviet of Broadway; only his best friends know of the money he gives away anonymously to sick chorus girls, and rum-dums, and broken actors. Once he heard that members of the baseball team of a stick town he was playing were ashamed to go on the diamond because they had no uniforms; he used a week's salary to get them the best suits, bats, gloves the could be bought. A week later he played polo with the Prince of Wales. ". . . Yes, I'm one of these movie fellers but I'm not a regular one. I've been married twenty years and I still have the same wife I started out with."

THE HOLLAND TUNNEL OPENED IN NEW YORK ■ BABE RUTH HIT HIS 60TH HOME RUN OF THE SEASON ■ PICTURES TALKED, WITH AL JOLSON IN "THE JAZZ SINGER" ■ JOSEPHINE BAKER RULED PARIS NIGHT LIFE ■ GRETA GARBO STARRED IN "FLESH AND THE DEVIL" ■ AND LINDBERGH CROSSED THE ATLANTIC IN "THE SPIRIT OF ST. LOUIS" . . .

1927

The electrocution of Sacco and Vanzetti underscored the spreading "Red Scare" — a preoccupation with the Communist threat that would continue for decades.

AERONAUTICS

Flight

The Atlantic in its immense indifference was not aware that man-made cables on its slimy bottom contained news, that the silent heavens above pulsed with news—news that would set thousands of printing presses in motion, news that would make sirens scream in every U. S. city, news that would cause housewives to run out into backyards and shout to their children: "Lindbergh is in Paris!"

Late one evening last week Capt. Charles A. Lindbergh studied weather reports and decided that the elements were propitious for a flight from New York to Paris. He took a two-hour sleep, then busied himself with final preparations at Roosevelt Field, L. I. Four sandwiches, two canteens of water and emergency army rations, along with 451 gallons of gasoline were put into his monoplane, *Spirit of St. Louis.* "When I enter the cockpit," said he, "it's like going into the death chamber. When I step out at Paris it will be like getting a pardon from the governor."

He entered the cockpit. At 7:52 a.m. he was roaring down the runway, his plane lurching on the soft spots of the wet ground. Out of the safety zone, he hit a bump, bounced into the air, quickly returned to earth. Disaster seemed imminent; a tractor and a gully were ahead. Then his plane took the air, cleared the tractor, the gully; cleared some telephone wires. Five hundred onlookers believed they had witnessed a miracle. It was a miracle of skill.

Captain Lindbergh took the shortest route to Paris—the great circle—cutting across Long Island Sound, Cape Cod, Nova Scotia, skirting the coast of Newfoundland. He later told some of his sky adventures to the aeronautically alert *New York Times* for syndication: "Shortly after leaving Newfoundland, I began to see icebergs . . . Within an hour it became dark. Then I struck clouds and decided to try to get over them. For a while I succeeded at a height of 10,000 feet. I flew at this height until early morning. The engine was working beautifully and I was not sleepy

at all. I felt just as if I was driving a motor car over a smooth road, only it was easier. Then it began to get light and the clouds got higher... Sleet began to cling to the plane. That worried me a great deal and I debated whether I should keep on or go back. I decided I must not think any more about going back....

"Fairly early in the afternoon I saw a fleet of fishing boats... On one of them I saw some men and flew down almost touching the craft and yelled at them, asking if I was on the right road to Ireland. They just stared. Maybe they didn't hear me. Maybe I didn't hear them. Or maybe they thought I was just a crazy fool.

"An hour later I saw land... I flew quite

MAN OF THE YEAR
"Well, here we are."

low enough over Ireland to be seen, but apparently no great attention was paid to me."

Captain Lindbergh then told how he crossed southwestern England and the Channel, followed the Seine to Paris, where he circled the city before recognizing the flying field at Le Bourget. Said he: "I had intended taxiing up to the front of the hangars, but no sooner had my plane touched the ground than a human sea swept toward it. I saw there was danger of killing people with my propeller

and I quickly came to a stop."

He had completed his 3,600-mile conquest of the Atlantic in 33 hours, 29 minutes, at an average speed of 107 $\frac{1}{2}$ miles per hour. His first words were, "Well, here we are. I am very happy."

Some of the crowd of 25,000 attempted to strip souvenirs from the *Spirit of St. Louis,* while the majority escorted Captain Lindbergh, on somebody's shoulders, to a nearby clubhouse. Then, there were congratulations from U. S. Ambassador Myron Timothy Herrick and French officials, a massage and some coffee (he had refused to take coffee on the flight), a motor trip through dense traffic to Paris and ten hours' sleep in the U. S. Embassy.

He is 25, more than six feet tall, rangy, handsome, blond. He knows flying as the barnstormer with a $250 plane and as the chief pilot for the St. Louis-Chicago air mail route. He is a prominent member of the Caterpillar Club, having four times become a butterfly and descended to earth in a parachute.

Not only did Captain Lindbergh win the $25,000 prize offered by Raymond Orteig, Manhattan hotelman, for the first New York-Paris non-stop flight, but he established for himself the immemorial right of extracting dollars from the hero-gaping U. S. public by appearing on the vaudeville stage, in the cinema, etc.

Fadeout

As one title on a cinema screen slowly fades out and another title slowly takes its place, so with the beginning of this week the name Lindbergh was gradually vanishing from the black, multi-column newspaper headlines. With the Lindbergh episode almost over, cynics may rise to call his ovations "hysteria," his receptions "sensationalism run riot." But back of the torn paper and the screeching headlines lay a very sincere and very spontaneous outburst of popular emotion.

SINCLAIR LEWIS

LEON TROTSKY

ROBERT LA FOLLETTE, JR.

1928

As nationalist tensions again took hold in Europe, the world's nations reaffirmed their desire for peace: 65 countries gathered in Paris to sign the Kellogg-Briand pact outlawing war.

HERBERT HOOVER WON THE PRESIDENCY IN A LANDSLIDE AGAINST AL SMITH ■ AMELIA EARHART MADE THE FIRST FLIGHT BY A WOMAN ACROSS THE ATLANTIC ■ "AMOS 'N' ANDY" DOMINATED RADIO ■ MICKEY MOUSE MADE HIS DEBUT AS "STEAMBOAT WILLIE" ■ AND EUGENE O'NEILL'S CLASSIC "STRANGE INTERLUDE" OPENED ON BROADWAY . . .

GOV. ALFRED E. SMITH

FLORENZ ZIEGFELD

MRS. CALVIN COOLIDGE

THEATRE

New Plays in Manhattan

Strange Interlude. Culture climbers, scattered seafaring men, drama devotees, Germans, George Jean Nathan, and common people eyed narrowly the first performance of the season's prodigy. Eugene Gladstone O'Neill's nine-acter was solemnized by the Theatre Guild. The play began at 5:15, ran until 7:30, took recess for hungry actors and audience, resumed at 9, discharged at 11:10.

The Acting. Earle Larimore, Glenn Anders and Tom Powers played husband, lover, friend, all acceptably. To Mr. Powers went the most irregular characterization and he played it with a curiously electric irregularity. Lynn Fontanne drew the desperately difficult duty of portraying Nina. Her performance, like the whole of the event, lacked perfection but came close to majesty in many a passage.

The Significance. The play was strange, not only by reason of its length. Playwright O'Neill re-introduced the aside, mainstay of earlier dramatists, long discarded by scornful realists. His people's words and actions he completed with their thoughts. Every few moments the action stopped completely while an immobile performer spoke what was rattling through his mind. The spoken word was often a direct denial of its companion thought. Suspicion, mastered grief, cynicism, inferiority—the raw matter of truth—were permitted and expressed. The author tried devotedly to give his hearers a third theatrical dimension. The strange convention, difficult at first to grasp, soon blended into the engrossing total.

Skeptics sniffed that O'Neill has simply pasted two or three plays together; sniffed harder that his elaborately recurrent asides would have been unnecessary had his dialogue and stage directions provided complete characterization.

Nearly every one agreed on the faults. The play dragged toward the end. As age smothered the characters their dramatic interest dwindled slightly. The asides were not always accurately and shrewdly handled; the new technique was necessarily a trifle coarse. Rose the inevitable foolish chorus that Nina was a vile female and should never have been written up at all. Some strove to discredit it with the growl that O'Neill had simply taken many findings of the psychoanalysts and copied them into his characters.

Beyond and above all these disturbances rose the conviction of many an acute observer that a great play had been delivered to the world. Writhing and not always sharply articulate in the labor of his composition, Playwright O'Neill has done no tidy job. Raw life does not arrive that way. Uncompromising, tiny and horribly large, mystic and yet inestimably exact, *Strange Interlude* sweats blood.

The Playwright. Eugene Gladstone O'Neill is the son of actor James O'Neill, famed across the U. S. in earlier days as Monte Cristo. With his trouping father and a devoted mother, not an actress, he spent staccato years in larger cities where James O'Neill was acting. After that, school days under Catholic and later conventional preparatory schoolmasters. Then a year at Princeton, whence he was fired for a "prank." Then an inordinate mixture of oddities. He worked in a mail order firm in Manhattan; went gold prospecting to Honduras; shipped as a common sailor to South American ports; was destitute, "on the beach," for a considerable period in Buenos Aires; played in vaudeville; became a reporter in New London, Conn. These years hacked his health to pieces and it was in a Connecticut sanitarium, defeating a faint touch of tuberculosis, that he stopped to think. Soon he wrote his first play and proceeded to George Pierce Baker's famed playwright's class at Harvard to achieve technique. In 1916 at the tiny Wharf Theatre in Provincetown, Mass., his first production came to life, a one-acter, *Bound East for Cardiff*. Henry Louis Mencken and George Jean Nathan, then editors of the rascally *Smart Set*, accepted three plays for publication. Critic Nathan, notorious, noisy, can always say, truthfully, he recognized the good wine of genius before the grape was ripe. He still ballyhoos O'Neill frantically.

A scattering of potent one-act plays flowed from the playwright's pen to the resolutely experimental Provincetown Theatre, in the shadows of Manhattan's Greenwich Village. In 1920 his long play *Beyond the Horizon* flung him to the front rank of U. S. dramatists. Since then there have been *The Emperor Jones*, *Anna Christie*, *The Hairy Ape*, *All God's Chillun Got Wings*, *Desire Under the Elms*, *The Great God Brown*, etc. O'Neill is, incomparably, the first playwright of our theatre.

Few know O'Neill. He is the shyest sailor that ever flung his pay across a dirty waterfront bar to escape the curse of life in liquor. In early days he was a potent drinker. It is said of him that he was no intruder in the underworld of which many of his plays treat, but part of it. Now, in easy circumstances he lives seclusively, seldom even eating in a restaurant if he can help it. He works unceasingly; exercises sternly to preserve his body; has never thought of writing when not strictly temperate. In company he sits restlessly silent, uninterested in trivialities, embarrassed by his fellow man. When matters close to life are in discussion his interest jumps, he expresses his opinion fiercely. *Strange Interlude* is life and his opinions on it.

The Title. Says Nina, thinking ". . . the only living life is in the past and future . . . the present is an interlude . . . strange interlude, in which we call on past and future to bear witness we are living."

TROTSKY WAS EXPELLED FROM THE U.S.S.R., AFTER LOSING THE STRUGGLE AGAINST STALIN ■ *ALL QUIET ON THE WESTERN FRONT* TOPPED BESTSELLER CHARTS ■ THE ST. VALENTINE'S DAY MASSACRE ROCKED CHICAGO'S GANGLAND ■ THE VATICAN WAS ESTABLISHED AS AN INDEPENDENT STATE ■ AND THE MARKET COLLAPSED WITH A CRASH . . .

1929

Modern art began to achieve mainstream acceptance with the opening of the Museum of Modern Art in New York; many in attendance viewed their first VanGoghs, Cezannes, and Gaugins.

BUSINESS & FINANCE

Bankers v. Panic

In Grand Central, Manhattan, Sydney Zolicoffer Mitchell dismounted from the *Twentieth Century* with a bad cold, went quickly to his office in the 2 Rector St. building. He telephoned a large Stock Exchange house, said he thought there would be trouble but "just call on me for anything you want." A few hours later stock of his gigantic Electric Bond & Share which had recently reached a high of 189, sold for 91. A few days later, it sold at 50.

Promptly at 10 a.m. on Thursday Oct. 24, sounded the gong of the New York Stock Exchange and 6,000 shares of Montgomery Ward changed hands at 83—its 1929 high having been 156.

For so many months so many people had saved money and borrowed money and borrowed on their borrowings to possess themselves of the little pieces of paper by virtue of which they became partners in U.S. Industry. Now they were trying to get rid of them even more frantically than they had tried to get them. Stocks bought without reference to their earnings were being sold without reference to their dividends. At around noon there came the no-bid menace. Even in a panic-market, someone must buy the "dumped" shares, but stocks were dropping from 2 to 10 points between sales—losing from 2 to 10 points before a buyer could be found for them. Sound stocks at shrunk prices—and nobody to buy them. It looked as if U.S. Industries' little partners were in a fair way to bankrupt the firm.

Then at 1:30 p.m., a popular broker and huntsman named Richard F. Whitney strode through the mob of desperate traders, made swiftly for Post No. 2 where the stock of the United States Steel Corp., most pivotal of all U.S. stocks, is traded in. Steel too, had been sinking fast. Having broken down through 200, it was now at 190. If it should sink further, Panic, with its most awful leer, might surely take command. Loudly, confidently at Post No. 2, Broker Whitney made known that he offered $205 per share for 25,000 shares of Steel—an order for $5,000,000 worth of stock at 15 points above the market. Soon tickers were flashing the news: "Steel, 205 bid." More and more steel was bought, until 200,000 shares had been purchased against constantly rising quotations. Other buyers bought other pivotal stocks. In an hour General Electric was up 21 points, Montgomery Ward up 23, Radio up 16, A.T.& T. up 22. How far the market would have gone downward on its unchecked

BROKER WHITNEY
Panic might leer

momentum is difficult to say. But brokers and traders alike agreed that the man who bid 205 for 25,000 shares of Steel had made himself a hero of a financially historic moment.

That hero, Richard Whitney, head of Richard Whitney & Co., was brother of George Whitney, Morgan Partner. Back of his action lay a noontime meeting held at No. 23 Wall St., Home of the House of Morgan. Head of the House John Pierpont Morgan was in Europe. It was Partner Thomas W. Lamont with whom conferred Charles E. Mitchell, National City Bank; Seward Prosser, Bankers Trust. These men controlled resources of more than $6,000,000,000. They met briefly; they issued no formal statement. But to newsmen, Mr. Lamont remarked that brokerage houses were in excellent condition, that the liquidation appeared technical rather than fundamental. He also conveyed, without specifically committing himself, the impression that the banks were ready to support the market. And the meeting was hardly over before Hero Whitney had become Heroic.

Despite the rapid Thursday afternoon recovery, the low point of the swinging pendulum cut off many a speculative head. Roaring was the business done by downtown speakeasies. Wild were the rumors of ruin and suicide. In Manhattan, one Abraham Germansky, realtor, was last seen tearing ticker tape. In Seattle, one Arthur Bathstein, finance company secretary, shot himself.

Market "Lesson"

Why then, did a Market which had broken on Oct. 23 demonstrate with a continued crash on Oct. 24 that the end of the Great Bull Market had really arrived? Apt appeared the analogy between the break on the market and a run on a bank. The Bank was U.S. Industry. Assets of the bank were the real assets of U.S. Industry. Stocks were the Paper money which the bank had issued. Now all banks, even the Federal Reserve System, issue more money in paper than they have gold in their vaults. Every bank would be broken if all its depositors simultaneously attempted to exchange paper for gold.

Why the crash came on Oct. 23, 1929, is as mysterious as why the World War chanced to begin on Aug. 4, 1914. Vital point is the undermining of popular confidence that ended in the crash. The September slump was of tremendous importance in its indication that a Market which could survive only by constant rises had reached the limits of its climb. Slowly the Market began to realize that 1929 might be an abnormal year, a high-water year instead of one more level in a still-rising tide. If this fear were well founded, what then of 1930, or 1931, of even more distant times?

ADOLPH ZUKOR

ALBERT EINSTEIN

PRINCESS ELIZABETH

THE WOMEN

"WHAT DO WOMEN WANT?" SIGMUND FREUD (A 1924 TIME COVER SUBJECT) FAMOUSLY ASKED. ARETHA FRANKLIN (A 1968 TIME COVER SUBJECT) SPELLED OUT THE ANSWER: R-E-S-P-E-C-T. IN ONE OF THE GREAT MOVEMENTS OF THE 20TH CENTURY, WOMEN GRADUALLY SEIZED THE RIGHT TO EQUAL OPPORTUNITY WITH MEN, THOUGH GLORIA STEINEM AND SUSAN FALUDI (1992 TIME COVER SUBJECTS) WOULD ARGUE THERE IS STILL MUCH ROOM FOR IMPROVEMENT. ONE MAN, AT LEAST, AGREED: NOBEL-PRIZE-WINNING AUTHOR GABRIEL GARCIA MARQUEZ TOLD TIME IN A SPECIAL ISSUE ON THE MILLENIUM, "THE ONLY NEW IDEA THAT COULD SAVE HUMANITY IN THE 21ST CENTURY IS FOR WOMEN TO TAKE OVER THE MANAGEMENT OF THE WORLD."

ELEANORA DUSE
1923

FRANCES PERKINS
1933

EVA PERON
1947

MARGOT FONTEYN
1949

BEVERLY SILLS
1971

NADIA COMANECI
1976

GERTRUDE STEIN
1933

EVE CURIE
1940

INGRID BERGMAN
1943

ELIZABETH ARDEN
1946

GRACE KELLY
1955

SYLVIA PORTER
1960

LEONTYNE PRICE
1961

JULIA CHILD
1966

SANDRA DAY O'CONNOR
1981

INDIRA GANDHI
1984

JACKIE JOYNER-KERSEE
1988

GLORIA STEINEM
SUSAN FALUDI
1992

1930s

What Price Peace?

Mrs. Chamberlain remained snug and cozy at No. 10 Downing Street last week and Mr. Chamberlain went fishing. It had been a titan's task to win brief leisure for this favorite recreation of Britain's best-known brother of the angle and Prime Minister. His method is to get things done by businesslike steps. First, he averted European war by Czechoslovak dismemberment. Second, he won a vote of confidence on this act last week, 366 to 144, in the House of Commons. Third, he averted strife in his Conservative Party by postponing indefinitely the annual Party Conference which was to have been held last week. And fourth, the Prime Minister went fishing in the River Tweed.

So vast were the issues broached at Munich that no man can say with firm assurance whether history will record it as a first great stride on the road to peace or as a first great step on the road toward world war. Any man could see last week, however, that in itself the Munich agreement was not a trade. To give a man a quarter to watch your car because you believe he will slash your tires unless you do is not a trade. At Munich it was impossible to call the police, as Neville Chamberlain would have done in the Municipality of Birmingham, if Adolf Hitler had offered to slash tires. There are no international police.
October 17, 1938

BRITISH COMBINE

Search Abandoned

On the other side of the world last week, the U.S. Navy's great search for Amelia Earhart Putnam and Navigator Fred Noonan, lost in mid-Pacific while flying round the world "for fun," was coming to its close. While its commanders gritted their teeth and hoped fervently for no mishaps, 60 of the aircraft carrier *Lexington's* complement of 62 planes took the air near the point where the International Date Line crosses the equator. Later the searching force was cut to 42 planes. One day the *Lexington's* 1,500 sailors roasted under a fierce sun and the aviators smeared their faces with protective grease; another day, tropical squalls sent planes scurrying back to the ship. At week's end, having swept an area roughly the size of Texas, the *Lexington* pointed home for San Diego.
July 26, 1937

99%

Adolf Hitler was reasonably happy last week. Behind him was a Germany so united on paper as to leave no outside doubt that he was its one & only master. Before him was a ring of sovereign powers who could not make up their common mind what to do about this fuzzy-lipped little man who had just spat in their respective faces.

Fortnight ago Adolf Hitler had collected 44,952,937 fresh pieces of paper purporting to show that 99% of German voters approve his three great steps toward FREEDOM AND PEACE. That these three steps had rashly violated Germany's most sol-

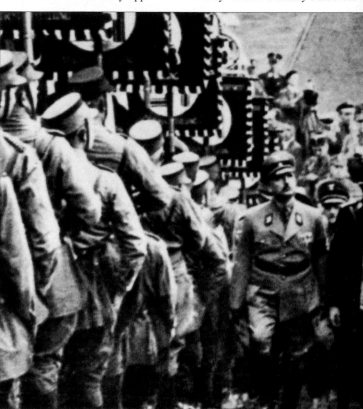

UPI

nn treaty obligations and had
ereby unbalanced the peace of Eu-
pe seemed to disturb no one inside
e Fatherland. Once again Germany
ad a real Army, with more than half
million men cocked and primed to
rike at a moment's notice. Once
gain a tough, hard-hitting German
Navy was in the making. Once again
the Rhineland, sacred soil to every
German, was back in the Fatherland's military fold, with German
guns and German gunners muzzling
the frontier. And once again Germany was virtually friendless in an
angry world.
April 13, 1936

"Scarface Al" Capone

No desperado of the old school
is "Scarface Al," plundering or murdering for the savage joy of crime.
He is, in his own phrase, "a business
man," who wears clean linen, rides
in a Lincoln car, leaves acts of
violence to his hirelings. He has an
eleven-year-old son noted for his
gentlemanly manners. Three years
ago newsmen called upon him at his
brick house at No. 7244 Prarie
Avenue in Chicago, the "little home"
which he used to give substance to
his story of being "out of the booze
racket." He opened the door to
them, wearing a pink apron, carrying
a pan of spaghetti.
March 24, 1930

Enshrined Violence

Spain's atrocity-spangled Civil
War burned and butchered into its
second month this week. At least
25,000 Spaniards had been killed and
less than half of these had died on
any battlefield. Night after night all
over Spain men were torn from their
weeping families, lined up and shot
for what were supposed to be their
political opinions. Scores of cities,
towns and villages had been bom-
barded and burned. More than 200
churches had gone up in flames and
over $40,000,000 in cash and Span-
ish Government bonds stripped from
clericals.

Atrocity of the week occurred in
the village of Buitrago in the
Guadarrama Mountains which form
the chief bulwark of Madrid on the
north. There some 80 children too
young to have any political opinions
were discovered hiding in a church.
Out they were dragged, to be lined
up, dispatched by firing squads and
left to rot on the ground.
August 24, 1936

Ulysses Lands

Watchers of the U.S. skies last week reported no comet or other celestial portent. In Manhattan no showers of ticker-tape blossomed from Broadway office windows, no welcoming committee packed the steps of City Hall. No overt celebration marked the day with red. Yet many a wide-awake modern-minded citizen knew he had seen literary history pass another milestone. For last week a much-enduring traveler, world-famed but long an outcast, landed safe and sound on U.S. shores. His name was *Ulysses*.

Strictly speaking, *Ulysses* did not so much disembark as come out of hiding, garbed in new and respectable garments. Since 1922, when the first edition of *Ulysses* was published in Paris, hundred of U.S. citizens have smuggled copies through the customs or bought them from bookleggers. But this week, on the strength of Federal Judge John Munro Woolsey's decision that *Ulysses* is not obscene, Random House was able to publish the first edition of the book ever legally printed in any English-speaking country.
January 20, 1934

Horse Feathers

Far more depraved than Groucho, more irrelevant than Chico, more implausible than Zeppo, is Harpo Marx. He never speaks, does not need to. His appalling brain ex-

Disney's Folly

Wary Hollywood, which scoffed at sound ten years ago, first scoffed at the *Snow White* project, referred to it as Disney's Folly. But skeptical Hollywood, that had wondered whether a fairy story could have enough suspense to hold an audience through seven reels, and whether, even if the plot held up, an audience would care about the fate of characters who were just drawings, was finally convinced that Walt Disney had done it again.

Snow White is as exciting as a Western, as funny as a haywire comedy. It combines the classic idiom of folklore drama with rollicking comic-strip humor. A combination of Hollywood, the Grimm Brothers, and the sad, searching fantasy of universal childhood, it is an authentic masterpiece, to be shown in theaters and beloved by new generations long after the current crop of Hollywood stars, writers and directors are sleeping where no Prince's kiss can wake them.
December 27, 1937

resses itself in a language more
disastrous than words. He pursues
women with the abandon of a satyr
and the stamina of a Paavo Nurmi.
Sofas and tables are his racetracks.

In Chicago, Harpo bought an old
harp. He tuned and played it to suit

himself. The harp became so dilapi-
dated that, when his train was
wrecked at Mobile, Harpo claimed
and received $250 on it although it
had been unhurt.
August 15, 1932

Surrealism

Surrealism would never have
attracted its present attention in the
U.S. were it not for a handsome 32-
year-old Catalan with a soft voice
and clipped cinemactor's mustache,
Salvador Dali. Artist Dali, who
wears a knitted Catalan liberty cap
whenever possible, takes surrealism
in dead earnest, but has a faculty for
publicity which should turn any circus pressagent green with envy. He
was taken up by swank New York
socialites and in his honor was held a
fancy dress ball that is still the talk of
the West Fifties. Mme. Dali wore a
dress of transparent red paper and a
headdress made of boiled lobsters
and a doll's head. Artist Dali wore a
glass case on his chest containing a
brassiere.
December 14, 1936

Me'n Paul

When he arrived at the Cardinals
training camp in Bradenton, Fla. last
year, Pitcher Dizzy Dean astonished
reporters by promising that he and
his Brother Paul would win 45
games. They won 49. This season
Pitcher Dean was a shade more cir-
cumspect. Said he, "Frankie Frisch
thinks he can win this pennant by
putting the halter on me'n Paul. He's
got the wrong idea."

As famed as his pitching prowess
are the eccentricities which are the
result of Dizzy Dean's semi-illiteracy
and shrewd self-aggrandizement.
When he first joined the Cardinals he
squandered his money so foolishly
that he was put on an allowance of $1
a day. He registered at three hotels,
slept in whichever one was nearest
when he felt tired. On a blistering
day in St. Louis last year, he lit a
bonfire in front of his team's dugout,
wrapped himself in a blanket, pre-
tended to be an Indian.
April 15, 1935

1930

Renewed German militarism alarmed Europe; in defense, France began construction of the Maginot Line.

THE DISCOVERY OF A NEW PLANET, PLUTO, WAS ANNOUNCED BY THE LOWELL OBSERVATORY ■ LONDON THEATRE-GOERS DELIGHTED IN NOEL COWARD'S "PRIVATE LIVES," WHILE DIETRICH DONNED TOP HAT IN "THE BLUE ANGEL" ■ THE U.S. POPULATION REACHED 122 MILLION ■ AND IN INDIA, MAHATMA GANDHI LED THE DRIVE FOR INDEPENDENCE . . .

AL CAPONE

JOSEPH STALIN

KING GEORGE V AND
QUEEN MARY

FOREIGN NEWS

INDIA

Declaration of Independence

In famed "Lahore the Golden," capital of the Punjab, ancient seat of the Mogul Sultan "Akbar the Magnificent," there stood on a muddy sidewalk last week, with a grin of amazement and recognition on his round red face, His Majesty's Mr. Constable Sean O'Rourke.

A wild familiar Irish tune was in the air. It shrilled and banged from the oriental instruments of an outlandish procession. First on a white charger rode Pandit Motilal Nehru, President of the Indian National Congress, followed by 20 elephants magnificently caparisoned. Next came famed Mahatma Gandhi, a wizened, self-starved little saint, wearing as his only garment a skimpy loin cloth—the most adored and potent man in India.

Following Mr. Gandhi came a rabble of marchers, many of them as reedy looking as the Mahatma, all stepping briskly to the stirring air which Mr. Constable Sean O'Rourke was now bellowing in a rich Dublin tenor:

. . . " 'Tis the most distrustful country That ever yet was seen! They're hanging men and women for the wearing of the green. "

What could be more appropriate? The Nationalists are in effect the Irish of India—except that they lack Irish brawn and humor.

Now they were marching 80,000 strong to "The Wearing of the Green" out of Lahore and along the green left bank of the River Ravi to an enormous, amazing Congress camp surrounded by a barricade consisting of 13,000 worn-out railway cars.

Even with 500 British special constables skulking outside, the 80,000 Nationalists (physically weak and mentally timid though they are) felt safe behind their barricade. They had met with the announced purpose of committing High Treason *en masse*, assembled as did 65 American colonists in 1776 to defy a British sovereign with a Declaration of Independence. Only 3,000 of them were official delegates but all 80,000 shrilled applause as Pandit Nehru cried: "We are now in open conspiracy to free India."

Year ago the Nationalists met in Calcutta and resolved this ultimatum: If the British Parliament does not grant India Dominion status with a legal Indian Parliament before Dec. 31, 1929, then the Indian National Con-

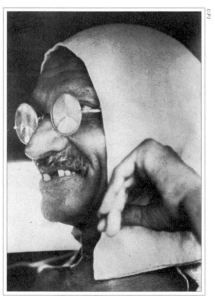

GANDHI
80,000 Irishmen would be different

gress will proclaim civil resistance to the British raj (rule).

Since that defy, despite the would-be liberal policy of James Ramsay MacDonald, the Prime Minister's hands have been tied by opposition in the House of Commons, and the British Government has in fact done nothing to meet Indian aspirations.

With their ultimatum in effect rejected, the Indian National Congress was at zero hour last week when Mr. Gandhi, attended by ascetic gentlemen in white loin cloths and lean ladies in pink girdles, squatted down cross-legged on the rostrum and announced that the executive committee of the Congress had adopted unanimously his draft Declaration of Independence and would put it to vote after suitable debate. As the debate began, the weather turned bitter cold. Mr. Gandhi drew a piece of cloth over his shoulders and sat quiet, knitting something woolen.

What was contemplated by Saint Gandhi was that the Congress should exhort 250 million Indians to stop paying taxes, stop buying British goods, indulge in a passive orgy of "non-violent non-cooperation."

If Indians stopped buying, Great Britain would lose more than one-eighth of her export sales, and if Indians stopped paying taxes, the people of Great Britain could not make up the deficiency necessary to maintain themselves as a great power. Because previous Indian boycotts have always broken down, British statesmen calmly faced the probability that before "non-violent non-cooperation" has gotten very far there will be enough casual rioting and bloodshed to justify the re-imprisonment of Mr. Gandhi (let out of jail in 1924), and the mowing down of a goodly number of gentlemen in white, ladies in pink.

Peace Terms

The "peace terms" offered by Mahatma Gandhi to the British Government were duly forwarded by Viceroy Lord Irwin to London last week. Nationalist demands were reported to be simply: "Give us Dominion status and we will abandon the civil disobedience campaign."

To foreign observers this demand seemed modest enough. The British Government has continually implied that it was maintaining India in tutelage only until she could be educated to Dominionhood. But the British lion last week roared his amazement at St. Gandhi's "diabolically clever" plan.

Oswald mosely organized the fascist party in britain ■ Al capone was jailed for income tax evasion ■ Dali startled the art world with his painting of limp watches, "the persistence of memory" ■ The cyclotron was invented ■ And the first new charlie chaplin film in two years was "city lights" . . .

1931

The worldwide depression continued to deepen; Britain abandoned the gold standard, while Germany was forced to close all banks.

CINEMA

The New Pictures

City Lights (United Artists). It is almost a law in publicity-loving Southern California that the two greatest personalities there present shall hobnob while the press & public loudly cheer or jeer. Usually this means William Randolph Hearst and whatever foreign personage happens to be visiting Hollywood. But last week it meant Charles Spencer Chaplin and Albert Einstein. All of Hollywood's police reserves turned out one evening to make tunnels through the populace so that Mr. Chaplin could escort Dr. Einstein and a party of scientists to see the first new Chaplin film in two years.

Hollywood is volatile, jealous and perhaps sinful. But it is intensely loyal to the little man whom it used to call Charlie before the wide world called him Charlot, Carlos, Cha-pu-rin and as many more variations as there are languages. Had *City Lights* been a failure, Hollywood would have been personally and bitterly depressed. But Hollywood was not depressed. Neither was it frightened. For though *City Lights* is a successful silent challenge to the talkies, its success derives solely from the little man with the battered hat, bamboo cane and black mustache. Critics agree that he, whose posterior would probably be recognized by more people throughout the world than would recognize any other man's face, will be doing business after talkies have been traded in for television.

City Lights is not silent in the strictest sense. Synchronized sound effects and music are used beginning with the very first sequence, where the talkies are burlesqued by horn sounds that make the actors seem to be talking with their mouths full of mush. Also there is an episode where Mr. Chaplin swallows a whistle. Each time he coughs he whistles and he cannot stop coughing. Taxis hurry up and stop, dogs overwhelm him. Hollywood also grew hysterical during a prizefight in which Charlie survives two rounds by dodging so briskly that the referee is always between him and his murderous opponent.

To thread together these and kindred quaint inventions the picture tells the story of a blind flower girl (Virginia Cherrill). He falls in love with her, encouraging her to believe he is a millionaire. His difficulties in getting funds to maintain this reputation in her unseeing eyes supply most of the complications. He finally acquires $1,000 for which he is promptly and

CHARLIE CHAPLIN

unjustly jailed. When he emerges she has regained her sight by the aid of the thousand. As the film fades she recognizes in the ragged helpless vagrant the wealthy prince she dreamed about in darkness.

A "running gag"* much admired by Hollywood is built up in a millionaire who, when drunk, is Chaplin's dearest friend; when sober, has him thrown out of the house. A new gag: Chaplin trying to light his cigar but suc-

---
*A piece of business or dialogue often repeated.

ceeding only in lighting the cigar which another character is waving airily before his face. As in all Chaplin films there are touches of smut: Chaplin as a busy street cleaner seeing an endless troop of mules, hurrying in the opposite direction, only to meet an elephant; Chaplin acting girlish toward a prize fighter stripping for battle.

Cinema is primarily an industry, secondarily an art. Squat, tasteful red brick buildings in the heart of Hollywood are the physical evidences of Chaplin's supremacy as industrialist as well as artist. Chaplin finances his own pictures and shrewdly supervises their sale and distribution. He writes them, casts them, directs them. He works by mood. He shoots thousands upon thousands of feet of film, saving perhaps 50 feet that he feels is right. When things go wrong he stops work and plays tennis. Sometimes he works all night. He listens to a great lot of advice, disregards most of it. Sometimes his spasmodic working habits bewilder his subordinates. To ease their minds he has instructed a special studio watchman to keep a lookout for his big car and swiftly warn the workers of its approach. Thus laggards will not lose their self-respect by having the boss catch them in a poker game.

City Lights cost $1,500,000 to produce. Before release it had sold to a guaranteed booking of more than $4,000,000. Chaplin worked frantically to make it his greatest, to justify his faith in pantomime. Chance guests would be hauled into his projection room to see rushes of the film. They were asked to describe what they had seen. If they missed a point that was intended to be clear, Chaplin—feeling that his story must be understood by everyone, even the stupid or the distracted—would have the scene re-filmed. In rest intervals he would play "Violetera" on his harmonium and sing an imitation of Spanish words to it in the manner of Raquel Meller. One afternoon he nearly lost his mustache. He has had the same one for 15 years. A Manhattan theatrical barber picked it out for him. He says that if he ever loses it he will play smooth shaven. On this day he came in just in time to see a guest about to throw the mustache away, mistaking it for hair combings on Chaplin's make-up table.

WALTER LIPPMAN

ADOLF HITLER

JOHN NANCE GARNER

1932

The nation looked for a way out of its economic desperation, electing FDR with his promise of "a New Deal for the American people."

GANDHI WAS ARRESTED IN INDIA, AND THE INDIAN CONGRESS WAS DECLARED ILLEGAL ■ EAMON DE VALERA WAS ELECTED PRESIDENT OF IRELAND ■ JOHNNY WEISMULLER SWUNG THROUGH THE TREES AS TARZAN ■ THE RADIO PLAYED, "BROTHER, CAN YOU SPARE A DIME?" ■ AND IN WASHINGTON, THE RAG-TAG "BONUS EXPEDITIONARY FORCE" CAMPED OUT . . .

YEHUDI MENUHIN

NORMAN THOMAS

THE MARX BROTHERS

NATIONAL AFFAIRS

HEROES

Bonus Expeditionary Force

Last week the House of Representatives surrendered to the siege of the Bonus Expeditionary Force encamped near the Capitol. It voted (226 to 175) to take up the bill by Texas' Patman for immediate cashing of Adjusted Service Compensation certificates at a cost of $2,400,000,000 in printing-press money. This first test of the Bonus boosters' strength indicated that the House would probably pass the Patman bill and send it to the Senate. In that body 56 Senators—a majority—were said to be lined up against the Bonus. But even should the measure somehow get by Congress an insurmountable veto awaited it at the White House.

Largely ignorant of legislative processes, the B. E. F., bivouacked some 15,000 strong on the Anacostia mudflats, was delirious with delight at its House victory. Its tattered personnel, destitute veterans who had "bummed" their way to the Capitol from all over the country, whooped and pranced about among their crude shelters. Most of them had left hungry wives and children behind. They had gone to Washington because, long jobless, they had nothing better to do. In camp with their A. E. F. fellows again, they seemed to have revived the old ganging spirit of Army days as an escape from reality. They convinced themselves that they were there to right some vague wrong—a wrong somehow bound up in the fact that the Government had opened its Treasury to banks, railroads and the like but closed it to needy individuals. When the House voted to take up their bill, they slapped one another on the back and were quite sure they would be getting their money in a few days to take home.

During the week the B. E. F.'s ranks were more than quadrupled by the new recruits. Leaders predicted 50,000 more were on the march to Washington. Seven thousand of them paraded one evening in quiet order up Pennsylvania Avenue. The discipline at "Bonus City" continued good, despite the fears of alarmed Washingtonians who helped to spread unfounded Red scares. Crude shelters were built from old lumber, packing boxes and scrap tin, and thatched with old straw. Several hundred secondhand Army tents were provided. Company streets were laid out. Latrines were dug. Regular formations were held daily. Campers were organized for field sports to keep them out of mischief. Newcomers were required to register after proving that they were *bona fide* veterans with honorable discharge papers.

Credit for the B. E. F.'s good behavior went principally to 34-year-old Walter W. Waters, originator of the Washington march, who was selected last week as the B. E. F.'s commander-in-chief. Tall, lean, sun-burned, Waters first saw service on the Mexican border. Then he went overseas as a sergeant for nearly two years with the 146th Field Artillery. Mustered out, he married a blonde slip of a girl from Valparaiso, Ind., took her to Oregon where he worked as superintendent of a canning factory, had a house of his own, a car, two little daughters. Eighteen months ago he lost his job. His small savings melted. He led the B. E. F.'s first contingent of 300 from Portland across the continent last month. Now in command of 15,000 men, he became the sober, strict executive with headquarters and a staff in a deserted building on Pennsylvania Avenue. He directed the B. E. F.'s lobbyists, organized newcomers, arranged for food and shelter, maintained camp order and, above all, kept the Bonus uppermost in his followers' minds. Said he: "We're here for the duration and we're not going to starve. We're going to keep ourselves a simon-pure veterans' organization. If the Bonus is paid it will relieve to a large extent the deplorable economic condition."

Best Washington friend of the B. E. F. last week was Pelham Glassford, Superintendent of Police, onetime Army brigadier. He supplied the camp with food during its first hard days, later managed the money and supplies donated for its subsistence. He bought or borrowed tents, arranged for quarters in condemned Government buildings. He supplied trucks to take all who wanted to leave 50 miles from the Capitol. When no appreciable number accepted his free transportation offer, he dug in to make the B. E. F. as comfortable as possible. His kindness brought rumors that President Hoover, displeased, might summarily dismiss him on the ground that his activities encouraged more veterans to head for Washington.

Over Bonus City hung the constant threat of pestilence. Flies swarmed. Garbage lay half buried. The men bathed in the Eastern Branch (Potomac), virtually an open sewer. Twenty-three cases of communicable disease were spotted but were lost in the crowd. The air reeked with filthy smells. Eight men were reported to have died. Food was poor. Scabies broke out. Public health officers declared conditions were "frightful," warned of a "terrible epidemic" which might suddenly fan out from the camp across the city and country. A 24-hour quarantine was set up for new arrivals and a special camp with hospital facilities opened for the sick and diseased.

The B. E. F. was frowned upon by the American Legion, which has hushed its demand for Bonus cashing. At the National Republican Club in Manhattan last week Major General James Guthrie Harbord, retired, voiced one popular view when he declared: "Nothing so ominous or so nasty as the Bonus march has been seen since 1916 when organized labor forced through the eight-hour-day railroad law under threat of strike. Not since 1783 has an army of citizens marched on the Capitol with evil in their hearts. . . Something must be done to curb this movement. Otherwise it will spread and I don't know what may happen."

THE FIRST BASEBALL ALL-STAR GAME WAS HELD ■ CONGRESS VOTED INDEPENDENCE FOR THE PHILIPPINES ■ ROOSEVELT DECLARED A BANK HOLIDAY ■ JAMES HILTON DESCRIBED SHANGRI-LA IN *LOST HORIZON* ■ GERTRUDE STEIN PRESIDED OVER A PARIS SALON OF *ARTISTES* ■ AND FDR DECLARED "THE ONLY THING WE HAVE TO FEAR IS FEAR ITSELF" . . .

1933

The Nazi grip on Germany became absolute; all rival parties were banned, and the first concentration camps established.

NATIONAL AFFAIRS

THE PRESIDENCY

"We Must Act"

"O Lord, our Heavenly Father, the high and mighty ruler of the Universe, Who dost from Thy throne behold all the dwellers upon earth; most heartily we beseech Thee, with Thy favor to behold and bless Thy servant, Franklin, chosen to be the President of the United States . . ."

His face cupped in his hands Franklin Delano Roosevelt began the biggest day of his life with that prayer ringing in his ears at Washington's St. John's Episcopal Church across Lafayette Park from the White House. For the 20-minute service in the plain white chapel he had gathered about him his family, his Cabinet, a few close friends. At the altar in cassock & surplice stood his old schoolmaster, Groton's Dr. Endicott ("Peabo") Peabody who had married him to Anna Eleanor Roosevelt. From his heart, from the hearts of his little band of worshipers, from the heart of a stricken nation rose a wordless appeal for divine strength to right great ills. The President-elect stood up in his pew, squared back his shoulders. As he walked out of St. John's, a brief streak of sunlight shot down upon him through grey wintry clouds.

Meanwhile ten times ten thousand men, women & children had gathered before the inaugural platform on the East Front of the Capitol. They blackened 40 acres of park and pavement. They sat on benches. They filled bare trees. They perched on roof tops. But for all the flags and music and ceremony, they were not a happy, carefree crowd. Their bank accounts were frozen by what amounted to a national moratorium. Many of them wondered how they could raise the cash to get home. Their mass spirits were as somber as the grey sky above. Yet they remained doggedly hopeful that this new President with his New Deal would somehow solve their worries

ROOSEVELT AT INAUGURATION
"The only thing we have to fear is fear."

and send them away in brighter mood.

Ta-ta-Ta-ta-aa sounded a bugle. Through the great bronze doors that tell the story of Columbus, appeared the President-elect leaning on the arm of his son James. From the door to the platform had been built a special ramp, carpeted in maroon. Down this he shuffled slowly while the crowd cheered and the Marine Band played "Hail to the Chief."

President Roosevelt, without hat or overcoat in the chill wind, swung around to the crowd before him, launched vigorously into his inaugural address. His easy smile was gone. His large chin was thrust out defiantly as if at some invisible, insidious foe. A challenge rang in his clear strong voice. For 20 vibrant minutes he held his audience, seen and unseen, under a strong spell.

"My Friends!" He began. "This is a day of national consecration . . . The only thing we have to fear is fear itself—nameless, unreasoning, unjustified terror which paralyzes needed efforts to convert retreat into advance.

"This nation asks for action, and action now. Our greatest primary task is to put people to work. It can be accomplished in part by direct recruiting by the Government itself, treating the task as we would treat the emergency of war."

THE CONGRESS

Bank Bill

Called into special session on four days notice, the 73rd Congress, young and Democratic, sat momentously in the Capitol last week. President Roosevelt had summoned it to meet the banking crisis—Emergency Item No.1 of the New Deal. Not since War days had the Congressional temper been so grave, so unanimously bent on speedy action. The State of the Union was so serious that the most opinionated Senators and Representatives submerged their convictions in worried silence and took orders from the White House.

After Speaker Rainey had sworn in the membership with one thunderous oath and the President's message had been read, the House plunged headlong into *H.R. 1491*, "an act to provide relief in the existing national emergency in banking." So hastily had the bill been drawn up that no printed copies of it were yet available for members. Their only knowledge of what they were being asked to approve came from a clerk's sing-song reading of the lone text which still bore last-minute corrections scribbled in pencil. Chairman Steagall of the yet unorganized Banking & Currency Committee arose to explain to his bewildered colleagues how *H.R. 1491* gave dictatorial banking power to the President, authorized impounding of all gold, and provided for a new currency issue. Members were told that only by voting this measure could the nation's banks open on the morrow.

Precisely 38 minutes after it had taken up *H.R. 1491* the House passed it with a unanimous roar. Trusting their new President to do right, members voted it blind, without a single word's change. Under the Roosevelt spell the House's deliberative session became a ratification meeting.

NEVILLE CHAMBERLAIN

MARIE DRESSLER

HERMANN GÖRING

1934

A depressed nation forgot its problems at the movies; over 100 million tickets were sold each week.

STALIN INITIATED BLOODY PURGES OF THE RUSSIAN COMMUNIST PARTY ■ DRIVING TESTS WERE INTRODUCED IN BRITAIN ■ CHURCHILL ADDRESSED PARLIAMENT ON HIS FEARS OF A GERMAN AIR MENACE ■ VITAMIN C WAS SYNTHESIZED ■ AND IN CANADA, A FARM WIFE GAVE BIRTH TO FIVE BABY GIRLS . . .

ELSA SCHIAPARELLI

CECIL B. DEMILLE

UPTON SINCLAIR

MEDICINE

Quintuplets

The rough, nickel-loded, forest-fuzzed Canadian frontier at the east end of Lake Nipissing bulged large with spring's fertility last week. The full moon with Venus, Mars and Saturn accompanying swelled pompously across the midnight sky. And in a lamp-lit farmhouse near Callander a buxom French-Canadian woman of 24 whimpered with the unusual fullness of her womb. She, too, had three attendants — her aunt, another goodwife who had borne 17 children, and her husband Ovila Dionne. Upstairs in bed were the two boys and three girls of the Dionnes. Four years in his grave lay their sixth child.

Toward 4 a. m. things began popping in the uncarpeted downstairs bedroom where Elzire Dionne lay. *"Ça me fait mal,"* she wept. Ovila Dionne surmised that his wife was complaining about the swelling of her legs. But the goodwives knew that Elzire Dionne was on the verge of bearing her seventh child, perhaps twins. They dispatched Ovila down the rocky, forest-edged road to Dr. Dafoe's, placed kettles and pots of water to boil, laid out clean towels and a bottle of olive oil on the new bedroom bureau, lined a wicker clothesbasket with pads and sheets to receive the newcomer, washed their hands, and composed themselves to watch a labor which no one expected for at least another month.

Dr. Allan Roy Dafoe, a stocky little grey-haired practitioner who has delivered some 1,500 children in frontier Ontario, leaped nimbly into his clothes when Ovila timidly rapped at the door. In the doctor's Dodge they drove back to the Dionne house.

A premature baby girl was there ahead of them, and another was on the way before the doctor could remove his coat, roll up his sleeves and wash his hands. Like a football quarterback, Dr. Dafoe passed another girl to the dumbfounded goodwives and another and another and another. *"Mon Dieu, mon Dieu,"* sniffled Papa Dionne, fetching and pouring

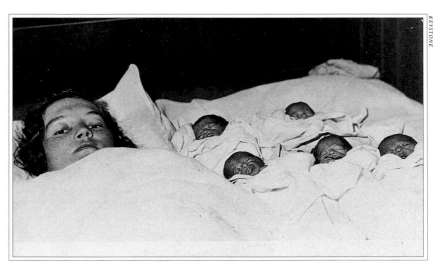

CECILE, YVONNE, MARIE, EMILY & ANNETTE DIONNE WITH MOTHER

hot water. Fearing that none of the 9-in. mites would live long enough for a priest to arrive, he baptized each one himself, as Dr. Dafoe passed them back.

With the birth of the fifth girl, who completed the 31st authentically known quintuplet in 500 years, Mrs. Elzire Dionne fainted. It all had taken place in 30 minutes.

Ovila Dionne wept: "I am ashamed of myself." He fetched a potato scales and weighed the lot in the clothesbasket: 13 lb. 6 oz.

The Dionne roosters were crowing for dawn while Dr. Dafoe washed up, eased his suspenders, donned his coat and drove back to his wifeless, book-filled home. He needed a little sleep, for later that day he expected another confinement.

Dr. Allan Roy Dafoe, 51, graduate of the University of Toronto, has been practicing at Callander for 26 years, is the district's medical officer and coroner. Obstetrics has always been a large part of his practice among the prolific French Canadians. His youngest mother was 13, his oldest 63. Once he delivered a two-headed monster. One of his pa-

tients has borne 23 children, only one of whom has died, and that one, said Dr. Dafoe last week when he had an opportunity to relax in the wicker easy-chair in his library, "was dead at birth. It was one of twins. I remember I was alone with the mother at the time. The father had left the farmhouse to hunt for his horse that had run away."

Dr. Dafoe is positive that the Dionne quintuplets are identical, *i.e.*, developed from a single ovum. That seemed incredible to many an obstetrician who telegraphed Dr. Dafoe for details of this rare and astounding example of multiple births.

Stout hearted Mme. Elzire Dionne, with eleven offspring, holds no record for prolificness. One recorded woman produced 59 children in 27 labors (twins, triplets, quadruplets). Another bore 30 children in 22 years by her first husband, 14 in three years by her second husband (triplets, quintuplets and sextuplets). Noteworthy was Dr. Mary Austin, Civil War nurse, one of whose sisters bore 41 children, another 26. Dr. Austin herself bore 13 twins, 6 triplets — a total of 44 children.

ALCOHOLICS ANONYMOUS WAS FOUNDED IN NEW YORK CITY ■ THE MOSCOW SUBWAY OPENED ■ THE NAZIS REPUDIATED THE VERSAILLES TREATY AND ENACTED ANTI-JEWISH LAWS ■ SINCLAIR LEWIS PUBLISHED *IT CAN'T HAPPEN HERE* ■ AND IN BATON ROUGE, LOUISIANA, "DICTATOR" HUEY LONG WAS SHOT DOWN . . .

1935

Fascist armed aggression began with the invasion of Ethiopia by Mussolini, undeterred by a League of Nations condemnation.

NATIONAL AFFAIRS

LOUISIANA

Death of a Dictator

One morning last week the New York *Herald Tribune* published a cartoon by Jay ("Ding") Darling captioned "The Fates Are Funny That Way." It pictured a wreck at a railway crossing ("36,000 Die in Auto Crashes Every Year!"); a scene in an operating room ("Prominent Senator Succumbs to Emergency Operation!"); a street accident ("Pedestrian Killed Crossing Street!"); a row of dead lying beside a table ("Poison Food Kills 469 at Old Settlers' Picnic!"); a volcano erupting ("Earthquakes, Floods, Cancer and Pestilence Kill Thousands Every Day!"). Beneath this billboard of horrors appeared a citizen, newspaper in hand, turning to his wife exclaiming, "But nothing ever seems to happen to Huey Long!"

Three days later in Baton Rouge something very serious happened to Huey Long. The seventh special session of Louisiana's Legislature was just getting down to the business of rubberstamping 39 bills devised by the Senator to tighten his one-man dictatorship over the State. On the floor there had been the customary brawling and cursing as the "Kingfish" strutted up & down the aisle giving orders to his henchmen. As the Legislature adjourned for the night, Senator Long marched out of the chamber and started down the corridor to Governor Allen's office, flanked, as always, by his bodyguards. A young man in a white suit, lurking in a corner, stepped out into the Senator's path, shoved a small revolver against his right side, pulled the trigger. There was a muffled explosion. One of the Long bodyguards grappled with the assassin. He fired again, searing the bodyguard's thumb. Then the young man in the white suit went down under a rain of sub-machine gun bullets.

Senator Long clapped his hand to his side, staggered down the corridor. Attracted by the crackle of gunfire, friends rushed forward, carried the wounded "Kingfish" out a rear door, put him into a car, started for Our Lady of the Lake Hospital. On the way Huey Long held his hand to his bleeding side, spoke only once: "I wonder why he did it."

Why a 29-year-old doctor named Carl Austin Weiss Jr. did it seemed fairly plain to local newshawks. Young Dr. Weiss, a Tulane Medical School graduate who practiced with his father in Baton Rouge, had married Miss Louise Yvonne Pavy. Mrs. Weiss was the daughter of Circuit Judge B. H. Pavy, a rabid anti-Longster in St. Landry Parish. One of the 39 bills up for passage by the Legislature was to gerrymander Judge Pavy's judicial district in such a way as to effect his ouster. Brooding darkly on this piece of petty politics, Carl Weiss apparently thought he was doing his father-in-law a favor by taking a potshot at Boss Long.

At the hospital the Senator was taken straight to the operating room. On examining his wound physicians found that the bullet had twice pierced his colon, made its way out through his back. On the operating table, the intestinal punctures were sewed up. Then Huey Long was put to bed and a mass vigil began: by his wife, daughter, two boys and three hastily reconciled brothers at the bedside; by his miscellaneous henchmen in the corridor outside; by a brigade of newshawks downstairs; by a truculent detachment of State troopers and bodyguards around the building who were ordered to shoot photographers on sight; and by a horde of onlookers who shuffled up & down in front of the hospital. While the Senator's political enemies buried Assassin Weiss with honor in a nearby Catholic cemetery next day, the Senator's doctors ordered five successive blood transfusions, adrenalin injections, an oxygen tent. Toward sunset, when his condition became hopeless, it was arranged that the lights would blink in the sickroom to signify the end to friends and kin on the porch below.

Men look smaller when dead, but Huey Long, who developed the traditional figure of the American backwoods demagogue to its fullest stature, was not likely to shrink in the estimates of his contemporaries for some time to come. Twenty years ago but a traveling-salesman, a peddler of baking powder and cotton seed oil, he married a girl who won a cake-baking contest which he staged. After seven months' study of the law, he was a lawyer, wangled himself a job on Louisiana's Railway Commission, and began building up a political following. He made the Governorship in 1928. In short time an effort was made to impeach him, but in vain. He "reached" 15 Senators, enough to forestall his ousting, and from that time on no one in Louisiana could stand against him. After he had himself elected to the U.S. Senate, he refused to go to Washington until he could arrange to leave Louisiana bound and gagged in the hands of a Long-chosen Governor. At the Democratic Convention in 1932, he was not only Senator but Dictator of Louisiana and with his vital votes Franklin Roosevelt was nominated. But President Roosevelt refused to pay the political debts which Huey Long thought Candidate Roosevelt had contracted. So Huey Long, the ex-drummer, was a pariah instead of a leader in the most powerful Administration in U.S. history.

A favorite saying of the dictator was: "I'm a smart man. There are very few men in the United States as smart as I am, and none in Louisiana." In truth, he left no successors, only stooges. These, Governor Allen, Lieutenant Governor Noe and Col. "Abe" Shushan, the machine's money-man, quit their leader's death bed in a panic. The best thing they could think of was to throw a cordon of police around the State House, hold troops ready in New Orleans to prevent a possible *"coup d'etat."* With equal melodrama, the suppressed anti-Long forces throughout the State began to serve threateningly and the Square Deal Association ominously warned the Legislature: "Heed the example of the man who has just passed away."

JEAN HARLOW

J. EDGAR HOOVER

JOSEPH P. KENNEDY

1936

The modern self-help movement was born, as Dale Carnegie wrote How To Win Friends and Influence People.

HAILE SELASSIE

JOHN L. LEWIS

CLARK GABLE

FOREIGN NEWS

Prince Edward

Dignity, like the Imperial mantle which is placed upon England's King at his Coronation, clothed Edward VIII and his every act last week after the decision of His Majesty to abdicate.

Scarcely anyone failed to tune in on Edward VIII as he took leave of his country or to read within a few hours the simple words with which His Royal Highness said good-by to very nearly all except "the woman I love."

Prince Edward was scrupulous not to betray his class, and to do and say all he could to uphold the Kingdom and the Empire, giving no opportunity to irresponsible groups of the masses to harm Britain. Long after His Majesty's instrument of abdication was signed, sealed, published and in course of certain enactment by Parliament one of the greatest mass gatherings in British history was still roaring outside of Buckingham Palace, "WE WANT EDWARD!" He was not there.

Neither as King Edward nor later last week as Prince Edward did the eldest son of the Royal House enter London. This idol of the British masses (for such His Majesty unquestionably was) vanished, and after a little space other idols (for such King George VI, Queen Elizabeth and crown princess Elizabeth will soon be) were substituted.

The basic English truth which emerged is that the Kingdom long ago became and is today neither a democracy nor a monarchy but an efficient oligarchy, more or less benevolent. Its symbol is the Crown, but the really effective British crowns are the top hats worn by Stanley Baldwin and a few hundred others. They rule over millions of British soft hats, tens of millions of caps and hundreds of millions of Indian noddles. Members of the British Royal Family have long had this basic reality embedded in their natures, and last week in King Edward VIII's hour of sorest indecision it tipped the scales. He left England as the eldest son who has locked a rattling

GEORGE V (25 YEARS), EDWARD VIII (325 DAYS) & GEORGE VI

skeleton in the Empire's closet and thrown away the key.

In his historic broadcast, Prince Edward did not defend either himself or Mrs. Simpson. That would have been undignified. The skeleton must not be jangled. Unmentioned therefore by Prince Edward was the clash of wills between himself and the Church of England over whether the Archbishop of Canterbury would refuse or consent to officiate at the Coronation and *consecration* of a King who intended to marry a woman such as Mrs. Simpson. In the House of Lords, the Archbishop spoke volumes when he said in a broken voice, "Of the motive which compelled the renunciation we dare not speak."

The Archbishop's motive had to do with a feature of the Coronation service scarcely noticed by laymen who suppose that the whole point of a coronation must be that somebody is crowned. There have been British coronations for 1,000 years and until comparatively recent generations the whole emphasis was on the "anointing" of the King, as a newly created bishop is anointed — thus making him a *persona mixta* or a "person of mixed nature,"

part layman, part priest. Queen Victoria was of the opinion that she was the head of the Church of England, virtually a female pope.

Although Prime Minister Gladstone gently dispelled this impetuous pretension, Her Majesty was far more right than she was wrong in the eyes of English churchgoers. The unspeakable dilemma in the case of Edward VIII in recent weeks has been: "Can there be consecrated, as a part-priest, or part-Pope, one who we all know has done everything to face us with the fact that he is resolved to marry a lady with a past, even if we did our best to keep him from making this known to us?"

Dignified Prince Edward, after dining for a last time with his Queen Mother, new King George VI, the Duke of Gloucester and the Duke of Kent, drove last week at great speed through night and fog to Portsmouth, intending to embark on the Admiralty Yacht. At the last moment this plan was changed; the name of the yacht is the *Enchantress*. It was dignified to sail instead on the British destroyer *Fury,* and "His Grace, the Duke of Windsor" debarked at Boulogne into a private car and a new life of wealth, ease and perhaps happiness.

THE "HINDENBURG" EXPLODED WHILE ATTEMPTING TO LAND IN NEW JERSEY ■ DUPONT INTRODUCED A NEW FABRIC: NYLON ■ CHAMBERLAIN BECAME PRIME MINISTER IN BRITAIN ■ PICASSO DEPICTED THE HORRORS OF MODERN WAR IN "GUERNICA" ■ AND ERNEST HEMINGWAY PUBLISHED HIS LATEST NOVEL . . .

1937

Japanese aggression reached new heights: troops seized major Chinese cities, including Peking, and planes sank a U.S. gunboat in Chinese waters.

BOOKS

"All Stories End . . ."

TO HAVE AND HAVE NOT—Ernest Hemingway—*Scribners* ($2.50)

In the eyes of the polite world, Ernest Hemingway has much to answer for. Armed with the hardest-hitting prose of the century, he has used his skill and power to smash rose-colored spectacles right & left, to knock many a genteel pretence into a sprawling grotesque. Detractors have called him a bullying bravo, have pointed out that smashing spectacles and pushing over a pushover are not brave things to do. As the "lost generation" he named have grown greyer and more garrulous, so his own invariably disillusioned but Spartan books have begun to seem a little dated; until it began to be bruited that Hemingway was just another case of veteran with arrested development and total recall.

Hemingway himself did little to encourage any other attitude. With *The Sun Also Rises* (1926), *Men Without Women* (1927) and *A Farewell to Arms* (1929), he had found himself in the unique position of being not only a best-seller but also a writer whom first-line critics intensely admired and respected. Younger writers all imitated him. Wielder of a style of unmatched clarity and precision, master of the art of conveying emotions, particularly violent ones, with an effect almost of first-hand experience, he seemed to have established himself as the most powerful direct influence on contemporary literature. After these three books, however, came the slump. Apart from *Winner Take Nothing* (1933), a volume of short stories, the eight succeeding years saw only two books, both failures. To most readers *Death in the Afternoon* (1932) was a verbose testimonial to the author's enthusiasm for bull-fighting. *Green Hills of Africa* (1935) was an exhaustive and exhausting account of a month's big-game shooting.

Overlooked, however, was the fact that Hemingway is far from being a run-of-the-mine writer. Disregarded also were certain further clues. *Death in the Afternoon* contains much information on its author's basic philosophy. "All stories," he remarked there, "end in death, and he is no true-story teller who would keep that from you. . . ."

Death forms the background of Hemingway's tenth and latest book, his only novel with a U. S. background. But readers of previous love & death stories by Hemingway will find in *To Have and Have Not* a maturity which reflects the more serious turn his personal life has taken in the last year. For the queasy, it should be added that many of the killings (twelve) in *To Have and Have Not* are

HEMINGWAY & AFRICAN KUDU
"A man alone ain't got no . . . chance."

perpetrated with much goriness; for the strait-laced, that the book brings to naked print practically all the four-letter words extant, contains scenes in which copulation and masturbation are impressionistically but vividly presented.

The scene of the book is Key West and Cuba. The story is a sort of saga, disconnected and episodic, of one Harry Morgan, burly, surly, hard-natured "conch" (as Key West natives call themselves), whose life has been spent in the single-minded effort to keep himself and his family on the upper fringes of the "have-nots." Owner of a fast motor boat, he charters it to big-game fishermen, also uses it for running contraband.

No picker and chooser of ways and means, he turns a neat trick on a bunch of Chinese by arranging to ferry them over from Cuba to the Keys, accepts their money, then kills their leader and abandons the rest. Then his luck turns bad. A flier at rum-running results in the confiscation of his boat and the loss of an arm. So the way is paved to the last, most desperate venture of all—an attempt to provide a get-away, in a borrowed boat, for a quartet of bank robbers fleeing from a hold-up at Key West. Morgan knows that unless he kills them first the four will most certainly kill him, as soon as his usefulness to them is ended. He kills them, but not before he has received his own death-wound. In the Coast Guard cutter that has picked him up, half-delirious, dying, he tries to voice the dictum that is the book's real motto: "No matter how, a man alone ain't got no bloody —— * chance."

Tall, heavily-built, dark-skinned and square-featured, Hemingway is still a bull-fight *aficionado* (fan), likes also big-game fishing, hunting, plays tennis regularly to keep his weight down. Divorced (1926) from his first wife, he was remarried a year later to Pauline Pfeiffer, then a Paris fashion writer for *Vogue,* has had by her two sons, Patrick and Gregory Hancock. Since 1930, he has made his home at Key West, living there in a thick-walled, Spanish-built house, its garden somewhat incongruously inhabited by peacocks. His 30-ft. launch *El Pilar* he uses for casual pleasure jaunts, trips to Cuba (90 miles away) and fishing. A Roman Catholic, he is also very superstitious: he never travels on Friday, touches wood constantly, is upset if a black cat crosses his path. Writing (in longhand), he works regular hours, revises conscientiously.

Such, at least, was his pleasant routine till a year ago, when the outbreak of the Spanish War touched off a hitherto well-hidden social consciousness, enlisted him violently on the Loyalist side. No longer big-incomed, he managed to raise $40,000 on his personal notes and dispatched the sum to buy ambulances for Madrid, followed soon after to film *The Spanish Earth.* But no matter what is to happen to Hemingway, U. S. readers last week could reassure themselves that U. S. writers still have a front rank and that he is still in it.

*Obscenity deleted.

THOMAS E. DEWEY

FIORELLO LaGUARDIA

LUNT & FONTANNE

1938

Desperate to avoid war, the world powers agreed to Nazi dismemberment of Czechoslovakia; German troops occupied Sudetenland and installed a puppet government.

A 40-HOUR WORK WEEK WAS ESTABLISHED IN THE U.S. ■ THOUSANDS PANICKED AT ORSON WELLES' RADIO BROADCAST OF *WAR OF THE WORLDS* ■ HOWARD HUGHES FLEW AROUND THE WORLD IN 3 DAYS, 19 HOURS ■ "OUR TOWN" WON THE PULITZER PRIZE FOR DRAMA ■ AND ARCHITECT FRANK LLOYD WRIGHT'S "COMEBACK" WAS IN FULL SWING . . .

BETTE DAVIS

RODGERS & HART

WALTER WINCHELL

ART

Usonian Architect

About four miles from Spring Green, Wis., the hills splay into two soft ranges to let a fast stream flow toward the Wisconsin River. Facing southwest over this valley a big, long house folds around the summit of one hill, its roof lines parallel to the line of ridges, its masonry the same red-yellow sandstone that crops out in ledges along the stream. Its name is Taliesin, a Welsh word meaning "shining brow." Its history is one of tragic irony. Its character is one of extraordinary repose. It is the home of Frank Lloyd Wright, the greatest architect of the 20th Century.

For the past five years Taliesin has been a workshop, farm and studio for more than a score of apprentices. During its first winter the Taliesin Fellowship spent most of its time cutting wood in two shifts to keep the fires going. Since then, its life has been less defensive. After nearly a decade, the master of Taliesin has again had work in hand. In California, Texas, Wisconsin, Minnesota and Pennsylvania superb new buildings have grown from his plans.

The valley in which Architect Wright lives was settled by his Welsh grandfather when it was wild. Wright was born there and grew up on the farm of one of his uncles. His first adventurous piece of architecture was a windmill. He felt and has developed a stronger sense of the earth's reality than most poets. "Man takes a positive hand in creation," he has said, "whenever he puts a building upon the earth beneath the sun."

An erect, impudent youngster of 18, Frank Lloyd Wright arrived in Chicago in the spring of 1887 with three years of engineering school behind him. No. 1 U. S. architect was an immaculate, brown-eyed little French-Irishman of haughty brilliance named Louis Henry Sullivan. Sullivan fathered the skyscraper.

While Louis Sullivan was working on public buildings, what few commissions Adler & Sullivan were given for private houses fell to Frank Lloyd Wright. In the next twenty years he designed and built, for clients scattered throughout the Midwest, nearly 100 houses for which no precedent existed anywhere. In leafy suburbs of Chicago these houses still look strangely civilized and sheltered, with low vistas and wide spreading eaves.

But though Wright had freed domestic architecture he did not feel himself free. Mak-

WRIGHT AND APPRENTICES
A house is more than a home

ing what provision he could for his wife and six children, he went to Italy with a woman named Mamah Borthwick Cheney. They were never married. On their return in 1911, he put all he knew of architecture into the building of Taliesin as a new home for them both. Changes of this kind are ill-fated by ancient superstition, but few have met such a fate as Frank Lloyd Wright's. In 1913, a Barbados Negro servant had run amok at Taliesin, murdered its mistress, her two children, an apprentice and three others, burned the living quarters to the ground. Wright buried his mistress alone, and lived there alone for months. Then he began to rebuild Taliesin.

After 1915, Wright's rebirth in architecture took the form of creative audacity on a grand scale. Commissioned in 1916 to build the new Imperial Hotel in Tokyo, he produced one of the marvels of modern construction. A vast, low building on a symmetrical plan, it was Wright's first ambitious use of the canti-

lever principle, which allowed him to rest each concrete floor slab on a central support, like a tray on a waiter's fingers. He roofed the building with light copper sheathing, made the centre of gravity low as a ship's. And like a ship, the Imperial was made to float. Instead of sinking deep piers, to bedrock, the architect rested his building on hundreds of slender, pointed 8-ft. piles, distributing the weight evenly on a 60-ft. pad of mud.

He had not been back at Taliesin long before the house again burned down, this time destroying hundreds of valuable things Wright had brought from Japan. Again he rebuilt Taliesin. Then his second wife, Miriam Noel, left him. Before he was able to marry Olgivanna, the soft-voiced, Montenegrin woman who is his present wife, they and their baby were incredibly harried by the newspapers, the Noel lawyers and the police, who jailed them in Milwaukee. Wright could get no work, could earn no money. Taliesin fell into the hands of a bank. Wright got it back only when a group of old clients and friends incorporated him in 1929

Since then, bobbing up for the third time, Frank Lloyd Wright has done perhaps his most amazing work. In Racine, Wis., Contractor Ben Wiltscheck is now finishing a business building for S. C. Johnson & Son which is unlike any other in the world. At Bear Run, Pa., Wright has just finished his most beautiful job, "Fallingwater," a house cantilevered over a waterfall.

Usonia is Frank Lloyd Wright's name for the U. S. A. He found it in Samuel Butler and, eclectic for once, appropriated it because he liked it. It is one of the tricks of speech and thought by which Wright links curiously old-fashioned Americanism to an Americanism which is still ahead of his time. He thinks of himself as in the "centre line" of Usonian independence that runs through Thoreau and Whitman. Whether or not that line is still central in U. S. culture, there can be little doubt that Frank Lloyd Wright is their worthy peer.

Pan am began regular flights between Europe and the U.S ■
Judy garland danced with munchkins in "the wizard of oz" ■ The
U.S. economy boomed with European orders for war equipment ■
Great britain instituted the draft ■ And hitler attacked poland,
beginning world war II . . .

1939

While the world sank into war, a different version of the future was on display at the New York World's Fair.

NATIONAL AFFAIRS

THE PRESIDENCY
Preface to War

The telephone in Franklin Roosevelt's bedroom at the White House rang at 2:50 a.m. on the first day of September. It was a ghastly hour, but operators knew they must ring. Ambassador Bill Bullitt was calling from Paris. He told Mr. Roosevelt that World War II had begun. Adolf Hitler's bombing planes were dropping death all over Poland.

That day Franklin Roosevelt's press conference was a grave business. One question was uppermost in all minds. Correspondent Phelps Adams of the New York *Sun* uttered it: "Mr. President, can we stay out of it?" Franklin Roosevelt sat in silent concentration, eyes down, for many long seconds. Then, with utmost solemnity, he replied: "I not only sincerely hope so, but I believe we can."

POLISH THEATRE
Grey Friday

World War II began last week at 5:20 a.m. (Polish time) Friday, September 1, when a German bombing plane dropped a projectile on Puck, fishing village and air base in the armpit of the Hel Peninsula. At 5:45 a.m. the German training ship *Schleswig-Holstein* lying off Danzig fired what was believed to be the first shell: a direct hit on the Polish ungerground ammunition dump at Westerplatte. It was a grey day, with gentle rain.

In the War's first five days, hundreds of Nazi bombing planes dumped ton after ton of explosive on every city of any importance the length & breadth of Poland. They aimed at air bases, fortifications, bridges, railroad lines and stations, but in the process they killed upward of 1,500 noncombatants. The Nazi ships were mostly big Heinkels, unaccompanied by pursuit escorts. Germany admitted losing 21 planes to Polish counterattack by pursuits and antiaircraft.

The broad outlines of Germany's assault began to take shape. Recapture of what was Germany in 1914 was the first objective: Danzig, the Corridor, and a hump of upper Silesia. It is believed that Adolf Hitler, if allowed to take this much, might have checked his juggernaut at these lines. When Britain & France insisted that he withdraw entirely from Polish soil, he determined on the complete subjugation of Poland.

POLISH VILLAGE ATTACKED
Hitler was a man perhaps mad

GERMANY
Hitler's Decision

All week sombre-faced Germans filed past the huge new building that Adolf Hitler built as a symbol of Germany's might. It was a housepainter's dream of a Reichschancellery, nearly a quarter-mile long, with marble chambers and vast, tapestry-hung halls and an immense study in which a man might feel alone with his destiny. For the seven most momentous days of Europe's modern history Adolf Hitler did not leave this building.

Alone in spirit, the man whose word meant peace or war pondered his decision. He slept little, ate little, spoke little. He rose promptly at seven o'clock each morning, put on his brown uniform, breakfasted on fruit, zwieback and a glass of milk. Throughout the day he conferred endlessly, stopping for 20-minute meals of vegetables, bread-&-butter and his special 1% beer. For half an hour in the morning, and again in the afternoon, he strolled through the Chancellery gardens, usually with Göring, Hess or von Ribbentrop. Until far into the night he talked with these confidants, leaving then for bed at four or five in the morning. Whenever a decision was needed, he went off to brood alone.

Thursday night the strange man whom no one understood sat alone in his study, a portrait of Bismarck looking down at him from the opposite wall. Outside, his lieutenants waited. Berlin grew sleepy, went to bed. Before the Chancellery two stiff sentries stood mute. The night wore on; milk wagons began to rattle through the streets. Through the long French windows leading from the study into the Chancellery garden blew an early morning breeze. Adolf Hitler picked up a pen. At 5:11 o'clock in the morning of Sept. 1 Germany was at war.

Slaves

The platform of the railroad station of Lublin, in German Poland, teemed. On it stood a forlorn, broken-spirited crowd of Jews who moved only when shoved. They were utterly destitute. All they had for baggage was here a knapsack, there a handbag, sometimes just a cloth bundle. Gradually the Jews were herded from the station and put to work twelve hours a day.

Lublin was recently chosen by Adolf Hitler as the site of his long-planned Jew-sump. By next April 1, according to a German government decree, 650,000 Jews must be evacuated to Lublin or other "reservations" like it.

ELEANOR ROOSEVELT

WENDELL WILLKIE

WINSTON CHURCHILL

THE WARRIORS

As today's news recedes into tomorrow's history, the face of warfare past takes on a romantic hue; words like valor and glory seem appropriate. General Pershing's pursuit of Pancho Villa plays in our minds like an episode from the Old West, and the great names of World War II (a term coined by TIME) have already assumed fixed places in a pantheon: Montgomery and Rommel, MacArthur and Yamamoto. But the implacable images of Generals William Westmoreland and Ho Chi Minh are still close enough in memory to stir mixed emotions, proof that only time can make old enmities — like old soldiers — fade away.

Gen. John Pershing
1924

Paul von Hindenburg
1926

Gen. Georgy Zhukov
1942

Claire L. Chennault
1943

Mauldin's "Willie"
1945

Josip Broz Tito
1946

GEN. FRANCISCO FRANCO
1937

ADMIRAL YAMAMOTO
1941

GEN. DOUGLAS MACARTHUR
1941

FIELD MARSHALL ROMMEL
1942

LT. GEN. GEORGE PATTON
1943

SIR BERNARD MONTGOMERY
1943

LT. GEN. OMAR BRADLEY
1944

MAJ. GEN. CURTIS LEMAY
1945

HO CHI MINH
1954

GEN. WILLIAM WESTMORELAND
1966

LANCE CPL. THOMAS JENKINS
1991

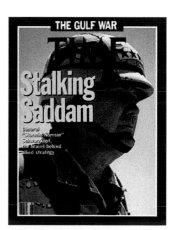

GEN. NORMAN SCHWARZKOPF
1991

1940s

CIT ARCHIVE

The Genius

Of all the strange things that the Easter Island idols have looked out upon through the ages, the strangest was preparing last week. A world, with the power of universal suicide at last within its grasp, was about to make its first scientific test of that power. During the earliest favorable weather after July 1, two atom bombs would be exploded at Bikini Island.

Against the peaceful backdrop of palm frond and pandanus, on this most "backward" of islands, the most progressive of centuries would write in one blinding stroke of disintegration the inner meaning of technological civilization: all matter is speed and flame.

Through the incomparable blast and flame, there will be dimly discernible, to those who are interested in cause & effect in history, the features of a shy, almost saintly, childlike little man with the soft brown eyes, the drooping facial lines of a world-weary hound, and hair like an aurora borealis. He is Professor Albert Einstein.
July 1, 1946

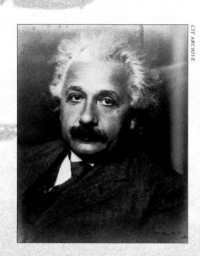

The Thirty-Second

Sam Rayburn had just poured the Vice President a drink of bourbon and tap water when there was a call from the White House. As he listened, Harry Truman's face turned pale. He left abruptly, saying not a word. But his sudden action spoke loudly enough. Every man in the room knew that Franklin Roosevelt's health had been swiftly declining. Said Sam Rayburn before the Vice President got to the door, "We'll all stand by you, Harry."

Harry Truman had been haunted for weeks by the prospect that he might one day soon be President. For more than a month he had had a secret service guard in case of the emergency that had now come.

Speeding down Pennsylvania Avenue in a White House car, Harry Truman, hard-working product of small-town Missouri, had little time to think of the sudden turn of fate. He had dreaded the burden that might be laid on him. Now it was here.
April 23, 1945

Battle of Britain

Winston Churchill is tough. The first important thing he does when he is awakened at 7:15 every morning is light a cigar. His mind requires and retains whole libraries of facts. His spirit loves good food, good drink, pretty and witty women. His body tolerates terrific burdens. He wears out whole squads of secretaries. He talks down platoons of men who have hated and now love him. He knows no fear. During air raids he often rushes into the gardens of No. 10 with no protection but a "battle bowler." He loves life and liberty so much that he has nearly killed and thoroughly enslaved himself a hundred times over in the past six months.

Winston Churchill is a Tory, an imperialist, and has been a strike-breaker and Red-baiter; and yet,

when he tours the gutted slums of London, old women say: "Gor bless you, Winnie."

As the Luftwaffe continued to come over in short nuisance raids and careful military attacks during the day, and in long merciless strangulation by night, Britain's leaders grew more & more concerned about the discomfort and discontent of little people. If anyone could hold their confidence, it was old Winnie. His fond grip on them grew every hour. Rich and poor alike paid him honor. Britain felt that it was cornered, but that Winnie would find a fence to climb over and a mine to hide in.
September 30, 1940

Promise Fulfilled

In the captain's cabin of the 77-ft. PT-41 he lay on the tiny bunk, beaten, burning with defeat. Corregidor was doomed and with it the Philippines, but one leading actor in the most poignant tragedy in U.S. military history would be missing when the curtain fell. Douglas MacArthur, Field Marshal of the Philippine Army, four-star General in the U.S. Army, had left the stage. It was the order of his Commander in Chief.

That was in mid-March 1942. The MacArthur who flew into Australia then was the picture of what had happened to the U.S. in the Pacific. But he was not really beaten. In Adelaide he made the promise that the U.S., bewildered and shaken by the Japs' victorious campaign, heard with renewed hope, "I came through — and I shall return."

Last week, on the flag bridge of the 10,000-ton, 614-ft. light cruiser *Nashville*, stood a proud, erect figure in freshly pressed khaki. He had slept well, eaten a hearty breakfast. Now with his corncob pipe he pointed over the glassy, green waters of Leyte (rhymes with 8-A) Gulf, where rode the greatest fleet ever assembled in the Southwest Pacific. Douglas MacArthur had come back to the Philippines, as he had promised.
October 30, 1944

The Groaner

Casual, talented, and loaded with Irish luck, Bing Crosby has shed a confusing new light on the problem of how to be a success. He has never studied music or voice or pounded the pavements looking for work; yet jobs kept turning up — each a little better than the last. He always falls uphill. Year after year he just sings, and people pay fortunes to hear him.

That Bing Crosby's voice is America's favorite depends upon the fact that it not only sounds good, but that Crosby sings every song as though he felt it was the best song ever written. And characteristically, the happy-go-lucky Groaner manages to convey the impression that anyone could do the trick. Says he: "A crooner gets his quota of sentimentality with half his natural voice. That's a great saving. I don't like to work."
April 7, 1941

Louis the First

Louis Armstrong and New Orleans jazz grew up together. Louis says: "Jazz and I grew up side by side when we were poor." The wonder is that both jazz and Louis emerged from streets of brutal poverty and professional vice — jazz to become an exciting art, Louis to be hailed almost without dissent as its greatest creator-practitioner. Playing without written arrangements, bending the melody around on his own, then blending in with the others when the clarinet or trombone soars off on the lead, Louis has wrung raves even from long-haired critics.

MARGARET BOURKE-WHITE

New Musical in Manhattan

Oklahoma! pretty much deserves its exclamation point. A folk musical laid in the Indian territory just after the turn of the century, it is thoroughly refreshing without being oppressively rustic. It boasts no musicomedy names and nothing much in the way of a book. But Composer Richard Rodgers (working for the first time in his Broadway career without Lyricist Lorenz Hart) has turned out one of his most attractive scores and Choreographer Agnes de Mille has created some delightful dances. Even run-of-de-Mille dances have more style and imaginativeness than most Broadway routines, while the best are almost in a different world. If, compared to Lorenz Hart's at their best, Oscar Hammerstein's lyrics lack polish, so after all did frontier Oklahoma.
April 12, 1943

A generation of quibbling, cult-minded critical *cognoscenti* has called New Orleans jazz many things, from "a rich and frequently dissonant poly-phony" to "this dynamism (which) interprets life at its maximum inten-sity." But Louis grins wickedly and says: "Man, when you got to ask what it is, you'll never get to know."

At London's Palladium, King George V did Armstrong the honor of attending in person. Louis repaid the compliment with a grinning bow to the royal box: "This one's for you, Rex."
February 21, 1949

Rookie of the Year

He looks awkward, but isn't. He stops and starts as though turned off & on with a toggle switch. He seems to hit a baseball on the dead run. Once in motion, he wobbles along, elbows flying, hips swaying, shoul-ders rocking — creating the illusion that he will fly to pieces with every stride. But once he gains momentum his shoulders come to order and his feet skim along like flying fish. He is not only jack-rabbit fast, but about one thought and two steps ahead of every base-runner in the business. In the toughest first season any ballplayer has ever faced, Jackie Roosevelt Robinson has made good as a major leaguer, and proved him-self as a man.
September 22, 1947

1940

The German onslaught seemed unstoppable; Norway, Denmark, and the Low Countries all fell, and air raids destroyed much of London.

PREHISTORIC WALL PAINTINGS WERE DISCOVERED IN LASCAUX, FRANCE ■ JACK DEMPSEY RETIRED FROM THE RING ■ FDR WAS REELECTED FOR AN UNPRECEDENTED THIRD TERM ■ LILLIAN HELLMAN'S "WATCH ON THE RHINE" WAS PRODUCED ■ AND MICKEY ROONEY LIT UP MOVIE SCREENS AS ALL-AMERICAN ANDY HARDY . . .

CORDELL HULL

ROBERT A. TAFT

MARTIN NIEMÖLLER

CINEMA

Success Story

Hollywood's No. 1 box office bait in 1939 was not Clark Gable, Errol Flynn, or Tyrone Power, but a rope-haired, kazoo-voiced kid with a comic-strip face, who until this week had never appeared in a picture without mugging or over-acting in it. His name (assumed) was Mickey Rooney, and to a large part of the more articulate U.S. cinemaudience, his name was becoming a frequently used synonym for brat.

Nevertheless, Mickey Rooney was no brat to some 24,000 movie exhibitors who (in the annual *Fame-Motion Picture Herald* poll) voted him the man whose pictures keep their houses best filled. Nor did Mickey Rooney seem a brat to his studio, Metro-Goldwyn-Mayer, for whom in 1939 he grossed a box-office total of $30,000,000. They saw Mickey Rooney in bread & butter terms, and as such he was the biggest actor of the year in pictures.

Sonny. Mickey Rooney was born Joe Yule Jr. some 19 years ago on the present site of the Brooklyn Telephone Company building. His mother, née Nell Carter, was a small-time Kansas City vaudevillian when she met up with dancing Joe Yule shortly before World War I, and married him.

Mickey was called Sonny and at seven months Sonny could walk around backstage. At one year he could already say "I'm not going to do that." He was ready to make his debut. He did so by interrupting a serious duet of Sid Gold and Babe Latour. Dressed in his backstage jeans, Mickey brought down the house by ambling out from the wings in the middle of their act and piping *Pal of My Cradle Days*. After that first performance Sonny was in the act.

At three Sonny was wearing specially tailored, midget-sized tuxedos that cost the Yules $5 a suit. At four Sonny was a has-been. Age was robbing him of his infantile cuteness. It took him almost a decade to get it back again.

Meanwhile the Yules separated. Mom, who kept Sonny, found the going hard. One

MICKEY ROONEY
"Sir, I am an actor!"

PETER STACKPOLE

day, with some six or eight other footloose vaudevillians, Mom bundled Sonny and luggage into two automobiles, headed for Hollywood. It was 1925. Sonny was five.

Joe Yule Jr. First effect of Hollywood on Mickey Rooney was to make him resume his rightful name, Joe Yule Jr. Mom got $15 knocked off her rent for taking charge of a bungalow court. Joe Yule Jr. got some small parts, sometimes made as much as $50 a week. But this was small change compared with the dreams Joe Yule Jr. was beginning to dream in the heady Hollywood air.

Afternoons off, Mom and her son, like two characters out of a Theodore Dreiser novel, would go for long bus rides through booming Beverly Hills. Joe promised his Mom a big house some day and a great big car "where you sit inside and the chauffeur sits outside and gets rained on."

Mickey McGuire. Through thick and thin Mom had always been a great newspaper reader. Combing the classified ads one day, she found one asked for a young actor to play black-polled Mickey McGuire in a series of shorts based on Cartoonist Fontaine Fox's *Toonerville Trolley* strip. Mom blackened little Joe's tow head with burnt cork and for the next seven years Joe Yule Jr. made 78 Mickey

McGuire pictures at $200 a picture. He also had his name legally changed to Mickey McGuire. But in 1932 Producer Larry Darmour shelved the series.

Without a job himself Mickey McGuire decided to put his name to work. He planned to take Mickey McGuire on a ten-week vaudeville tour. McGuire never went. For this time Mickey was not only jobless but nameless. Irate Cartoonist Fox had hauled him into court, forced Mickey to relinquish the name McGuire. But Fox could not make him give up Mickey. In a moment of inspiration Mom suggested that Mickey take the surname Looney. Mickey changed it to Rooney.

Mickey Rooney. In 1937, MGM bought a play by Aurania Rouverol called *Skidding*. It was a mild little piece about a small town U.S. family, named Hardy, whose ups and downs were intended to rouse no deeper emotion in theatre-goers than a tender smile through a film of happy tears. MGM proposed to turn *Skidding*, with title changed to *A Family Affair*, into a picture on a rock-bottom budget of less than $200,000.

Mickey had been an MGM contract player ($250 a week top) for a year, and his pert ways and brassy cackle had lent themselves to shows like *Ah Wilderness, A Midsummer Night's Dream, The Devil Is a Sissy*. It did not look to anybody as if the part of Andy Hardy in *A Family Affair* would buy Mom's big car. It was a B picture and got a normal B response. But serials were being done. So MGM made another Hardy picture, and another. The fourth one, *Love Finds Andy Hardy*, was made by the kind of reflex that keeps studios grinding them out.

Nobody was more surprised than MGM officials to wake up one night to find that *Love Finds Andy Hardy* was being enthusiastically received in all the best movie houses. Here was MGM with a serial gold mine on its hands and a surprising new star, an appealing Irish rough-neck who had twined his boyish fingers around the heart strings of U.S. movie-goers.

GARBO MADE HER LAST MOVIE, WHILE RITA HAYWORTH AND GARY COOPER WERE RISING HOLLYWOOD IDOLS ■ THE NATIONAL GALLERY OF ART OPENED IN WASHINGTON ■ RUDOLPH HESS WAS IMPRISONED AFTER A QUIXOTIC FLIGHT TO ENGLAND ■ AND A SQUADRON OF JAPANESE BOMBERS ATTACKED AMERICAN FORCES AT PEARL HARBOR, HAWAII . . .

1941

On advice from Einstein, the U.S. government launched the Manhattan Project of intensive atomic research.

THE U. S. AT WAR

Dec. 7, 1941

It was Sunday midday, clear and sunny. Many a citizen was idly listening to the radio when the flash came that the Japanese had attacked Hawaii. In Topeka they were listening to *The Spirit of '41* and napping on their sofas after dinner. In San Francisco they were listening to the news, the Philharmonic and *Strings in Swingtime.*

Out on the Pacific the great drama of U.S. history was coming to a climax. There was an unanswered question: What would the people, the 132,000,000, say?

The U.S. met the first days of war with incredulity and outrage, with a quick, harsh, nationwide outburst. But the U. S. knew that its first words were not enough.

National Ordeal

The Government and People of the United States declared war on the Japanese Empire at 4: 10 p.m. Monday, Dec. 8, 1941. At dawn the day before, the Japanese had attacked savagely all along the whole great U.S. island-bridge which stretches to the Orient. It was premeditated murder masked by a toothy smile. Instantly on the news from Pearl Harbor, President Roosevelt ordered the Army and Navy: "Fight Back!"

At noon next day the President sat back in the deep cushions of his big closed car, adjusted his big dark Navy cape. The gravel spattered from the driveway, the car moved off slowly around the south lawn, and up the long clear stretch of Pennsylvania Avenue toward the looming dome of the Capitol.

The President moved slowly into the House of Representatives. In the packed, still chamber stood the men & women of the house, the Senate, the Supreme Court, the Cabinet. The heavy applause lingered, gradually began to break into cheers and rebel yells.

Mr. Roosevelt gripped the reading clerk's stand, flipped open his black, loose-leaf schoolboy's notebook. He took a long, steady look at the Congress and the battery of floodlights, and began to read.

"Yesterday, Dec. 7, 1941—a date which will live in infamy—the United States of America was suddenly and deliberately attacked by naval and air forces of the Empire of Japan."

The President left the House. Members began roaring impatiently: "Vote! Vote! Vote!" The Speaker gaveled for order. The Senate left.

The President had arrived at 12:12 p.m. At 1 p.m. exactly the Senate passed the declaration of war, 82-to-0. The House received with

ROOSEVELT IN CONGRESS
"A date which will live in infamy."

a whoop the identical Senate bill. The vote: 388-to-1.

Tragedy at Honolulu

The Japs came in from the southeast over Diamond Head. Civilians' estimates of their numbers ranged from 50 to 150. They whined over Waikiki, over the candy-pink bulk of the Royal Hawaiian Hotel. Some were big four-motored jobs, some dive-bombers, some pursuits. All that they met as they came in was a tiny private plane in which Lawyer Ray Buduick was out for a Sunday morning ride.

They riddled the plane with machine-gun bullets, but the lawyer succeeded in landing. By the time he did, bombs were thudding all around the city. The first reported casualty was Robert Tyce, operator of a civilian airport near Honolulu, who was machine-gunned as he started to spin the propeller of a plane.

Torpedoes launched from bombers tore at the dreadnoughts in Pearl Harbor. Dive-bombers swooped down on the Army's Hickam and Wheeler Fields. All the way from Pacific Heights down to the center of town the planes soared, leaving a wake of destruction.

Obvious to onlookers on the Honolulu hills was the fact that Pearl Harbor was being hit hard. From the Navy's plane base on Ford Island (also known as Luke Field), in the middle of the harbor, clouds of smoke ascended. One citizen who was driving past the naval base saw the first bomb fall on Ford Island.

Said he: "It must have been a big one. I saw two planes dive over the mountains and down to the water and let loose torpedoes at a naval ship. This warship was attacked again & again. I also saw dive-bombers coming over in single file."

When the first ghastly day was over, Honolulu began to reckon up the score. It was one to make the U.S. Navy and Army shudder. Of the 200,000 inhabitants of Oahu, 1,500 were dead, 1,500 others injured. Washington called the naval damage "serious," admitted at least one "old" battleship and a destroyer had been sunk, other ships damaged at base. Meanwhile Japan took to the radio to boast that the U.S. had suffered an "annihilating blow."

CHARLES DEGAULLE

JOE LOUIS

RITA HAYWORTH

1942

Now commonly referring to themselves as the "United Nations," the 26 Allies pledged not to make separate peace treaties with Axis enemies.

ENRICO FERMI SUCCEEDED IN SPLITTING THE ATOM ■ 487 DIED IN THE COCONUT GROVE NIGHTCLUB FIRE IN BOSTON ■ GREER GARSON INSPIRED MILLIONS AS "MRS. MINIVER" ■ MAJ. GENERAL DOOLITTLE BOMBED TOKYO ■ BING CROSBY SANG "WHITE CHRISTMAS" ■ AND DETROIT SWITCHED FROM MANUFACTURING AUTOMOBILES TO TANKS . . .

CHIANG KAI-SHEK

JAMES DOOLITTLE

PIERRE LAVAL

THE U.S. AT WAR

PRODUCTION

Detroit: New Era Begins

At 3:18 of a snowy afternoon, in Flint, Mich., a little knot of men stood around a shiny black Chevrolet coupe in Assembly Plant Number Two. Someone had scrawled on its rear window in white crayon: last Chevrolet off Jan. 30, 1942. A reporter and a veteran Chevrolet workman climbed into the car. The reporter stepped on the starter, drove off the assembly line, turned the lights on & off, honked the horn. The strident little beep, echoing through the acres of suddenly silent machinery, signaled the end of an epoch in U.S. industrial history.

The men grinned, joked, washed up and wandered outside to line up before the pay window. A passing workman gave the last Chevrolet an affectionate kick in the rear — as if he might be a farmer slapping an old horse. They knew that a chapter in their lives was over. Some current of emotion—half-abashed, self-conscious, a sentiment that seemed a little ridiculous when dedicated to inanimate machinery — moved through the crowd, finding its outlet in the horseplay, the offhand talk, the what-the-hells with which American workmen cover up what they feel.

It was the same thing at Dodge, at Plymouth, at Pontiac. Throughout the vast automobile industry, except for a few isolated plants still winding up their quotas, civilian manufacture had ended — and no one knew when it would begin again.

This end meant also a beginning, of something greater than anything Detroit has seen in the 40-odd years of the motor industry. The industry had literally died and was being reborn—new, bigger, and completely different.

For 200,000 or 250,000 auto workers it meant a layoff before arms production could employ them — and last week Detroit argued about how long that would be. The workmen themselves, used to seasonal layoffs, confident of the power of the industry to re-hire

IN DETROIT
Workmen wheel the last passenger auto from the Plymouth assembly lines, as the auto industry clears its floors for the war production program ahead

them, were not greatly worried — their estimates ran from two weeks to two months.

Except to eyewitnesses, except by translating statistics that could not even be quoted in wartime, it was impossible to communicate the extent of the change that was sweeping Detroit.

Last week some 20 top-flight newspapermen rushed from plant to plant to view the outward evidences of that change. From 9 in the morning until dusk they raced from plant to plant in cars that moved at 70 m.p.h. They grabbed lunch on the way from the tank arsenal to the River Rouge plant. They saw, on the outskirts of Detroit, where a cornfield flourished a few months ago, a tank factory where huge sections of armor plate and steel castings moved down a production line five miles long.

Ernest Kanzler, onetime Ford production chief, last week held his first press conference. It was unexciting. Said Mr. Kanzler: "I am here only to serve as the catalyst" — which means, said hard-boiled newspapermen, that he would be the gadfly to spur dunderheaded laggards into speed-up. Much of the U.S. public had expected Kanzler to announce resoundingly that the automobile industry would

forthwith be converted to defense. But Detroit knew that the industry was already converted.

General Motors expects to employ 450,000 persons (previous top: 303,000); Ford — 200,000, including 25,000 women among the 100,000 employees of its bomber plant; Chrysler — 130,000 compared to its previous high of 65,000. The correspondents wrote about production lines miles long . . . Chrysler making at least $675,000,000 worth of tanks, planes, and guns in 1942 . . . Ford with eleven miles of airplane runways at Willow Run . . .

Detroit knew that the war production effort was succeeding. In the arms factories, where morale was high, the men knew that so many tanks already had been built, so many planes, so many guns. But it was Detroit's misfortune that the rest of the country did not know and could not be adequately told the terrific things that Detroit was doing. Before Pearl Harbor, the nation had been given cruelly revealing figures about how badly production had gone. After Pearl Harbor, with industry taking seven-league strides, the figures of accomplishment were military secrets. Industry had taken the past blame, but it was not given the credit it now deserves.

HEPCATS WORE ZOOT SUITS AND DANCED THE JITTERBUG ■ THE U.S. INITIATED WIDESPREAD FOOD RATIONING ■ BETTY SMITH POIGNANTLY DESCRIBED CITY CHILDHOOD IN *A TREE GROWS IN BROOKLYN* ■ ITALY SURRENDERED AND ENTERED THE WAR AGAINST GERMANY ■ AND BOB HOPE BEGAN A LEGENDARY CAREER OF "ENTERTAINING THE TROOPS" . . .

1943

The tide turned for the Allies: Germans surrendered at Stalingrad and the RAF raided Berlin.

THE THEATER

Hope for Humanity

For fighting men, this grimmest of wars is in one small way also the gayest. Never before have the folks who entertain the boys been so numerous or so notable; never have they worked so hard, traveled so far, risked so much. In the Middle East last week were Jack Benny, Larry Adler and his harmonica, Al Jolson with a harmonium; Ray Bolger was in the South Pacific, Judith Anderson in Hawaii. A while back Martha Raye went to the fox-holes of Tunisia; and in New Guinea a show went on within earshot of the Japs. From the ranks of show business have sprung heroes and even martyrs, but so far only one legend.

That legend is Bob Hope. It sprang up swiftly, telepathically, among U.S. servicemen in Britain this summer, traveling faster than even whirlwind Hope himself, then flew ahead of him to North Africa and Sicily, growing larger as it went. Like most legends, it represents measurable qualities in a kind of mystical blend. Hope was funny, treating hordes of soldiers to roars of laughter. He was friendly — ate with servicemen, drank with them, read their doggerel, listened to their songs. He was indefatigable, running himself ragged with five, six, seven shows a day. He was figurative — the straight link with home, the radio voice that for years had filled the living room and that in foreign parts called up its image. Hence boys whom Hope might entertain for an hour awaited him for weeks. And when he came, anonymous guys who had had no other recognition felt personally remembered.

Head & Heart

This tearing trip — about 250 camp and hospital shows in eleven weeks — was no floodlighted 100-yd. dash, but just a fast lap in a very long race. In 1941 Hope got an Oscar "for humanity," for a record-breaking 562 benefits in two years. Probably the first entertainer to work with the armed forces, Hope has also been the most frequent. Using trains, cars, trucks, tanks, jeeps, Hope has played in virtually every U.S. camp, last fall hopped off with his USO team (Singer Frances Langford, Guitarist Tony Romano, Comic Jerry Colonna) to tour Alaska. When, at the last moment, it looked as if the tour would fall through Hope wired Lieut. General Simon B. Buckner: WE SING, DANCE, TELL STORIES; HAVE TUXEDOS; WILL TRAVEL; CAN WE PLAY YOUR CIRCUIT? They played it straight through to tiny posts in the Aleutians, where men almost never get leave.

But the British circuit was tougher, with Hope & Company (Comic Jack Pepper substituting for Jerry Colonna) "resting" from camp shows by bobbing up in hospitals, dropping in on ack-ack crews, sloshing across rain-swept heaths to entertain soldiers on maneuvers. Hope's gags got around so fast he had to keep changing them, and he and Scriptwriter Hal Block ground out new ones in bumpy transit, or in hotel rooms long past midnight.

There was one camp Hope did not get to — so to catch his performance 600 men tramped ten miles across the moors, could not get within earshot, started tramping back again. After the show Hope heard about them, tossed his gang into jeeps, overtook the hikers, and, in a drenching downpour, clowned for 40 minutes.

Last week Hope was back home again to resume another life in which he is tops. Between radio and cinema, he bests all rivals as a double-draw; the name Hope has become a radio synonym for Tuesday night, has helped make the *Road to Morocco* almost as famous as the *Road to Mandalay*. Yet his huge mike-and-movie success is less than a lustrum old. And it is so huge it obliterates all memory of Hope as a vaudeville headliner and a Broadway star.

But vaudeville is the key to Hope, even though he has recently had the lock changed. He is first & foremost a gag man, with a gag man's brash ability to keep moving, ad-lib, hit back; above all, with a gag man's sense of timing. Says Hope: "I was born with timing and coordination." Artistically he was born with little else — no special trick of speech, gift of pantomime, sense of character. Quite intrinsically, indeed, he was born with a kind of strenuous averageness — which paradoxically has managed to set him apart.

MADAME CHIANG

POPE PIUS XII

DWIGHT D. EISENHOWER

© 1942, SAMUEL GOLDWYN, ALL RIGHTS RESERVED

DOROTHY LAMOUR & BOB HOPE

GERMAN OFFICERS ATTEMPTED THE ASSASSINATION OF HITLER ■ ALLIES LANDED ON D-DAY ■ THE LAST MAJOR NAZI OFFENSIVE OCCURRED AT THE BATTLE OF THE BULGE ■ TENNESSEE WILLIAMS' "THE GLASS MENAGERIE" WAS STAGED ■ V-1 AND V-2 ROCKETS WERE FIRED ON ENGLAND ■ AND PENICILLIN PROMISED A MEDICAL REVOLUTION . . .

OVETA CULP HOBBY

ERNIE PYLE

EDGAR BERGEN AND CHARLIE MCCARTHY

MEDICINE

20th Century Seer

Medical news last week vied with news of the days before an invasion. Under the aspect of eternity, the medical news might even be more important than the military. The War Production Board announced that the wonder drug penicillin, for three years practically a monopoly of the Army & Navy, was now being manufactured in such quantity that it can be issued to civilians. Some 1,000 hospitals will be allowed to buy generous monthly quotas for distribution to patients and other hospitals. For impatient sufferers (many of them dying), the good news came none too soon. Penicillin (sometimes rhymes with villain, sometimes with whistle in) is the best treatment for all staphylococcic infections, all hemolytic streptococcic infections, pneumococcic infections (of the lining of the skull, spinal cord, lung and heart surfaces), pneumococcic pneumonia that sulfa drugs will not cure, all gonococcic infections (including all gonorrhea that sulfa drugs will not cure). Diseases against which penicillin is effective but not fully tested: syphilis, actinomycosis, bacterial endocarditis.

The man who made possible this incalculable alleviation of human suffering is Dr. Alexander Fleming, discoverer of the antibacterial effect of the mold from which penicillin is made. He is a short (5 ft. 7 in.), gentle, retiring Scot with somewhat dreamy blue eyes, fierce white hair and a mulling mind, which, when it moves, moves with the thrust of a cobra. Until time's solvent has dissolved the human slag, it will be hard to say who the great men of the 20th Century are. But Dr. Alexander Fleming is almost certainly one of them. For he belongs in the tradition of the scientific seers, which includes Galileo watching the swing of a lamp in the Cathedral of Pisa and deducing from it the law of the pendulum, and Isaac Newton watching the fall of an apple and deducing from it the law of gravity. For thousands of years men looked at the crypto-gamic mold called *Penicillium notatum*, but Dr. Fleming was the first to see its meaning. His discernment, restoring to science the creative vision which it has sometimes been held to lack, restored health to millions of men living and unborn.

The story of his discovery is legendary.

PENICILLIN IN THE MAKING
Like Galileo watching the lamp

Back in 1928 Alexander Fleming taught bacteriology at St. Mary's Hospital Medical School, University of London. In his small, old-fashioned laboratory, he grew staphylococci in petri plates (flat glass culture dishes). One day he found that mold had spoiled one of his cultures. Staphylococci grew on only half of the plate. A blue-green mold spotted, but did not cover, the other half. He noticed that the mold had cleared a wide, bacteria-free area between itself and the staphylococci—perhaps had killed them.

Next year what Dr. Fleming knew about the mold's bacteria-baiting by-product appeared in the British *Journal of Experimental Pathology*. He had found out that the mold was some kind of Penicillium (from the Latin for pencil—the shape of the magnified mold). He named its by-product penicillin. Having made his great discovery, Dr. Fleming went on to other work. He was engaged in many other experiments—no scientist knows just which of his bottles contains the Nobel Prize.

By 1938 when World War II loomed, a good internal and external antiseptic was still to seek. But at Oxford's Sir William Dunn School of Pathology, the man who was to make Dr. Fleming's discovery save human lives was already at work on the problem. He was Dr. Howard Walter Florey, 45, an Australian-born professor of pathology.

At first, Dr. Florey's researchers got only about a gram of reddish-brown powder (the sodium salt of penicillin) from 100 liters of the mold liquid. But at last, after heroic chemical cookery, they accumulated enough penicillin to test the drug on living creatures.

Eight mice were inoculated with a deadly strain of streptococci. Says Dr. Florey: "We sat up through the night injecting penicillin every three hours into the treated group. I must confess that it was one of the more exciting moments when we found in the morning that all the untreated mice were dead and all the penicillin-treated ones alive." The first human guinea pig was a policeman dying of staphylococcus septicemia(blood infection). After five days on penicillin, he "felt much improved."

To Dr. Fleming, whose pioneer mind has reverted to watching and waiting, penicillin is not an end, but a beginning. There are at least 100,000 molds and fungi, any one of which may one day yield a drug with which to cure many plagues penicillin leaves untouched. "It would be strange indeed," says Dr. Fleming, who is hard at work on other antibiotics, "if the first one described remained the best."

A B-25 BOMBER STRUCK THE EMPIRE STATE BUILDING ■ WAR IN EUROPE ENDED DAYS AFTER HITLER'S SUICIDE IN BERLIN ■ FDR DIED AND WAS SUCCEEDED BY TRUMAN ■ ROCKY GRAZIANO WAS NAMED "BOXER OF THE YEAR" ■ THE NUREMBURG WAR-CRIMES TRIALS BEGAN ■ AND WITH THE DROPPING OF BOMBS OVER JAPAN, THE WORLD'S ATOMIC AGE BEGAN . . .

1945

The full extent of Nazi atrocities was revealed, with the estimate of concentration camp deaths placed at 10 million.

THE U. S. AT WAR

THE PEACE

The Bomb

The greatest and most terrible of wars ended, this week, in the echoes of an enormous event—an event so much more enormous that, relative to it, the war itself shrank to minor significance. In what they said and did, men were still, as in the after shock of a great wound, bemused and only semi-articulate, whether they were soldiers or scientists, or great statesmen, or the simplest of men. But in the dark depths of their minds and hearts, huge forms moved and silently arrayed themselves: Titans, arranging out of the chaos an age in which victory was already only the shout of a child in the street.

With the controlled splitting of the atom, humanity, already profoundly perplexed and disunified, was brought inescapably into a new age. The race had been won, the weapon had been used by those on whom civilization could best hope to depend; but the demonstration of power against living creatures instead of dead matter created a bottomless wound in the living conscience of the race. The rational mind had won the most Promethean of its conquests over nature, and had put into the hands of common man the fire and force of the sun itself.

Was man equal to the challenge? In an instant, without warning, the present had become the unthinkable future. Was there hope in that future, and if so, where did hope lie?

When the bomb split open the universe and revealed the prospect of the infinitely extraordinary, it also revealed the oldest, simplest, commonest, most neglected and most important of facts: that each man is eternally and above all else responsible for his own soul.

My God!

The run was short and straight. At 9:15 a.m. Major Thomas Ferebee pressed the toggle and the single bomb was away, down through the substratosphere. Colonel Paul Warfield Tibbets, the pilot, took back the controls and ten pairs of eyes strained at the plexiglass windows as Tibbets turned the plane broadside to the city of Hiroshima.

It took less than 60 seconds. Then the brilliant morning sunlight was slashed by a more brilliant white flash. It was so strong that the crew of the Superfortress *Enola Gay* felt a

ATOMIC BOMB OVER JAPAN
The most Promethean of conquests

"visual shock," although all wore sun glasses.

A few seconds after the flash, the shock wave from the blast reached the *Enola Gay,* several miles away, and rocked it like a giant burst of flak. From the men who had rung up the curtain on a new era in history burst nothing more original than an awed "My God!"

Hiroshima had once harbored 344,000 people. Reconnaissance photographs showed 4.1 square miles—60% of the city's built up area—destroyed by fire and blast. There was no crater in which the blast effect would have been largely wasted; the bomb had exploded well above ground. How many tens of thousands of Hiroshima's people had perished was not yet and might never be known.

Three days later, the Superfort *Great Artiste* was out on a similar mission. Major Charles W. Sweeney had a rough trip to Japan in bad weather; his primary target was socked in. Over the second choice target, Nagasaki, he had just enough gas left for one run. This bomb was even more powerful than the one dropped on Hiroshima, so much of an improvement that the first bomb was obsolete.

We Interrupt This Program . . .

When the first news of Japan's surrender came to the fighting fronts, G.I.s yelled wildly, pounded backs, fired guns, drank hoarded whiskey. On Okinawa the night was lighted by millions of tracer bullets as men fired rifles, machine guns, antiaircraft guns. Green and yellow flares glared in the darkness. Ships off shore, fearing a *Kamikaze* attack, laid down a smoke screen, opened up with antiaircraft guns. Veterans had seen nothing like it during the whole battle for the islands. The celebration had tragic consequences: six men were killed, 30 wounded.

Manila echoed as soldiers drove jeeps and trucks madly through the dusty streets, blowing horns, beating on fenders with iron pipe. Over the din sounded the shrill voices of children screaming: "Beectory . . . beectory . . ."

The great Cunard liner Queen Elizabeth approached New York harbor with a captured Nazi flag flying at her main mast, an effect achieved by laughing, shouting soldiers. Manhattan's excitable garment workers threw tons of paper and cloth shreds into the streets.

SERGEI PROKOFIEV

EMPEROR HIROHITO

WALTER REUTHER

1946

As governments in Eastern Europe fell one by one to Communist rule, Churchill delivered his "Iron Curtain" speech.

THE U.N. GENERAL ASSEMBLY HELD ITS FIRST SESSION IN LONDON ■ TRUMAN CREATED THE ATOMIC ENERGY COMMISSION ■ ETHEL MERMAN WORE BUCKSKINS IN "ANNIE GET YOUR GUN" ■ AN "ELECTRONIC BRAIN" WAS ASSEMBLED AT PENNSYLVANIA UNIVERSITY ■ AND A PEERLESS VOICE WAS HEARD IN THE OPEN AIR AT THE LINCOLN MEMORIAL . . .

CARDINAL SPELMAN

DANNY KAYE

HENRY WALLACE

RELIGION

In Egypt Land

Go tell it on the mountain,
Over the hills and everywheah;
Go tell it on the mountain,
That Jesus Christ is aborn.

At Salzburg, backdropped by magical mountains, where Austria's great musical festivals were held before the war, and where he first heard Marian Anderson sing, Arturo Toscanini cried: "Yours is a voice such as one hears once in a hundred years."

Toscanini was hailing a great artist, but that voice was more than a magnificent personal talent. It was the religious voice of a whole religious people — probably the most God-obsessed (and man-despised) people since the ancient Hebrews.

White Americans had withheld from Negro Americans practically everything but God. In return the Negroes had enriched American culture with an incomparable religious poetry and music, and its only truly great religious art — the spiritual.

This religious and esthetic achievement of Negro Americans has found profound expression in Marian Anderson. She is not only the world's greatest contralto and one of the very great voices of all time, she is also a dedicated character, devoutly simple, calm, religious.

Up from Philadelphia. Thanks to the ostracism into which they are born, Negro Americans live very deeply to themselves. They look out upon, and shrewdly observe, the life around them, are rarely observed by it. They are not evasive about their lives; many are simply incapable of discussing them.

The known facts about Marian Anderson's personal life are few. She was born (in Philadelphia) some 40 years ago (she will not tell her age). Her mother had been a schoolteacher in Virginia. Her father was a coal & ice dealer. There were two younger sisters.

When she was twelve, her father died. To keep the home together, Mrs. Anderson went to work. Miss Anderson says that the happiest moment of her life came the day that she was able to tell her mother to stop working. Later she bought her mother a two-story brick house on Philadelphia's South Martin Street. She bought the house next door for one of her sisters.

Miss Anderson's childhood seems to have been as untroubled as is possible to Negro Americans. In part, this was due to the circumstances of her birth, family, and natural gift. In part, it was due to the calm with which she surmounts all unpleasantness. If there were shadows, she never mentions them. Perhaps the most characteristic fact about her childhood is that Marian disliked bright colors and gay dresses as much as her sisters loved them.

Shortly after her father's death, Marian Anderson was "converted." Her mother is a Methodist. But Marian was converted in her father's Union Baptist Church, largely because the late Rev. Wesley G. Parks was deeply interested in music, loved his choirs and encouraged any outstanding singer in them. At 13, Marian was singing in the church's adult choir. She took home the scores, and sang all the parts (soprano, alto, tenor, bass) over & over to her family until she had learned them. Since work is also a religion to her, Miss Anderson considers this one of the most important experiences of her life. She could then sing high C like a soprano.

At 15, she took her first formal music lesson. At 16, she gave her first important concert, at a Negro school in Atlanta. From then on, her life almost ceases to be personal. It is an individual achievement, but, as with every Negro, it is inseparable from the general achievement of her people. It was the congregation of the Union Baptist Church that gave Miss Anderson her start. Then a group of interested music lovers gave a concert at her church, collected about $500 to pay for training her voice under the late Philadelphia singing teacher, Giuseppe Boghetti.

In 1924, she won the New York Stadium contest (prize: the right to appear with the New York Symphony Orchestra). In 1930, she decided that she must study in Germany. When she had perfected her lieder, songs by Schubert, Brahms, Wolf, she gave her first concert on the Continent. It cost her $500 (the Germans explained that it was customary for Americans to pay for their own concerts). She never paid again.

Applause followed her through Norway and Sweden. In Finland, Composer Jean Sibelius offered her coffee, but after hearing her sing, cried: "Champagne!" In Paris, her first house was "papered." From her second concert, enthusiasts were turned away in droves. She swept through South America.

The Trouble I've Seen. In the U.S. the ovation continued. Only one notably ugly incident marred her triumph. In Washington, the management of Constitution Hall, owned by the Daughters of the American Revolution, announced that it would be unable to lease the hall on the date which Sol Hurok, Miss Anderson's manager, had asked for. The refusal resulted in Eleanor Roosevelt's resignation from the D.A.R. and an enormous ground swell of sympathy for Miss Anderson and her people. Miss Anderson, who has carefully kept herself and her art from being used for political purposes, said nothing.

But Washington heard her. She sang, first in the open air in front of the Lincoln Memorial. Later, the D.A.R. leased her Constitution Hall, and she sang to a brilliant white and Negro audience. She had insisted only that there should be no segregation in the seating. Nobody knows the trouble that an incident like this one causes to a spirit like Marian Anderson's. No doubt such things are in her mind when she ways, with typical understatement: "Religion, the treasure of religion helps one, I think, to face the difficulties one sometimes meets."

INDIAN INDEPENDENCE TOOK EFFECT ■ CONGRESS PASSED THE TAFT-HARTLEY ACT, RESTRICTING LABOR UNION RIGHTS ■ *THE DIARY OF ANNE FRANK* WAS PUBLISHED ■ THE DEAD SEA SCROLLS WERE DISCOVERED ■ THEATRE AUDIENCES WERE CAUGHT UP IN THE MAGIC OF "BRIGADOON" ■ AND THE MARSHALL PLAN PROMISED POSTWAR ASSISTANCE TO EUROPE . . .

1947

The modern age of electronics was born, as scientists at Bell Laboratories announced the invention of the transistor.

NATIONAL AFFAIRS

FOREIGN RELATIONS

Challenge & Response

An outrage! The words were President Harry Truman's. He meant the Communist seizure of Hungary. It was no ill-considered, uncalculated outburst. The President had a week to prepare his answer to Russia's challenge of the Truman Doctrine. Warned the President: the U.S. will not stand idly by.

Before the day was out, George Marshall struck at one of Russia's most sensitive nerves. At Harvard's commencement exercises, where he accepted an honorary doctorate of laws, the Secretary of State answered the Russian challenge by urging an economically integrated Europe. Europe must get together on its needs. Henceforth, U.S. help would be on a Europe-wide, not a nation-by-nation, basis.

Said Marshall: "Our policy is directed not against any country or doctrine but against hunger, poverty, desperation and chaos. Its purpose should be the revival of a working economy in the world . . . Such assistance must not be on a piecemeal basis as various crises develop.

"Any government that is willing to assist in the task of recovery will find full co-operation on the part of the U.S."

"With Both Hands"

"When the Marshall proposals were announced," said Ernie Bevin in Britain last week, "I grabbed them with both hands."

So did Europe.

To the French, Marshall's intimation that the U.S. was at last going to seek "a cure rather than a . . . palliative" for Europe's troubles was the best news since the Allies landed in Normandy. It mattered little that *le plan Marshall* was vague. "Today there is something new in the lives of Frenchmen," breathed President of the Republic Vincent Auriol.

As for the Russians, they seemed to be in a box, for once. If they joined Britain, France,

and the rest of Europe in really working for a continental recovery plan, they would be conforming to U.S. initiative; if they stalled and sabotaged, the responsibility for a divided and impoverished Europe would fall on the Kremlin.

For three hours last week Bevin and British Ambassador Duff-Cooper sat in low armchairs overlooking the British Embassy gardens in Paris, comparing notes. Then Premier Paul Ramadier and dapper, London-tailored Foreign Minister Georges Bidault arrived with their experts. Eleven French and eleven Brit-

SECRETARY MARSHALL OFFERS HOPE
"Against hunger, poverty, chaos."

ons got their heads together over the veal, adjourned to the garden veranda later for whiskey, brandy, and more happy talk.

Bevin flew back to London two days later and [made] a memorable speech in the House of Commons. Pounding a dispatch box with his heavy hands, Bevin said: "'The reply of the Soviet Government is awaited . . . [but] I shall not be a party to holding up the economic recovery of Europe by the finesse of procedure." The immediate problems of Europe were "food, coal, transport, houses, opportunities for a decent life."

Pas de Pagaille!

The committees to study Europe's needs and resources under the "Marshall approach" got down to work this week in the Grand Palais, one of the few really ugly buildings in the center of Paris.

Coal was the central issue at Paris. And coal meant the Ruhr and Germany. Without Ruhr coal, and without the German industrial output which depends on Ruhr coal, the rest of Europe cannot recover. To help remedy that paralysis, the U.S. last week issued a new directive to Germany's occupation chief, General Lucius D. Clay, superseding joint Chiefs of Staff Directive 1067 (which had directed the U.S. commander to take "no steps looking toward the economic rehabilitation of Germany"). The new directive said: "An orderly, prosperous Europe requires the economic contributions of a stable and productive Germany." The U.S. suggested that the permissible level of industry in Western Germany be raised by boosting steel production from 5.8 to 12 million tons a year.

When they heard that, the French promptly raised the roof, almost threatened to sabotage the Paris conference. The Communists hastened to aggravate these fears; *L'Humanité* cried: "Let French Mothers Again Tremble!" The British made difficulties too. They did not like a U.S. suggestion that their plans to socialize Ruhr mines be postponed.

Last week, it looked as though many Europeans were far ahead of their own leaders in understanding that it was more important to make the "Marshall approach" work than to keep Germany down. Said Henri-Albert Joinville, 46, a road repair man: "The Marshall plan was quite simple when it started and now the politicians are trying to make it complicated. It is still simple for me. We are in trouble. If we don't get help, there may be anarchy in France. Now let's get ahead. *Pour l'amour de Dieu, pas de pagaille!* [For God's sake, let's not mess around!]."

FRED ALLEN

JACKIE ROBINSON

HAROLD STASSEN

1948

In a move that was to signal an era of Cold War, Soviets halted all surface traffic into Berlin; U.S. and allies responded with an airlift of supplies.

GREAT BRITAIN NATIONALIZED ITS RAILROAD SYSTEM ■ *THE KINSEY REPORT* ON SEXUAL BEHAVIOR WAS PUBLISHED ■ CONGRESS PASSED THE MARSHALL PLAN, PLEDGING $17 BILLION IN AID TO EUROPE ■ THE WORLD COUNCIL OF CHURCHES WAS ORGANIZED IN AMSTERDAM ■ AND A NEW COUNTRY—THE STATE OF ISRAEL—WAS BORN IN THE MIDDLE EAST . . .

GEORGE GALLUP

JOE DI MAGGIO

DR. ROBERT OPPENHEIMER

FOREIGN NEWS

MIDDLE EAST

Birth of a Nation

Boast not thyself of tomorrow for thou knowest not what a day may bring forth.
—Proverbs 27:1

Between one pink dawn and another over the Moabite hills last week came The Day. It brought forth events sufficient to crowd aside the worries of tomorrow. To the Jews of Palestine this day brought a state of their own, the first in 1,878 years. To the British it brought the loss of a 10,460-square-mile base in the Mediterranean and relief from a burden they had snatched up with imperial optimism 31 years ago. To the Arabs, it brought a tautening of determination and a more sober assessing of their chances for victory.

Shortly after sunrise on May 14, the Union Jack flapped down from its staff over Government House, on Jerusalem's Hill of Evil Counsel. Without farewells from Jew or Arab, the British Governor General, tired-looking General Sir Alan Gordon Cunningham, flew to Haifa in an R.A.F. plane. There, at 10:05 a.m., he stepped into a naval launch and was sped out to the light cruiser *Euryalus*. On the dock, a bagpiper skirled the melancholy tune of *The Minstrel Boy*. Precisely at midnight, the *Euryalus* passed the three-mile limit of Palestine's territorial waters. From Royal Navy headquarters atop Mount Carmel a flare shot up, arched slowly, and fell flaming among the tall dark cypresses on the mountain slope. The British mandate had ended.

A few hours after Cunningham left the docks at Haifa, 400 Jews gathered at the Tel Aviv Museum under the watchful eyes of *Haganah* Bren-gunners. The 13 men who would rule the new Jewish state sat down at a long table on a raised dais. Over their heads were white Zionist flags bearing two pale blue stripes and a blue Star of David.

A stocky man with a halo of electric white hair, dressed in a light blue suit and tie and white shirt, fiddled nervously with his glasses and papers, looked frequently at his watch. On the dot of 4 p.m., David Ben-Gurion, first Prime Minister of the Jewish state, banged the table with his fist and began to read. As he reached the words proclaiming "the establishment of the Jewish State in Palestine, to be called Israel," the audience cheered and wept.

RIOTING IN JERUSALEM
An ancient longing fulfilled

In the two hours that remained before sundown, when the Jewish Sabbath would begin, Tel Aviv's jubilant people danced in the streets, paraded with blue-&-white streamers and Star of David flags, prayed in their synagogues, with tears and cheers waved off truckloads of *Haganah* youths headed for the frontiers.

Unhindered now by the British, the refugee ship *Andria* brought 360 immigrants into Haifa. Other ships brought war supplies to Tel Aviv. The new government announced its adherence to the principles of the U.N. Charter. At 21 minutes past midnight, Palestine time, President Truman announced: "The U.S. Government recognizes the provisional government as the *de facto* authority of the new state of Israel."

The long awaited deadline was not greeted by everyone with cheers. Abdullah Ibn-Hussein, King of the Hashimite Kingdom of Transjordan, watched his Arab legion assemble. With the first glimmer of dawn, the troops began to wind down the road to the Jordan Valley in tanks, armored cars and trucks. Their first operations were to occupy villages north and south of Jerusalem.

Still other Arab contingents were on the move. In southern Palestine, Egyptian troops crossed the border into the sandy wastes of the Negeb Desert to seize Jewish settlements on the road to Gaza. In northern Palestine, where *Haganah* was trying to secure the Galilee region, Syrian and Lebanese detachments attacked Jewish settlements. Egyptian air force planes swooped over Tel Aviv in the first strafing and bombing raids of the war. Palestine's native Arabs were panicky, almost leaderless.

Moderate Zionists wanted to make a settlement which would let them go back to the job of building Israel, free of Arab attacks. Already, however, some extremists have been advising the Jews to grab what they could. Last week, *Irgun* Commander Menachim Beigin said that he would stop underground activities in Israel, but he warned that his soldiers would fight for "all" of Palestine including Transjordan, "until the Jewish flag will fly over the Tower of David in Jerusalem and Jewish peasants will work in the fields of Gilead [in Transjordan]." He warned the Israelite government not to make "further concessions" to the Arabs. Arab leaders, for their part, have not yet shown any willingness to live with the accomplished fact of a Jewish nation. Said Egypt's King Farouk last week: "I cannot and will not tolerate, a Zionist state in the Middle East."

Both sides last week contained men who felt compelled to boast of tomorrow. Whatever hope there was of an understanding between Israel and the Arab states, short of years of debilitating conflict, lay in the fact that there were some who were boasting as little as possible.

Ireland was proclaimed a republic ■ Broadway audiences hummed "bali ha'i" ■ The german federal republic was established at bonn ■ Hungary's cardinal mindszenty was imprisoned for treason ■ Ballroom dancers discovered the samba ■ And 460 million chinese lost their leader of two decades . . .

1949

In an attempt to institutionalize racial division, South Africa established the legal system of apartheid.

FOREIGN NEWS

CHINA

What Can Li Do?

Defeated and helpless, Chiang Kai-shek, for 22 years the dominant figure in China, stepped down last week. His retirement symbolized one of the great shifts in the 20th Century's turbulent history: some 460 million Chinese, a quarter of the human race, were passing under the domination of Communism.

When Chiang told Communist officials to support Vice President Li Tsung-jen, one of his hearers asked: "What can Li do?" Everybody in China, including Li, knew the answer.

The Communist Boss Mao Tse-tung had won the war; he could dictate the terms of peace. What Mao wanted was power to put China in the Communist bloc. That he already had. He could proceed along the path of compromise and coalition certain that, with Chiang's passing, the back of anti-Communist resistance in China had been broken.

Mao's victory made a major change in the political and strategic world picture on the western shore of the Pacific. From Bering Strait to the Gulf of Tonkin Communism was now the major force. The western world merely held sentinel positions in Japan, the Philippines and Indonesia. Indo-China, Malaya and Burma—all three in turmoil—lay beneath the Communist threat.

Not since Hitler had stood on the French coast looking west across the Atlantic had the danger been so great.

Sunset

From dusty Nanking streets, sleek limousines converged on a plain brick residence in the spacious Ministry of National Defense compound. It was Friday afternoon; by 2 o'clock Generalissimo Chiang Kai-shek's small drawing room was jammed with ranking Kuomintang officials. Tense and silent, they waited.

Clad in a simple khaki uniform without insignia, China's Commander in Chief and President rose to his feet from a sofa in the corner of the room. Slowly, without show of emotion, he made the announcement that all had expected: he would leave Nanking and go to his native home. Then in his choppy Ningpo accent he read from a formal statement: "With the hope that hostilities may be brought to an

Mao & Commander Chu-teh
"Annihilate all who resist."

end and the people's suffering relieved, I have decided to retire."

Next day, after an early morning flight to Ningpo's carefully guarded airport, Chiang bounced and jostled by auto over a one-lane dirt road some 40 miles to Fenghwa, his home town, in the knob-topped Sze Ming Mountains. Nestled on a pine and laurel-covered slope is the Gimo's one-story, four-room retreat. A few feet up the slope is a wood and stone arch inscribed with the legend: "Road to Mother Chiang's Tomb." Through it passes a wide-stepped pebble and flagstone walk.

Chiang ascended the steps and went immediately to his mother's grave, a simple mound of grass-covered earth surrounded by a wall of brown sandstone where he meditated for 20 minutes. He then turned, entered his retreat.

A Holiday Spirit

More than a fortnight ago, the Gimo wrote Nationalist General Fu Tso-yi in Peiping of his decision to retire. The letter instructed Fu to make his own plans for North China. Last week, a typical Chinese solution ended the 40-day Communist siege of China's ancient capital.

Peiping's massive gates swung open and through them General Fu ("I will defend this city to the last!") marched 100,000 troops for "reorganization." At Peiping, Nationalists and Communists signed an agreement designed to "shorten the civil war, satisfy the public desire for peace and . . . prevent the vitality of the country from sinking any further." The agreement did not mention "surrender."

On Sunday, the first full day of peace, there was a holiday spirit among Peiping's 2,000,000 residents. Bazaars were crowded as prices dropped. In preparation for the Chinese New Year, firecracker makers started working around the clock catching up on time lost during the siege. Said a shopkeeper on Flower Street: "Now we can have plenty of *chaotse* (steamed meat dumplings) on New Year's night."

Swift Disaster

It was a week of stunning, swift disaster in China. Nearly a million Communist troops along a 400-mile front poured across the broad Yangtze, Nationalist China's last great defensive barrier, and swept government positions aside like puny earthworks in a raging tide. In four days they took Nanking, cut off Shanghai, and captured half a dozen cities.

In a joint order of the day, Communist Boss Mao Tse-tung, and Communist Commander in Chief Chu-teh, said: "Advance boldly, resolutely, thoroughly; cleanly and completely annihilate all . . . in China who dare to resist."

At most the Nationalists could hope to fall back, into the vast reaches of south China and onto the island of Formosa. But barring a miracle, they had no prospect of stopping the Red tide.

Perle Mesta

Cardinal Mindszenty

Capt. Charles Yaeger

THE PEACEMAKERS

THEY ARE FEWER IN NUMBER THAN THE WARRIORS, BUT THEIR BRAVERY IS PERHAPS GREATER. LIKE A WHISPER IN THE NIGHT, THEIR MESSAGE OF PEACE AND RECONCILIATION HAS SPREAD THROUGH THE TWENTIETH CENTURY, OVERCOMING BOUNDARIES OF GEOGRAPHY AND LANGUAGE, PASSING FROM NATION TO NATION WHEREVER OPPRESSION IS DARKEST, FROM WOODROW WILSON TO MARTIN LUTHER KING, JR., FROM DAG HAMMARKSJØLD TO ANWAR SADAT. THE PEACEMAKERS: IMPATIENT FOR THE KINGDOM OF HEAVEN ONCE PROMISED THEM, THEY HAVE TRIED TO BRING IT TO EARTH.

WOODROW WILSON
1923

FRANK B. KELLOGG
1925

DAG HAMMARKSJØLD
1955

MARTIN LUTHER KING
1957

MOTHER TERESA
1975

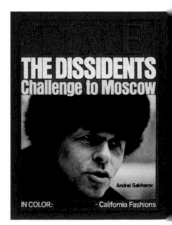

ANDREI SAKHAROV
1977

CORDELL HULL
1933

GEORGE C. MARSHALL
1948

ALBERT SCHWEITZER
1949

ELEANOR ROOSEVELT
1952

THE DALAI LAMA
1959

WILLY BRANDT
1959

ALEXANDER DUBÇEK
1968

PHILIP AND DANIEL BERRIGAN
1971

SADAT AND BEGIN
1978

JIMMY CARTER
1978

POPE JOHN PAUL II
1984

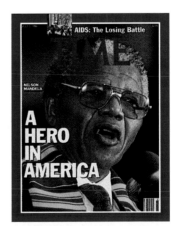

NELSON MANDELA
1990

The Race to Come

The dim streak across outer space exploded on man's consciousness in a profusion of meanings. To the three young University of Alaska scientists who became the first Americans to see it, the Soviet satellite appeared "like a star and brighter than Jupiter." To Washington's Democratic Senator Henry Jackson, it was a partisan reason for proclaiming a "week of shame and danger." To hundreds of U.S. scientists, it was a marvelous scientific-technical achievement, a triumph of mind over universal matter — and at the same time, a last-chance signal to beware onrushing Russian technology.

Communism had all but lost the ideological cold war in satellite Hungary, 1956; Communism had all but lost the economic cold war in the contrast between the prosperity of Western Europe and the poverty of Eastern Europe, 1957. But now the Communists were exploiting their brand-new Sputnik to achieve their old objectives. "People of the whole world are pointing to the satellite," crowed Nikita Khrushchev. "They are saying that the U.S. has been beaten."
October 21, 1957

NORDISK PRESSEFOTO

The Vengeful Visionary

The executioner's rifle cracked across Cuba last week, and around the world voices hopefully cheering for a new democracy fell still. The men who had just won a popular revolution for old ideals — for democracy, justice and honest government — themselves picked up the arrogant tools of dictatorship. As its public urged them on, the Cuban rebels shot more than 200 men, summarily convicted in drumhead courts, as torturers and mass murderers for the fallen Batista dictatorship.

The only man who could have silenced the firing squads was Fidel Castro Ruz, the 32-year-old lawyer, fighter and visionary who led the rebellion. And Castro was in no mood for mercy. Castro himself is egotistic, impulsive, immature, disorganized. A spellbinding romantic, he

The Tension of Change

One of the most important changes on the U.S. scene in September 1955, as the nation's children trooped back to school, was the astounding progress of racial desegregation. In Kansas City, Mo., and Oklahoma City, in Oak Ridge, and Charleston, W.Va., white and Negro children for the first time sat together in classrooms. This simple fact, part of a vast and complex social revolution, resulted from a legal victory: the U.S. Supreme Court's decisions of May 17, 1954, and May 31, 1955, holding segregated schools contrary to the 14th Amendment.

The name indelibly stamped on this victory is that of Thurgood Marshall, 47,

can talk spontaneously for as much as five hours without strain. He hates desks — behind which he may have to sit to run Cuba.
January 26, 1959

We like Ike

BETTMANN ARCHIVE

ounsel for the National Association for
e Advancement of Colored People.
e is at his sincerest and loudest (and
at is very sincere and quite loud) in
eclaring that he is only one of the mil-
ons, white and Negro, whose courage,
weat, skill, imagination and common
ense made the victory possible.
eptember 19, 1955

The Voyage of Privateer Joe

On Feb. 9, 1950, an obscure U.S. Senator told a Wheeling (W. Va.) audience that he had a list of 205 Communists employed by the State Department. With that, Joe Mc-Carthy launched one of the most spectacular political voyages in U.S. history. He charged often, proved seldom, never named his 205; in fact, he insisted he had said 57. But, because he had a sensitive issue, he became a big man. His bitterest foes were his best friends; Truman & Co. inflated his sails by exaggerating his importance.

But all along, McCarthy's ship has been trailed by its own kind of albatross, a bird called "McCarthy's methods." His albatross has brought him big headlines, but it has also brought him bitter criticism. This week, in his battle with the Army, he had built the smallest of molehills into one of the most devastating po-litical volcanoes that ever poured the lava of conflict and the ash of dismay over Washington.
March 8, 1954

The Little Man Who Dared

By midnight, stencils had been cut, and Press Secretary Joe Short gave the switchboard orders to summon the regular White House reporters at 1 a.m. The press got the mimeographed sheets: "With deep regret, I have concluded that General of the Army Douglas MacArthur is unable to give his wholehearted support to the policies of the United States government... it is fundamen-tal that military commanders must be governed by the policies and directives issued to them in the manner provided by our laws and the Constitution."

As the reporters scrambled for their phones to flash the news to an unsuspecting world, Blair House was dark. Harry Truman had gone to bed.

In Tokyo, just a little after 3 o'clock in the afternoon, General MacArthur was eating a chicken leg at a late lunch when an aide handed him a note. It was a radio news flash. Holding the drumstick in one hand and the note in the other, MacArthur read the news. His mouth opened in astonishment. Abruptly, the luncheon ended. It was 20 minutes later that he got the offi-cial dispatch informing him of the President's decision. Seldom had a more unpopular man fired a more popular one.
April 23, 1951

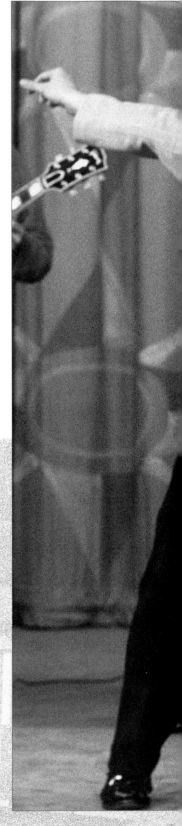

Cardiff Giant

On camera, Ed Sullivan has been likened to a cigar-store Indian, the Cardiff Giant and a stone-faced monument just off the boat from Easter Island. He moves like a sleepwalker; his smile is that of a man sucking a lemon; his speech is frequently lost in a thicket of syntax; his eyes pop from their sockets or sink so deep in their bags that they seem to be peering up at the camera from the bottom of twin wells. Sullivan is about the longest shot ever to have paid off in show business. Envious NBC President Pat Weaver is as baffled as anyone else by the riddle of Sullivan's popularity. Currently he subscribes to the theory that Sullivan never lost his appeal because he never had any to start with.
October 17, 1955

The Flame Heard Round the World

Night after night in New Orleans' 16,000-capacity Pelican Stadium, this gaunt young man with the Hickey-Freeman clothes and the eagle-sharp manner is bringing men and women down from the packed stands and up the length of the baseball field to make "decisions for Christ." This would be news enough in that tamed but still sin-ridden city of blues and bourbon. But the flame that is searing New Orleans is also burning greater and greater swaths across the whole U.S. and around the world. Billy Graham is the best-known, most talked-about Christian leader in the world today, barring the Pope.
October 25, 1954

Teener's Hero

Without preamble, the three-piece band cuts loose. In the spotlight, the lanky singer flails furious rhythms on his guitar, every now and then breaking a string. In a pivoting stance, his hips swing sensuously from side to side and his entire body takes on a frantic quiver, as if he had swallowed a jackhammer. Full-cut hair tousles over his forehead, and sideburns frame his petulant, full-lipped face. His style is partly hillbilly, partly socking rock'n'roll. His loud baritone goes raw and whining in the high notes, but down low it is rich and round. As he throws himself into one of his specialties — *Heartbreak Hotel*, *Blue Suede Shoes*, or *Long Tall Sally* — his throat seems full of desperate aspirates ("Hi want you, hi need you, hi luh-huh-huh-huv yew-hew") or hiccupping glottis strokes, and his diction is poor. But his movements suggest, in a word, sex.

The perpetrator of all this hoopla is Elvis Aaron Presley, a drape-suited, tight trousered young man of 21, and the sight and sound of him drive teenage girls wild. All through the South and West, Elvis is packing theaters, fighting off shrieking admirers, filling letters-to-the-editor columns with cries of alarm and, from adolescents, counter-cries of adulation.
May 14, 1956

Figure of a Fantasy

Offscreen as on, the face looks a little too beautiful to be true, like the kind of adolescent daydream served up in the comic strips. The cut of the face is Betty Boop, but the coloring and expression are Daisy Mae. The eyes are large and grey, and lend the features a look of baby-doll innocence. The innocence is in the voice, too, which is high and excited, like a little girl's.

She bears, in fact, a sharp resemblance to the airbrush Aphrodite known in the 30s as the Petty Girl. And like the Petty Girl, the Monroe is for the millions a figure of fantasy rather than of flesh. She offers the tease without the squeeze, attraction without satisfaction, frisk without risk. In Hollywood's pagan Pantheon, Marilyn Monroe is the Goddess of Love.
May 14, 1956

1950

The television era had arrived: 1.5 million sets were now counted in the U.S., with 15 million one year later.

ALGER HISS WAS SENTENCED FOR PERJURY ■ SCI-FI FANS READ *THE MARTIAN CHRONICLES* ■ POLAND AND EAST GERMANY FORMALIZED NEW BORDERS ■ CHINESE TROOPS OCCUPIED TIBET ■ MOVIEGOERS LEARNED "ALL ABOUT EVE" ■ BRINK'S WAS ROBBED ■ AND IN KOREA, AMERICANS LOOKED DEFEAT IN THE EYE . . .

TED WILLIAMS

EDDIE RICKENBACKER

HARRY S. TRUMAN

NATIONAL AFFAIRS

THE NATION

Defeat

The U.S. and its allies stood at the abyss of disaster. The Chinese Communists, pouring across the Manchurian border, had smashed the U.N. army, and this week were clawing forward to pursue and destroy its still-organized fragments. Caught in the desperate retreat were 140,000 American troops, the flower of the U.S. Army—almost the whole effective Army the U.S. had.

It was defeat—the worst defeat the U.S. had ever suffered. Even though the U.N. forces might still have the luck, skill and power to slow the Communist drive and withdraw in good order from the devastated peninsula, it was a defeat that could not be redressed in Korea. If this defeat were allowed to stand, it would mean the loss of Asia to Communism.

The only way the statesmen could save the U.N. forces would be through a plea for an armistice, or acceptance of a deal with the Communists. By any such deal, Communism would emerge triumphant. The alternative was war—that is, a recognition of the terrible fact that the U.S. and Communist China were already in a state of war. That would mean, inescapably, a campaign against the mainland of China by sea and air.

That war would have to be pursued in the full knowledge that it might go on for years. The war would have to be begun in the knowledge that Russia might come in too, which would lead to the atomic horrors of World War III.

There was no sign of where or how the enemy onrush could be stopped.

As Chinese hordes poured around the Eighth Army's open right flank, the 24th, 2nd and 25th Divisions fell back to the Chongchon and began crossing at Sinanju where a valuable airfield was lost, Anju and Kunu farther upriver. It was obvious that General Walker would have to keep his whole Eighth Army moving south if it was not to be trapped.

The Communist drive down the center of Korea's waist broke all contact between the Eighth Army and General Almond's X Corps, sprawled out over northeastern Korea. At the Changjin reservoir, Major General Oliver Prince Smith's 1st Marine Division had made a vain try to cut in behind the Chinese attacking the Eighth. Now Smith's men were attacked by ten Communist divisions, which threw an iron ring around the reservoir.

The three marine regiments, which had been in separated positions, around the reser-

WOUNDED MARINES IN RETREAT
"We'll make it somehow."

voir, finally fought their way through to junction in Hagaru, to the south, after running into bloody ambushes along the roads. The Communists fired on them comfortably at steep grades and hairpin turns, where the marines' vehicles slowed to a crawl. A dreadful indication of the casualties in this sector was that 1,200 wounded were flown out in the first two days.

Retreat of the 20,000

"Retreat, hell!" snapped Major General Oliver Prince Smith of the 1st Marine Division. "We're not retreating, we're just advancing in a different direction."

Said Colonel Lewis ("Chesty") Puller, battle-scarred commander of the 1st Marine Regiment: "We'll suffer heavy losses. The enemy greatly outnumbers us. They've blown the bridges and blocked the roads but we'll make it somehow."

The running fight of the marines and two battalions of the Army's 7th Infantry Division from Hagaru to Hamhung—40 miles by air but 60 miles over the icy, twisting, mountainous road—was a battle unparalleled in U.S. military history. It had some aspects of Bataan, some of Anzio, some of Valley Forge.

Assembled in Hagaru, south of the frozen, bloodstained beaches of the Changjin Reservoir, the 1st Marine Division and the 7th had already suffered heavy casualties. They had heard the screams of their comrades when the Reds lobbed phosphorous grenades into truckloads of U.S. wounded. When the order came to start south, the enemy was already closing in on Hagaru's makeshift airstrip, whence thousands of wounded had been flown out. The last plane waited an extra hour for one desperately wounded man. The marines abandoned none of their disabled men, but bulldozers pushed the dead into mass graves by hundreds.

The fight to Koto, six miles down the road, was the worst. The crawling vehicles ran into murderous mortar, machine-gun and small-arms fire from Communists in log and sandbag bunkers. The U.S. answering fire and air attacks killed thousands of the enemy and held the road open. When the lead vehicles reached Koto, the rearguard was still fighting near Hagaru to keep the enemy from chewing up the column from behind.

At week's end some 8,000 marines broke through the last thin crust of enemy resistance and poured into Hamhung. More kept coming in every hour as tanks brought up the rear. Frantic photographers called to the bedraggled men, asked them to "wave and look happy." They obliged. The triumph was marred by more than 30% casualties, but the bulk of the marine division's and the 7th's survivors reached safety.

THE 22ND AMENDMENT RESTRICTED THE PRESIDENCY TO TWO TERMS ■ TRUMAN RELIEVED GENERAL MacARTHUR OF HIS FAR EAST COMMAND ■ A PEACE TREATY WITH JAPAN WAS SIGNED ■ NORTH KOREAN FORCES CAPTURED SEOUL ■ NUCLEAR-GENERATED POWER LIT UP ARCON, IDAHO ■ AND A NEW TYPE OF BROADCAST TELEVISION MADE ITS APPEARANCE: *COLOR . . .*

1951

American culture embraced the model of alienated youth, as readers spent a weekend with Holden Caulfield in Salinger's The Catcher in the Rye.

BUSINESS & FINANCE

COMMUNICATIONS

The General

The public scored David Sarnoff's Radio Corp. of America with a lost round last year in the great color TV fight with Columbia Broadcasting System. Sarnoff did not stay down. Last week he showed the television industry a new tube that receives clear, true color, and he showed the public that RCA's color system can do what CBS's can not: color programs broadcast by RCA can be received in black & white on present sets without any change. It looked as if radio's miracle man had not run out of miracles.

For months, Wall Street speculators have been betting on Sarnoff. So far this year, RCA stock has risen from 16 3/8 to 21 1/2, CBS fallen from 33 to 25 1/2. This trend is the more remarkable because six months ago RCA was apparently caught flat-footed when the Federal Communications Commission decided to license the CBS "whirling disc" system for commercial broadcasting. RCA promised a much better system, one that existing TV sets would receive in black & white (unlike the CBS method) without any change in the sets. But the color RCA showed FCC last fall was mushy and CBS's was clear. FCC decided not to wait.

Even then, old radiomen kept their eyes on Sarnoff. He is the man who put radio in the home — and never forgets it for a waking moment. He is boss of RCA with its 52,000 employees (including those of the 238-station NBC radio and television network), of 13 manufacturing plants which turn out millions of radios, TV sets and hundreds of different electronic gadgets, and of a research staff which year in & year out develops new wonders. Would Sarnoff, who boasts that he was born about the same time that the electron was discovered (as if they were somehow twins), allow himself to be bested in the next great advance of the industry that he has led for two decades? Those who knew Sarnoff's vast ability — and has vast pride — thought not.

NANETTE FABRAY & RCA COLOR BROADCAST
Lovebirds flapped unblurred wings

They listened when, coldly eyeing the FCC decision, he said: "We may have lost the battle, but we'll win the war."

Secret Weapon. To get the weapon he needed, Sarnoff prodded RCA, not a nimble organization, into an amazing burst of speed to improve its color system. Last week, in his Radio City Exhibition Hall, Sarnoff put on a demonstration for some 200 radio and television reporters, who saw a 20-minute program starring Nanette Fabray and Singer Yma Sumac on RCA's new color tubes. There was no blurring or running of colors, even in the fastest movement, *e.g.*, a pair of performing lovebirds flapping their wings. As a show topper, an RCA mobile unit focused on a swimming pool near New York where a troupe of swimmers and divers performed. The outdoor telecast, which RCA explained could just as well be a football game or boxing match, came through almost as clearly as the studio show.

Within two months, RCA will start putting on similar public color demonstrations on 100 receivers which will be moved from city to city all over the U.S. By broadcasting its color show last week on its regular channel, RCA also showed TV set owners that its system is

compatible, *i.e.*, it could receive the broadcasts in black & white. The new tube's performance was so impressive that such TV competitors as Allen B. Du Mont, who has opposed any form of color up till now, changed their minds. Said Du Mont: "The RCA picture was good enough to start commercial programs immediately."

Sarnoff is far more cautious. He says: "Commercial color television on a big basis is still two to five years away. Material shortage, NPA cutbacks on TV production and defense orders will delay it. On top of that, it will take a long time to get the bugs out of mass production of the color tube."

Whatever technical or bureaucratic difficulties may lie ahead of RCA's color system, it was clear from last week's demonstration that Sarnoff was fighting his way out of a tough spot.

For more than 50 of his 60 years, Sarnoff has been doing just that. Driving through obstacles is his habit, his joy, his bitter necessity. He says: "There are three drives that rule most men: money, sex, and power." Nobody doubts that Sarnoff's ruling drive is power. Says a deputy: "There is no question about it; he is the god over here."

MARGARET TRUMAN

SUGAR RAY ROBINSON

JOE McCARTHY

1952

The sun was setting on the British Empire, as riots erupted in Egypt and the Mau Mau rebellion terrorized Kenya.

GEORGE VI DIED IN ENGLAND AND WAS SUCCEEDED BY ELIZABETH II ■ "THE MOUSETRAP" BEGAN ITS RUN IN LONDON ■ ALBERT SCHWEITZER WAS AWARDED THE NOBEL PEACE PRIZE ■ ARGENTINA MOURNED THE DEATH OF EVA PERON ■ AND RICHARD NIXON SPOKE TO THE COUNTRY ABOUT A COCKER SPANIEL NAMED "CHECKERS" . . .

ADLAI STEVENSON

ESTES KEFAUVER

BISHOP FULTON J. SHEEN

NATIONAL AFFAIRS

REPUBLICANS

The Trial

In the three-room suite on the fifth floor of Los Angeles' Ambassador hotel, the tension grew with each turn of the second hand. At 6:30 that Tuesday night, Dick Nixon was to face the television cameras to explain to the nation why he had drawn on an $18,000 private fund to pay some of his political expenses as a U.S. Senator. Telephone calls poured into the hotel from G.O.P. bigwigs across the nation. Some told him to fight, others told him that for the good of the party he must resign. Three hours before his broadcast Nixon sent his advisers away and ordered his telephone cut off. "I don't want to talk to anybody," he snapped as he closed his door.

The fact that weighed most heavily on Dick Nixon was that he was a man on trial, and strictly on his own. At stake were the campaign chances of the Republican Party, and his own political future. He had expected that Ike Eisenhower would make it clear to the nation that he was 100% behind Nixon. Ike had not done so. It was up to Nixon to clear himself with the people by presenting facts & figures. Until he did, Ike would not give him complete vindication.

Just before 6:30 Nixon sat down behind a desk in an NBC television studio in Hollywood, a sheaf of papers at his elbow. He had no written script, and the television crews were so uncertain of his plans that they warmed up two extra cameras in case he should walk out of range of the primary camera. Nixon's wife Pat sat in an armchair a few feet from the desk. When the announcer cued Nixon to start talking, not even Pat knew precisely what Nixon was going to say.

The Accounting. "My fellow Americans," said Nixon, as his earnest face loomed up on the nation's TV screens, "I come before you tonight as a candidate for the vice presidency and as a man whose honesty and integrity has been questioned." His voice was level and he showed no sign of the strain.

Was it "morally wrong" for him to have drawn on the $18,000 fund for political expenses? No, said Nixon, since the 76 contributors asked no special favors, expected none and got none. The fund was not really secret at all. And "not one cent of the $18,000, or any other money of that type, ever went to me for my personal use. Every penny of it was used to pay for political expenses that I did not think should be charged to the taxpayers of the U.S."

Nixon's voice took on a compelling note

NIXON & CHECKERS
From Texas, a contribution to keep

of seriousness as he launched his bold counterstroke: "And so now, what I am going to do — incidentally, this is unprecedented in the history of American politics — I am going at this time to give to this television and radio audience a complete financial history, everything I've earned, everything I've spent, everything I owe, and I want you to know the facts."

Most of his early life was spent in his family's grocery store in East Whittier, he said. "The only reason we were able to make it go was because my mother and dad had five boys and we all worked in the store.

"I worked my way through college and to a great extent through law school. And then, in 1940, probably the best thing that ever happened to me happened. I married Pat, who is sitting over here." The TV camera followed Nixon's cue, turned for the first time to Pat,

sitting in profile with her eyes on her husband. "I practiced law," said Nixon as the cameras picked him up again, "and she continued to teach school."

Package from Texas. Then, while he served with the Navy in the south Pacific, his wife worked as a stenographer, he said. Their joint savings at the end of the war were "just a little less than $10,000." Since then, he and Pat have inherited about $4,500; he has drawn $1,600 from cases which were in his law firm before he went into politics. He has made an average of $1,500 a year "from non-political speaking engagements and lectures." And he has had his salary as a Representative and Senator ($12,500).

"What do we have today to show for it? This will surprise you because it is so little . . . We've got a house in Washington which cost $41,000 and on which we owe $20,000. We have a house in Whittier, Calif. which cost $13,000 and on which we owe $10,000. My folks are living there at the present time. I have just $4,000 in life insurance, plus my G.I. policy, which I've never been able to convert and which will run out in two years . . . I own a 1950 Oldsmobile car. We have our furniture. We have no stocks and bonds of any type. We have no interest of any kind, direct or indirect in any business. I owe $4,500 to the Riggs Bank in Washington . . . I owe $3,500 to my parents . . . and then I have a $500 loan . . . on my life insurance."

Nixon had one postscript to his accounting. "One other thing I probably should tell you, because if I don't they'll probably be saying this about me too — we did get something, a gift, after the election. A man down in Texas heard Pat on the radio mention the fact that our two youngsters would like to have a dog, and believe it or not, the day before we left on this campaign trip, we got a message from the Union Station in Baltimore, saying they had a package for us . . . It was a little cocker spaniel dog . . . and our little girl Tricia, the six-year-old, named it Checkers. And you know the kids . . . love that dog, and . . . regardless of what they say about it, we're going to keep it."

Sir edmund hillary scaled mt. everest ■ An armistice in korea was signed at panmunjom ■ Stalin died and khrushchev began his ascendancy in the soviet hierarchy ■ The musical question was "how much is that doggie in the window?" ■ And julius and ethel rosenberg were executed for "a crime worse than murder" . . .

1953

The modern feminist movement found its intellectual grounding with the publication of Simone de Beauvoir's The Second Sex.

NATIONAL AFFAIRS

ESPIONAGE

The Last Appeal

It was Monday, the last day of judgment before the U. S. Supreme Court recessed for summer vacation. It was also, or so it seemed, the last hope before the bar of justice for Julius and Ethel Rosenberg. For the sixth time, the mousy little engineer and his wife, waiting in Sing Sing's death house, had petitioned the highest tribunal, this time for a stay of execution and review of their trial. For the sixth time, a majority of the nine Justices rejected a Rosenberg appeal.

Across town at the White House gate, hundreds of picketers marched with pro-Rosenberg placards; opposing demonstrators carried signs that read "Kill the Dirty Spies." A stream of mail from every quarter of the globe flowed to the President's desk. The Red campaign to "save the Rosenbergs" may have inspired the pleas, but many of them came from non-Communist clergymen and scientists, from liberals and humanitarians, from those who thought it bad politics to let the Communists have "martyrs" for their propaganda. At the focus of pressure, Dwight Eisenhower did not flinch.

Then, as the clock ticked on toward 11 p.m. Thursday, the hour of death for the spies, Supreme Court Justice William Douglas acted alone. Unexpectedly, the court having recessed for the summer, he granted the stay of execution that the full court had denied.

Last Scene

The stay of execution won from Douglas was short-lived — it was lost within 24 hours in the Supreme Court, and had gained less than a day of life for the Rosenbergs. The hour of death was moved to 11 p.m. Thursday from 8 p.m. Friday in order to avoid an execution on the Jewish Sabbath, which begins at sundown on Friday.

Julius entered first into the presence of the ugly, brown-stained oak chair. As he walked through the glaring light of Sing Sing's white-

walled death chamber, the three newsmen allowed as witnesses noted that his mustache had been shaved off, that he wore a white T-shirt, and that his feet were shod in cloth slippers. The prison chaplain, Rabbi Irving Koslowe, intoned the 23rd Psalm. Just before the chair, Julius seemed to sway. Guards quickly placed and strapped him in the seat, then dropped the leather hood over his face.

THE ROSENBERGS
By the most solemn judgment of U.S. courts

N.Y. JOURNAL AMERICAN INTERNATIONAL

Three shocks of 2,000 volts each flung his body convulsively against its bonds. Listening with stethoscopes to the heart under the T–shirt, attending doctors pronounced Julius Rosenberg dead.

The body was gone only a few minutes when Ethel Rosenberg entered the chamber. She wore a dark green print dress with white polka dots. Cloth slippers were on her feet, too, and her hair had been cropped close on top for the electrode's contact. The rabbi intoned the 15th Psalm. Just before the chair, the prisoner shook hands, then impulsively brushed a kiss on the cheek of a matron accompanying her. She sat down with taut composure, wincing only slightly as the electrode was applied to her head.

What They Did

In 177 years of U.S. history, the Rosenbergs were the first native-born Americans to be executed by order of a civilian court for espionage. Sentencing them in April 1951, Federal Judge Irving Kaufman stigmatized their crime as "worse than murder."

The crime had ideological roots. Children of East European immigrants who settled in Manhattan's lower East Side, both Julius Rosenberg and his future wife Ethel Greenglass took to Communism in their adolescent years. In so doing, they rejected the Jewish faith of their parents (a sore blow to Julius' father, a garment worker who yearned for his son to be a rabbi). So ardent was 19-year-old Ethel's devotion to the cause that she began indoctrinating her 13-year-old brother David. Then she found a comrade and a beau in Julius, two years her junior and an electrical engineering student at City College of New York.

They were married; World War II was under way, and Julius was working as a civilian engineer for the Army's Signal Corps (a good spot for spying on East Coast defense plants) when his Communist Party membership came to the attention of Army authorities. He was dropped from the Signal Corps but he became more valuable than ever to Moscow. He went underground. He became part-owner and operator of a Manhattan machine shop, but secretly he ran an apparatus of spies and informants who passed scientific and technical data to Russian agents.

The most precious, and most damning, piece of information came in 1945 from Ethel's younger brother David Greenglass, then employed as a machinist in the supersecret atomic bomb laboratory at Los Alamos, N. Mex. Ethel had used older-sister cajolery, and Julius had given money, to persuade David and his confused wife Ruth to join the treasonable conspiracy. At the Rosenberg trial, a U.S. atomic expert examining a sketch drawn by Greenglass and passed to the Russians, testified that it showed the atom bomb substantially as perfected.

MAMIE EISENHOWER

KONRAD ADENAUER

MICKEY MANTLE

1954

The Supreme Court laid the legal groundwork for the modern Civil Rights movement by declaring school segregation to be unconstitutional.

SEN. JOE McCARTHY WAS CENSURED FOLLOWING A TELEVISED WITCH-HUNT ■ QUEEN ELIZABETH BEGAN A TOUR OF THE COMMON-WEALTH ■ ARNOLD PALMER WON THE U.S. AMATEUR GOLF CHAMPION-SHIP ■ FILM FANS STARED OUT OF HITCHCOCK'S "REAR WINDOW" ■ AND THE FIRST NEWPORT JAZZ FESTIVAL ENLIVENED A SUMMER NIGHT . . .

GEORGE BALANCHINE

H-BOMB OVER THE PACIFIC

BILLY GRAHAM

MUSIC

Cats by the Sea

At Newport, the weathering old mansions of the rich still brood by the sea, and outsiders half expect to meet ladies in ankle-dusting tennis skirts escorted by blades in gaily banded boaters. But last week Newport's narrow streets were thronged with loud-shirted young bookie types from Broadway, young intellectuals in need of haircuts, crew-cut Ivy Leaguers, sailors, Harlem girls with extravagant hairdos, and high-school girls in shorts. They were cats. From as far away as Kansas they had come to hear a two-day monster jazz festival.

The Newport wingding was further evidence that jazz is enjoying its biggest boom in years, with record sales soaring and nightclubs sprouting new jazz acts all over the country. A crowd of 6,000 fans jammed into Newport's dingy old open-air Casino for the first-night concert. There was a clear moon overhead as Old-timer Eddie Condon, a little ill at ease in all the fresh air, stamped his foot four times and swung into *Muskrat Ramble*, sweeping along his bang-up Dixieland outfit, including Clarinetist Pee Wee Russell, Trumpeter Wild Bill Davison, Pianist Ralph Sutton. The music was hot, and the crowd warmed to it with shouts of "Go! Go!"

Up to the Stars. From the oldtime start, the music came gradually up to date. Things really began to hum when Bop Trumpeter Dizzy Gillespie took the stage with his quintet. Looking bemused and gesturing wildly, he set his cocked trumpet to his lips and played Gabriel-like tones that sent chills up the listeners' spines. "See, that's a square bend," he explained, pointing to the upswept angle. "Well, I get a sort of square note out of there. When you say 'Pow-w-w,' it comes out like a pounding — like a pounding of bricks."

When Pianist Oscar Peterson and his trio gave a fast-fingered version of *Tenderly* sprinkled with suave dissonances, the modernist crowd was ready to call it the high point of the festival. But the younger set shrieked louder when hollow-cheeked Gerry Mulligan

bellowed and coaxed *The Lady Is a Tramp* through his big baritone sax. The concert finally ended after midnight with a 20-man jam session that sent the strangest sounds ever heard in Newport floating up to the stars.

Topnotch *Tannhäuser*

One conductor slammed down his baton, grumbled "*auf Wiedersehen*," and walked out. Leading singers caught colds in the wet July weather. Technicians scrambled to lighten the murky stage so that the audience could see more of what was going on. After six weeks of preparing the season, Wieland and Wolfgang Wagner last week raised the curtain on the opening production, their grandfather's *Tannhäuser*. Despite all crises, the production turned out topnotch.

Bayreuth had not dared do *Tannhäuser* since Toscanini's unforgettable version 24 years ago. But brothers Wieland and Wolfgang, who will dare anything, decided the old Venusberg needed some drastic new landscaping. They hired fast-rising, Kiev-born Conductor Igor Markevitch, who had never done Wagnerian opera before, then replaced him with Germany's Joseph Kielberth. When the trumpets announced curtain time one afternoon last week, nobody at Bayreuth quite knew what to expect.

Musically, the production proved to be more than adequate despite the fact that Tenor Ramon Vinay and pretty Soprano Gre Brouenstein showed signs of strain. The chorus, one of the world's finest, performed brilliantly. But the chief attraction, as usual, was the staging. Wieland sees Tannhäuser as a harried misfit in a world of rigid conventions. Dressed in a black cloak, he moves among stiff, almost mechanized people of the court. Preparing for the crucial song contest in the second act — usually staged with casual confusion — uniformly dressed men and women march into the hall in stiff military style. But the orgiastic Venusberg scene, set in flowing concentric circles of light, is heavily sensual; the ballet flings itself into bumps and grinds that rival the old Minsky's.

After the final curtain, half of the Bayreuth audience seemed in tears, clapped for 15 minutes. With *Tannhäuser*, the Bayreuth brothers have now redraped all the standard Wagner works in their new, bare, dramatically lighted dress. Their style has become a prototype for new Wagner productions in most major opera houses. Notable exception: New York's Metropolitan, whose Wagner producers seem never to have heard of Bayreuth's lighting, let alone Minsky's.

NEWPORT JAM SESSION
From a crooked trumpet, a pounding of bricks

TIME

WEST GERMANY WAS ADMITTED TO NATO ■ BLACKS IN MONTGOMERY STAGED

A SUCCESSFUL BUS BOYCOTT ■ AUSTRIA REGAINED INDEPENDENCE

■ MARILYN'S SKIRTS BILLOWED IN "THE SEVEN YEAR ITCH" AND A BRONX

BUTCHER FOUND LOVE IN "MARTY" ■ JULIE HARRIS WAS "JOAN OF ARC" ■ AND

THE SALK VACCINE OFFERED HOPE FOR AN END TO POLIO . . .

1955

Conformity and social regimentation became concerns in the 1950s, personified by Sloan Wilson's The Man in the Gray Flannel Suit.

MEDICINE

It Works

The big news came in three words: "The vaccine works."

That was how the University of Michigan started off its terse summary of the verdict of the Salk polio vaccine. The reading of the report itself took longer, and the setting in the university's Rickham auditorium was elaborate. Under the klieg lights set up for TV and newsreel cameras, surrounded by microphones and 150 reporters, sat the unquestioned hero of the occasion: Dr. Jonas Edward Salk, 40, the determined, youthful-looking virologist who for five years had battled in his University of Pittsburgh laboratory to lick polio. Next to him sat the University of Michigan's Dr. Thomas Francis Jr., 54, one of the U.S.'s most eminent epidemiologists, who had been chosen by the National Foundation for Infantile Paralysis to evaluate last year's nationwide tests of the Salk vaccine. For an hour and a half, Dr. Francis read his report in an even, matter-of-fact tone. The gist:

* The vaccine is up to 90% effective.

* The vaccine causes a minimum of undesirable side effects—all, apparently, minor.

* Results were most favorable from the areas where conditions were best for accurate appraisal.

Dr. Francis stopped when he finished telling what had been done. Dr. Salk, who rose to a standing ovation from 500 usually undemonstrative scientists, took a peek into the future: the vaccine, he suggested, might be made almost 100% effective. This does not mean that polio will be suddenly abolished. But it could mean that as vaccination becomes universal for children, whole generations will grow up free of the paralysis that has condemned so many to enfeebled limbs or iron lungs. Eventually, polio can become as rare as smallpox—which U.S. doctors now rarely get a chance to identify.

The test vaccine was given in 127 areas, deliberately picked because they had had a high polio-attack rate for several years. This was to make sure that there would be enough cases for the epidemiologists and their statistical machines. No fewer than 1,830,000 children were studied in the trials (440,000 were inoculated with the vaccine, 210,000 got a dummy substance, 1,180,000 were merely observed as "controls").

Among these children, there were only 1,013 cases reported as polio (in the U.S. as a whole there were 38,000 cases in 1954).

Six big U.S. pharmaceutical firms are now producing Salk vaccine or hurrying to get

POLIO FIGHTER SALK
Generations will grow up free

into production. The vaccine works on a principle that has already provided protection against such traditional plagues as smallpox and yellow fever. When they attack human beings or other mammals, most viruses stimulate the invaded system to manufacture tiny protein particles called antibodies. If the system under assault does not have enough of these antibodies or cannot manufacture them fast enough, the victim may die or, with polio, suffer permanent crippling.

Polio virus is unusual in that there are three main types. All can cause paralysis, but one type causes more than the others combined. Within each type there are many different strains. The Salk vaccine is made by taking a representative strain of each type and growing it—till it reaches many times its original strength—in a broth made with snips of monkey kidney. (To keep production going, 4,000 monkeys a month are flown in from India and the Philippines.) Then the virus in each deadly brew is killed with formaldehyde. Strangely, although the virus particles now lose their power to multiply or to cause disease, they keep their power to stimulate a higher animal to produce antibodies. Because in the Salk formula the virus types are mixed, the Salk vaccine is really three vaccines in one, effective against all known polio strains.

Never before in history had a medical development been big, instantaneous news over a large part of the world. Ironically, poliomyelitis has always been a relatively uncommon disease with a comparatively low death rate. Polio is actually less of a public-health problem than rheumatic fever and some forms of cancer which single out the young. But, largely because of its long-term crippling effects, no disease except cancer has been so widely feared in the last three decades. With polio's dramatic defeat, as the *Detroit Free Press* wrote, "The prayers and hopes of millions . . . in all parts of the world were answered."

President Dwight Eisenhower ordered the State Department to transmit information on the Salk vaccine and its effectiveness to 75 nations through U.S. Ambassadors, and the World Health Organization planned to duplicate this effort. Actually, relatively few countries have facilities to make the vaccine; only a few areas in the world have a serious polio problem, for clinical polio is a disease that goes with high standards of hygiene and sanitation. Highest recent incidence abroad: Canada, New Zealand, Scandinavia. The six firms making the vaccine are selling it at cost to the National Foundation for Infantile Paralysis, but will otherwise sell it for normal profit, an average $1.50 per shot.

THURGOOD MARSHALL

GEORGE MEANY

ANTHONY EDEN

1956

Elvis swiveled to the tune of "Hound Dog" and American music, youth, and popular culture were never the same.

KHRUSHCHEV DENOUNCED STALIN IN HIS "SECRET SPEECH" TO THE COMMUNIST PARTY CONFERENCE ■ EISENHOWER CLAIMED A SECOND VICTORY AGAINST ADLAI STEVENSON ■ JAPAN WAS ADMITTED TO THE UNITED NATIONS ■ THEATRE-GOERS MET "AUNTIE MAME" ■ AND FREEDOM-HUNGRY HUNGARIANS REBELLED AGAINST RUSSIAN DOMINATION . . .

MARILYN MONROE

DWIGHT D. EISENHOWER

DAVID BEN-GURION

FOREIGN NEWS

WORLD CRISIS

Appalling Events

With anxiety and bewilderment, the world watched an appalling eruption.

In Hungary a gallant, leaderless rebellion against Russia's iron rule gave promise of success—until Russia turned its retreating tanks around and set out to crush the revolt.

Israel, taking advantage of Russia's difficulties (and taking for granted U.S. preoccupation with a presidential election), invaded Egypt. Great Britain and France, aggression-bound, moved in, determined to overthrow Gamal Abdel Nasser and recover the Suez Canal.

War in the Middle East gave Russia the chance to muffle the sounds of its own savage conduct in Hungary. With bland cynicism, it lectured Britain and France on aggression, proposed joining with the U.S. in fighting Egypt's invaders (a proposal the U.S. called "unthinkable"), and talked of using "force to crush the aggressors" in the Middle East.

The possibility that Russia might rush into the Middle East gave urgency to the efforts of peacemakers. The U.S. and Britain and France got back together again, after a week tragically apart. U.N. Secretary General Dag Hammarskjöld announced that Britain and France had agreed to a cease-fire.

HUNGARY

Revolution!

The magic chemistry of courage, anger and desperation that makes men wager their lives for an ideal fired Hungary into revolution last week. Unarmed, unorganized, unaided from outside, the Hungarian people rolled back the tide of Communism. They overthrew a government. They took on the Soviet army. In six days the Hungarian people made history—six days that shook the world. After the week's events, the Communist empire could never be the same. The rest of the world could only look on with a catch in its heart, while thousands who must have known they could

expect no outside aid chose, in Jefferson's phrase, to refresh the tree of liberty with blood.

Poland's break with Russia was the spark. Hungarian students got permission to express sympathy with the Poles by gathering silently before Budapest's Polish embassy. Then the Communist Central Committee canceled the

BANNERS OF FREEDOM IN BUDAPEST
A magic chemistry of courage and anger

permit. Party Leader Erno Gero wanted no demonstrations. At noon there were angry student meetings in every college. Budapest came out to see the fun. Said an old woman: "We have been silent for eleven years. Today nothing will stop us."

In a solemn but peaceful mood, the students went to pay their respects to Poland. Ten abreast down the broad Danube quays they marched to Petofi Square A student and workers' delegation went to the radio station, requested that its demands be made public. Security police arrested the delegation. The crowd stormed the building, but the police opened fire, killing several attackers.

Seven heavy tanks, manned by Hungarian soldiers, rumbled into the area around midnight. Soldiers, students and workers fraternized. A tank bearing Hungarian colors came through the crowd. Cried the Hungarian colonel standing in the open hatch: "We are unarmed! We came to join you, not to oppose the demonstration." Soon students and workers were flourishing Tommy guns. "The army is with us!" they shouted. Barricades were built in the street that night. Carnival had become revolution.

Budapest (pop. 1,750,000) woke early next morning to the sound of machine-gun fire as a column of 80 Soviet tanks rolled into the city and took up positions covering all bridges, boulevards and public buildings. Other tank forces ringed the city. At dawn martial law was imposed on the whole country, a 24-hour curfew on Budapest. Trains and streetcars stopped running, telephone communication with the outside world was cut.

Around noon a crowd began gathering in front of the huge neo-Gothic Parliament building facing the Danube, intending to present Premier Nagy with a petition demanding the withdrawal of all Soviet troops. Soviet tanks and a phalanx of security police blocked all entrances to the building. Trigger-sensitive young Russian tankists became unnerved by the milling crowd around them and began firing indiscriminately into the mass of unarmed people. In a few minutes hundreds of men and women were lying dead or wounded on the ground.

The massacre in Parliament Square sent Budapest mad. The Soviet embassy was raided, Soviet automobiles fired, the contents of a Soviet bookshop burned. Workers fought their way into an arms depot at outlying Fot, got themselves machine guns. Others made gasoline bombs out of wine bottles. Soon Soviet armored cars were burning in the streets.

On the sixth day of Hungary's people's revolution, rebels were in control of much of the countryside, but Soviet tanks, withdrawing to the outskirts of Budapest, left behind a crushed city, ringed by Soviet steel.

THE SUEZ CANAL REOPENED AFTER EGYPT'S NASSER SEIZED IT ■ THE
AFL-CIO EXPELLED HOFFA'S TEAMSTERS' UNION ■ AN INTERNATIONAL
GEOPHYSICAL YEAR WAS PROCLAIMED BY 67 NATIONS ■ RIVAL STREET GANGS
FOUGHT IN BROADWAY'S "WEST SIDE STORY" ■ AND THE NATIONAL GUARD
MARCHED INTO LITTLE ROCK TO ENFORCE DESEGREGATION . . .

1957

In the first concrete steps toward European unity, six nations signed the Treaty of Rome, envisioning a Common Market.

NATIONAL AFFAIRS

THE NATION

The Meaning of Little Rock

"Some people say it's like a dream — it can't be happening here," mused Presbyterian Minister Dunbar H. Ogden Jr., President of the Greater Little Rock Ministerial Association, as he contemplated the fate that had befallen his city. "But I haven't felt like that. This is real."

It was grimly real: a segregationist mob had ruled Little Rock for an ugly moment in U.S. history. Now the face of the law was that of a young U.S. Army paratrooper in battle gear outside Central High School. Little Rock was a name known wherever men could read newspapers and listen to radios, a symbol to be distorted in Moscow, misinterpreted in New Delhi, painfully explained in London.

More Drastic Talk. Arkansas Governor Orval Faubus was not one of these. He had drawn the battle lines. President Eisenhower had patiently tried to avoid direct conflict, but when forced to the issue, he had acted quickly and decisively. Now, at week's end Faubus — like Joe McCarthy before him — was trying to regain the initiative by even more drastic talk, slandering his political opponents and musing about the possibility of calling a special session of the Arkansas legislature to abolish the public school system. And the President of the U.S. would return to Washington this week to confer with a delegation of five Southern governors.

The governors typified the dilemma in which Orval Faubus had placed the South. Only one, Georgia's Marvin Griffin, was a rabble-rouser of the Faubus stripe. The four others, Florida's LeRoy Collins, Tennessee's Frank Clement, North Carolina's Luther Hodges, and Maryland's Theodore Roosevelt McKeldin, were moderates. But the emotional turmoil of the South had forced Collins, Clement and Hodges toward the side of Demagogue Faubus, even though most of them privately blamed him for the trouble. In Washington, they hoped to find a way to get federal troops

NEGRO STUDENTS & FRIENDS
From young hearts, heart

out of Little Rock. President Eisenhower was more than willing to listen to their arguments. But he made it clear in advance that he would not barter away his authority under the Constitution and statutes of the U.S., to put down mob rule wherever it arose.

The Inevitable Governor. It was small wonder that many of the ordinary citizens of Little Rock thought of their situation as a dream — a nightmare — in which they had played no part. But Presbyterian Ogden pointed up the meaning for ordinary citizens and would-be extremists alike. "This had to happen someplace in the South," said he. "It was inevitable that there was going to be a plan, worked out, approved, and accepted, for gradual integration. It was inevitable that somewhere a governor under pressure of extreme segregationists, was going to stop integration by calling out the National Guard.

Quick, Hard & Decisive

The President of the U.S. looked once more at the reports arriving in his vacation office near Newport. The weeks of patient working toward peaceful solution were over; a mob, stirred by the governor of Arkansas, still stood in the way of nine Negro youngsters

who, by court order, were entitled to join 2,000 whites at Little Rock Central High School. Two aides and a secretary watched silently as President Eisenhower, his decision made, picked up a pen and signed a historic document; it ordered Secretary of Defense Charles Wilson to use the armed forces of the U. S. to uphold the law of the land in Little Rock.

The Pentagon was ready: informed that the President's order was on the way, Wilson rapped out his own instructions. The ground and air forces of the Arkansas National Guard were placed in federal service, safely out of the hands of Governor Orval Faubus, who had used them to defy the U.S. Government.

That night, just eight hours after President Eisenhower signed his orders, the first trucks of the 101st Airborne drove up to Central High. It was one of the nation's most painful moments, and the first use of U.S. troops in a Southern racial crisis since Reconstruction days. Explained the President in a radio-TV speech to the nation: "The very basis of our individual rights and freedoms rests upon the certainty that the President and the executive branch of Government will support and insure the carrying out of the decisions of the federal courts, even, when necessary, with all the means at the President's command."

LEONARD BERNSTEIN

EARL WARREN

EDWARD R. MURROW

1958

The space race was on: while the Soviets prided themselves on Sputnik III, Americans made a failed attempt to send a rocket to the moon.

CARDINAL RONCALLI WAS ELECTED POPE JOHN XXIII ■ ALASKA ADDED A 49TH STAR TO THE FLAG ■ THE SOVIET UNION GRANTED FUNDS TO BUILD THE ASWAN DAM ■ READERS SAVORED *BREAKFAST AT TIFFANY'S* ■ MIYOSHI UMEKI STARRED IN "FLOWER DRUM SONG" ■ AND *WUNDERKIND* PIANIST VAN CLIBURN CHARMED AUDIENCES IN MOSCOW . . .

WERNHER VON BRAUN

JACK PAAR

BORIS PASTERNAK

MUSIC

American Sputnik

The chandeliered, high-windowed concert hall of Moscow's Tchaikovsky State Conservatory echoed last week to the rubbery beat of *Blue Moon* and the striding chords of *Embraceable You*. Then a reedy Texas voice rose above the piano: "A-a-ah've got you un-dah mah skin!" The singer was long-legged, tousled Van Cliburn, 23, prize-winning pianist at the Tchaikovsky International Piano and Violin Festival, who had got under the Russian skin as no foreign artist had done in modern memory.

With his impromptu Rodgers-Gershwin-Porter recital, Cliburn warmed up to play the last movement of the Tchaikovsky *First Piano Concerto* at a concert of the leading prize winners on the evening his victory was announced. He was called back for three encores, finally retired to shouts of "more" in English. As soon as the hall was empty, technicians scurried in, kept Cliburn at the keyboard until the early hours of morning while they reproduced his triumph on film.

"Vanyusha." So it went all through the week of triumph. He was besieged by professional offers and trailed by adoring crowds that recognized him on sight, calling him first "Vanya" (Little Van) and later "Vanyusha," an even more intimately endearing diminutive. His arrivals and departures at the conservatory set off small riots. Girls sent fresh blossoms to his practice room, and when word got around that he had lost weight and that he suffers from colitis, platoons of females turned up with bags of oranges. One determined girl even popped up in his room at the Hotel Peking in the middle of the night.

Official Russia, with an eye cocked to the propaganda values of Cliburn's triumph, was just as ecstatic. At a Kremlin reception, squat Premier Nikita Khrushchev threw his arms around Van's beanpole, 6-ft.-4-in. frame, asked him why he was so tall. Grinned Van: "Because I'm from Texas." At a second Kremlin reception, Khrushchev bore down on Cliburn

with hands outstretched, jovially introduced him to his son, daughter, and granddaughter. When a waiter appeared with champagne, teetotaling Van shifted from one foot to another, murmured "I really don't care for any," finally took a glass, clinked, sipped and dis-

CLIBURN WARMING UP
He's got them under their skin

carded it. Even Nikolai Bulganin was at the party; with grave courtesy, Van addressed him as "Mr. Molotov."

$2,500 a Concert. Near exhaustion, Cliburn found time to chat for 40 minutes by phone with his parents back home in Kilgore, stop by the conservatory to have a life mask made for its collection. Then he traveled to Klin to play Tchaikovsky's piano, played by the greatest pianists on Tchaikovsky's birthday only. For Van they moved the birthday up several weeks. Finally, he played a solo recital at the conservatory auditorium to thunderous cheers, boarded the Red Arrow train to Leningrad, on the first leg of a tour to Riga, Kiev and Minsk.

From Europe and the U.S. the offers were pouring in: Dowager Queen Elisabeth of Belgium personally invited him to play at the Brussels World's Fair (he may do so, with the Philadelphia Orchestra); Impresario Sol Hurok, who once passed him up, tried unsuccessfully to get Cliburn under option; Ed Sullivan put in his bid for Cliburn's first Stateside TV appearance. Columbia Artists announced plans to bring over Moscow Conductor Kirik Kondrashin to accompany Cliburn on May 19 in a Carnegie Hall duplication of his prizewinning concert, with later performances in Philadelphia and Washington. Cliburn's concert fee jumped in a week from a top of $1,000 to $2,500 plus.

Ghosts & Feathers. What chiefly confounded the Americans in Moscow who have followed Van's career, *e.g.*, Juilliard Dean Mark Schubart, Pianist Norman Shetler, is that he is playing significantly better in Russia than he was able to play in the U.S. He has always had the technical equipment: the twelve-note span, the bravura style, the big percussive attack. But in preparation for his Moscow trip (which he says was revealed to him a year ago in a séance as a journey to "an agrarian country" where he would win a gold medal), Cliburn put in a grueling two months of six-to-eight-hours-a-day practice. During this period he may have sharpened some of the qualities that confounded Moscow critics: emotional nuances and inflections such as are normally heard only from string players; the special ghostly sonority that he can draw from the piano, as in the first movement of Rachmaninoff's *Concerto No. 3*; fast passages that combine a feathery sound with perfect, unblurred articulation.

Cliburn himself thinks that he was playing better in Moscow than he ever has before. Certainly it was his first hearing before such a knowledgeable big-time audience. Trying last week to account for Van's sudden starry appearance in the musical firmament, a Radio Moscow interviewer put it this way: "He is the American Sputnik — developed in secret."

1959

The Cuban Revolution succeeded under Castro — dictator Batista fled, and U.S.-owned property was confiscated.

NATIONAL AFFAIRS

DIPLOMACY
The Elemental Force

"Nikita Sergeevich, I salute you on American soil," said the U.S.S.R.'s Ambassador Mikhail Menshikov at Andrews Air Force Base, Md. last week — and there he was. There on American soil was Nikita Khrushchev, short, bald and portly, wearing a black suit, Homburg and three small medals, bowing down the receiving line, accepting a 21-gun salute, parading past a guard of honor. There on his one hand stood his pleasant, shy wife Nina Petrovna, his daughters Julia, 38, and Rada, 29, his studious-looking son Sergei, 24, and a retinue of 63 officials and bureaucrats. There on his other hand stood President Eisenhower. "Permit me at this moment to thank Mr. Eisenhower for the invitation," Khrushchev said graciously, responding to the President's coolly proper speech of greeting. "The Soviet people want to live in friendship with the American people."

But Nikita Sergeevich Khrushchev was not five minutes into his speech or 15 minutes into the U.S. before he sounded a prideful note of power that was to echo, sometimes blaring, sometimes muted, as the dominant theme of his trip. "Shortly before this meeting with you, Mr. President," he said, "the Soviet scientists, technicians, engineers and workers filled our hearts with joy by launching a rocket to the moon. We have no doubt that the excellent scientists, engineers and workers of the U.S.A. will also carry the pennant to the moon. The Soviet pennant, as an old resident, will then welcome your pennant."

The Facts of Life. Thus began what was, from Washington to Manhattan to Los Angeles to San Francisco, not so much a move to reduce world tension as a historic and tireless one-man campaign to cajole, flatter, wheedle, shame, threaten, and defy the U.S. into changing its way of looking at the world. Khrushchev defined it most bluntly in Washington: "There are only two nations which are powerful — the Soviet Union and the U.S. You people must

KHRUSHCHEV MOTORCADE ON MANHATTAN'S 34TH STREET
Big pitch for the ruling circles

accept the facts of life. You must recognize that we are here to stay." Khrushchev's argument: the U.S. must accept that fact and concede a "status quo" or "thaw" or "peace." It must close down its worldwide deterrent bases and disarm. It should reap the golden harvest of trade with Communist nations. It should leave to a furious peacetime competition the settlement of the classic feud between Communism and capitalism. Ultimately, he declared cockily, Communism would win anyway.

Nikita Khrushchev, sleeping as little as three hours a night, scarcely bothering to look out the windows of cars, trains, planes, pressed his message in brief private talks with the President, with U.S. diplomats and business executives, and in public question-and-answer debates with U.S. businessmen and newsmen before TV crowds of millions. And as the trip piled climax upon climax, it was Khrushchev himself — with his peasant's roughhewn politeness and witty proverbs and knack of making others laugh; with his politician's adeptness at choosing which questions to answer, dodge, or bull through; with his dictator's unpredictable pace changes from toothy grins to sudden shouts; with his

Marxist's 19th-century-model sureness that capitalism, like feudalism, was doomed by a simple process of history — it was Khrushchev who was at all times the embodiment of the elemental challenge. With an expansive smile he proclaimed to the U.S.: "You wanted to see what kind of man Khrushchev is! Well here I am!"

"Nearer My God." Khrushchev, his wife and the President of the U.S. rode 13 miles in the President's open-top Lincoln from Andrews Air Force Base to Blair House, the President's guest house across Pennsylvania Avenue from the White House. As the motorcade swung behind blaring brass bands into downtown Washington, the crowds lining the streets stood silent and somber, did not respond to Khrushchev's doffs and waves of his Homburg. A skywriting plane traced a big cross in the sky, and the carillon of St. John's Episcopal Church, across Lafayette Square from the White House, pealed *Nearer My God to Thee*. A Russian aide reported to Khrushchev that it was all a capitalist plot; a car, he said, had gone through the streets just before the arrival bearing a sign instructing the crowds not to applaud. The Moscow press and radio reported a triumphal turnout.

FIDEL CASTRO

CHRISTIAN A. HERTER

JAMES R. HOFFA

THE
HEALERS

In the age of AIDS —"Invincible AIDS," TIME called it in a 1992 cover story — it is easy to forget the strides that medicine has made in the past 70 years. Our century has seen the birth of psychoanalysis, the founding of landmark clinics, the commonplace use of what we once called "wonder drugs," the development of the artificial heart, the unlocking of the genetic code. The achievements of these visionary researchers remind us that polio and heart disease seemed, once upon a time, as invincible as AIDS seems today.

Frederick G. Banting
1923

Sigmund Freud
1924

Jonas Salk
1954

Carl Jung
1955

Christiaan Barnard
1967

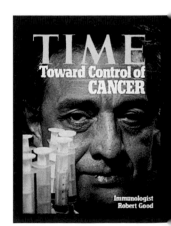
Robert A. Good
1973

CHARLES H. MAYO
1925

ALEXANDER FLEMING
1944

WILLIAM C. MENNINGER
1948

GEORGE W. MERCK
1952

IRVINE H. PAGE
1955

JOHN R. HELLER
1959

LEONARD W. LARSON
1961

MICHAEL DeBAKEY
1965

JOHN H. LARAGH
1975

WILLIAM DeVRIES
1984

DISEASE DETECTIVES
1989

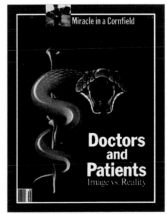

DOCTORS AND PATIENTS
1989

Man of the Year

By launching the Ecumenical Council called Vatican II, Pope John XXIII set out to adapt his church to the revolutionary changes in science, economics, morals and politics that have swept the modern world: to make it, in short, more Catholic and less Roman. Heading an institution so highly organized that it has been called "the U.S. Steel of churches," he has demonstrated such warmth, simplicity and charm that he has won the hearts of Catholics, Protestants and non-Christians alike.

When Jacqueline Kennedy came to visit, John asked his secretary how to address her. Replied the secretary: "'Mrs. Kennedy,' or just 'Madame,' since she is of French origin and has lived in France." Waiting in his private library, the Pope mumbled: "Mrs. Kennedy, Madame; Madame, Mrs. Kennedy." Then the doors opened on the U.S. First Lady and he stood up, extended his arms and cried, "Jacqueline!"
January 4, 1963

The Cruise of the *Vostok*

From Leningrad to Petropavlovsk, the U.S.S.R. came to a halt. Streetcars and buses stopped so that passengers could listen to loudspeakers in public squares. Factory workers shut off their machines; shopgirls quit their counters. Somewhere above them, a Soviet citizen was arcing past the stars, whirling about the earth at 18,000 miles an hour, soaring into history as the first man in space.

Vostok was not an un-manned satellite — impersonal, cold, emotionally empty. It had carried an ordinary man soaring across the face of the heavens, and mankind's imagination had soared with him.

As Washington awoke to its propaganda defeat, the proper people said the proper things. President Kennedy congratulated the Russians. But behind the cheerful and gracious phrases were frustration, shame, sometimes fury. U.S. spacemen had been beaten again.
April 21, 1961

Trigger of Hate

Far out at sea, mariners puzzled over a molten glow in the eastern sky. Over the roar of the freeway, motorists heard the unmistakable crack of rifle fire, the chilling stutter of machine guns. Above city hall, billowing smoke from 1,000 fires hung like a cerement. From the air, whole sections of the sprawling city looked as if they had been blitzed.

The atmosphere reminded soldiers of embattled Saigon. Yet this, last week, was Los Angeles — the City of Angels, the "safe city," as its boosters like to call it, the city that has always taken pride in its history of harmonious racial relations.

At 103rd Street and Compton Avenue, a mob methodically sacked a whole row of shops. As soon as any store was bare, it was set afire. One rallyiing cry never failed: "We're paying Whitey back!" Even women, children and grandparents joined the orgy of rapine. A little boy of eight or nine sat sobbing his heart out on a pawnshop shelf. Every time he took a radio, he whimpered, somebody bigger snatched it away from him.

August 20, 1965

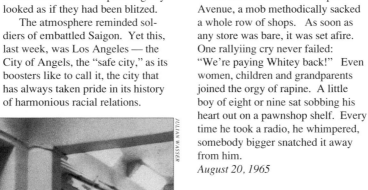

JULIAN WASSER

AP

AP

Arlington

Long after nightfall, the funeral train arrived in Washington. Along the lamplit streets, past a lumines-cence of sad and silent faces, the cavalcade wound through the federal city and across the Potomac, where in a green grove up the hill in Arling-ton, John Kennedy's grave looks out over the city and the river. The moon, the slender candles, the eternal flame at John's memorial — 47 feet away — and the floodlights laved Robert Kennedy's resting place beneath a magnolia tree. It was 11 o'clock, the first nighttime burial at Arlington in memory. There was no playing of taps, no rifle volley. After a brief and simple service, the coffin flag was folded into a triangle for presentation to Ethel, and the band played *America the Beautiful*.

June 14, 1968

The Grinding Bind

As the American jets flew high overhead, bypassing Hanoi for other targets, the enemy below was waiting. In the streets, grim-faced boys snapped through the manual of arms with wooden rifles while pretty girls in pantaloons hurled mock grenades through automobile tires, many of them scoring two hits out of three over 25 yards. Hanoi was ready for total war. So was Ho Chi Minh, the goat-bearded god of Viet-namese Communism. Ho was making his last and most steely stand, and his young country seemed ready to win or die with him.

Last week 8,000 more marines landed at Danang, raising the total of Americans in South Viet Nam to 63,000, and President Johnson told a press conference that another 10,000 U.S. troops will soon arrive. Experts in Saigon foresaw 150,000 men by year's end. The President was blunt about what the built-up U.S. forces face. Said he: "We expect it will get worse before it gets better."

July 16, 1965

1960s

JOHN ZIMMERMAN

New Leader

Win or lose, Arnold Palmer, with his daring, slashing attack, is fun to watch. Coldly precise in his study of the game, Palmer is anything but stolid during a round: he mutters imprecations to himself, contorts his face, sometimes drops his club and wanders away in disgust at a botched shot.

Since World War II the golfing era has been characterized by a crew of salty-talking, hard-driving pros who got their formal education in caddy shacks and found their relaxation at the bar-bunkered 19th hole. The Palmer breed, now taking over, is that of the college-trained family man with an agent to line up fat endorsements and a cooler in the auto trunk for baby's bottle.

May 2, 1960

Highs & Lows of Hippiedom

San Francisco's Haight-Ashbury district — a throbbing three-eighths of a far-from-square-mile — is the vibrant epicenter of the hippie movement. Fog sweeps past the gingerbread houses of "The Hashbury," shrouding the shapes of hirsute, shoeless hippies huddled in doorways, smoking pot, "rapping" (achieving rapport with random talk), or banging beer cans in time to ubiquitous jukebox rhythms. The tinkle of Indian elephant bells echoes from passing "seekers"; along the Panhandle of Golden Gate Park, hollow-cheeked flower children queue up for a plateful of stew, dispensed from the busy buses of the Diggers, a band of hippie do-gooders. Last week the sidewalks and doorways were filling with new arrivals — hippies and would-be hippies with suitcases and sleeping bags, just off the bus and looking for a place to "crash" (sleep)

July 7, 1967

an in Motion

Now on the eve of a three-month
urn tour of the U.S. with Britain's
oyal Ballet, Rudolf Nureyev stands
t as one of the most electrifying
ale dancers of all time. When he
aves the theater, hordes of glaze-
ed females of all ages have been
own to surround his car and fall on
eir knees chanting, "Thank you,
ank you." The admiration extends
ckstage as well. Whenever he
rforms, dancers crowd the wings
watch and learn.

If this were not enough, Nureyev
s been further blessed with a clas-
partner — Dame Margot
nteyn. They have about them the
agic makings for a fairy-tale ro-
ance. He is 27, a moody, mysteri-
s Tartar bristling with savage
arm. She is 45, an alabaster
auty of elegant refinement. He
the glittering young prince in the
st bloom of creative life. She is
e dying swan in the last flutter of
hining career.
ril 19, 1965

Good Grief

Comics have espoused many
causes; the strips have been crammed
with all kinds of propaganda. But
Peanuts is the leader of a refreshing
new breed that takes an unprecedented interest in the basics of life.
Love, hate, togetherness, solitude, the
alienation in an age of anxiety —
such topics are so deftly explored by
Charlie Brown and the rest of the
Peanuts crew that 60 million readers
who would not sit still for a sermon
readily devour the sermon-like car-
toons. Cartoonist Charles Schulz
owns up to making his *Peanuts*
mean because he believes that kids
are born mean.
April 9, 1965

1960

Presidential campaign politics were permanently altered when candidates Nixon and Kennedy appeared before the cameras in a nationally televised debate.

BELGIUM GRANTED INDEPENDENCE TO THE CONGO ■ NEO-NAZI POLITICAL GROUPS WERE BANNED IN GERMANY ■ THE U.S. LAUNCHED THE FIRST WEATHER SATELLITE, *TIROS I* ■ THE WORD "LASER" ENTERED THE VOCABULARY ■ TEENAGERS LEARNED TO TWIST ■ AND AMERICAN FRANCIS GARY POWERS WAS TRIED IN RUSSIA FOR ESPIONAGE . . .

JACQUES-YVES COUSTEAU

ARNOLD PALMER

JOHN F. KENNEDY

FOREIGN NEWS

RUSSIA

The Boy from Virginia

Q. What is your profession?
A. Pilot.
Q. What place of work?
A. Detachment 10-10 at Adana, Turkey.
Q. When did you receive the order to fly over Soviet territory?
A. On the morning on May 1.

Thus, in the flat accents of Pound, Va., U-2 Pilot Francis Gary Powers began to describe his part in one of history's most celebrated — and until his mishap, most successful — espionage operations.

The many-columned courtroom where Powers was brought to trial after 108 days in solitary confinement had seen history made before: in the days when it was still the Noblemen's Club, Pushkin and Tolstoy relaxed there; later the bodies of Lenin and Stalin lay there in state. But Powers seemed unmindful of history, and the faraway cities of which he talked were apparently little more than dots on the map to him. A man who by his testimony belonged to no political party and had never voted, Powers was simply an expert airplane chauffeur describing his trade. "I don't know," he said when asked about the workings of the U-2's phenomenal electronic brain. "I just turned on the switches." How did he get into the spy game? "I felt lucky to get such a good job — flying service with a big salary."

Showpiece. To demonstrate to the world through this uncomplicated flyer the "insane aggressiveness" of the U.S., Nikita Khrushchev had set up a show trial that evoked memories of Stalin's purge productions of the 1930s. All morning long in the cold Moscow rain, the black ZIM limousines rolled up to the court to disgorge Soviet Russia's Reddest-blooded aristocrats, including Khrushchev's daughter Elena. Out of the unaccustomed luxury of one of the ZIMs stepped Powers' wife, Barbara, 25, poised and cool in black, flanked by her mother and two lawyers. From another emerged her father-in-law, Oliver Powers, a 55-year-old cobbler whose last trip out of his hill country had been a visit to Atlanta and Washington in 1935. Hopelessly, Powers tried to comfort his wife Ida. "They'll know he's a good boy like he's always been," he said. "We'll have him back real soon."

Inside, under brilliant chandeliers, a theater bell called the audience to their seats, just as for the concerts that often fill the hall. As Powers mounted the six steps to the stage and stood gripping the wooden slats of the

THE POWERS FAMILY HEARING VERDICT
"They'll know he's a good boy."

defendant's box, his wife, at the opposite end of the hall, buried her face in her hands. But Powers, despite his baggy, Russian-made double breasted suit, looked fit and to all appearances unbrainwashed.

Powers began his birthday by pleading "Yes, I am guilty" to a 4,000-word indictment. Acknowledged as a spy by his own Government, he obviously saw cooperation with his captors as the only path to survival and dutifully professed his penitence. In jail, he had been allowed to talk to no one but his captors, had seen no Americans. "I understand that as a direct result of my flight, the summit conference did not take place," he said, "and President Eisenhower's visit was called off. I am sincerely sorry I had anything to do with this."

Socialist Humanitarianism. The summing up was the predictable set propaganda piece — one that the London *Times* dismissed as "crude stuff" and a "characteristic mistake by the Russians." To prosecutor Rudenko, the trial "unmasked completely the criminal aggressive actions of the U.S. ruling quarters" and the "savage, man-hating ethics of Allen Dulles & Co., placing the dollar, this yellow devil, higher than human life."

By way of defense, Powers' court-appointed attorney, Mikhail Grinev, who makes a good living losing cases he is expected to, tried to outdo the prosecution in attacking the U.S. Powers, he said, "should be joined in the dock by his masters, who attend this trial invisibly." Grinev in friendly fashion had told Powers' parents that "social factors are very important with our judiciary" and in his argument he stressed the family's hardscrabble hill-country life. Powers, he said, went to work for the CIA only because of "mass unemployment" in the U.S. Against Rudenko's suggested sentence of 15 years, Grinev asked for the minimum sentence, seven years.

At the end Powers himself got a brief chance to plead and said that he had never felt "any enmity whatsoever toward the Russian people." His voice was clear and strong. He did not join in his counsel's attack on the U.S., but neither did he disavow it. Apparently not aware that in Russia his defense attorney was as much the agent of the state as the prosecutor, he had let himself be persuaded to be pictured as a helpless tool of forces beyond him. Having made its case, having denounced the act while seemingly showing its charity to the defendant, the court quickly sentenced Powers to ten years, which it called an example of "socialist humanitarianism." By no coincidence, the trial wound up in exactly the three days for which the hall had been leased by the court.

ALAN SHEPARD BECAME THE FIRST AMERICAN IN SPACE, FOLLOWING SOVIET COSMONAUT GAGARIN ■ THE SENATE EXAMINED ACTIVITIES OF THE JOHN BIRCH SOCIETY ■ BOBBY FISCHER, 17, WON THE U.S. CHESS CHAMPIONSHIP FOR THE FOURTH TIME ■ AND IN JERUSALEM, NAZI WAR CRIMINAL ADOLF EICHMANN WAS SENTENCED TO DEATH BY HANGING . . .

1961

The world had a new symbol of totalitarianism when the Berlin Wall was hastily erected by East Germany to stem the exodus of refugees.

FOREIGN NEWS

ISRAEL

Judgment Day

From the moment that Israeli agents in Argentina flashed home the coded message 19 months ago, "The beast is in chains," there has been no doubt over the verdict in the case of Adolf Eichmann. Last week, as a chill rain fell on the deserted streets outside Jerusalem's *Beit Haam* (House of the People), the three Israeli judges returned to the courtroom in which, for four months, they heard 1,350,000 words of testimony. The crowd expected to hear first a detailed, legalistic defense of Israel's right to try Eichmann. Instead, Presiding Judge Moshe Landau (like his two colleagues a refugee from Nazi Germany) ordered Eichmann to attention in his glass, bulletproof cage, and bluntly told the accused: "The court finds you guilty."

Block of Ice. For the next 17 hours, taking turns reading their 100,000-word opinion, which has been four months in the writing, the judges explained why Eichmann was found guilty on all 15 counts (crimes against humanity, crimes against the Jewish people, war crimes, and membership in Nazi organizations) because, far from being "a puppet in the hands of others, he was among those who pulled the strings . . . This block of ice . . . this block of marble . . . closed his ears to the voice of his conscience, as was demanded of him by the regime to which he was wholeheartedly devoted, and to which he had sold himself body and soul. Thus he sank from one depth to another, until, in the implementation of the 'final solution,' he reached the nether hell."

The former Gestapo colonel's excuse that he had only rounded up Jews for deportation to death camps, and had not killed any himself, was rejected by the court.

"The legal and moral responsibility of him who delivers the victim to his death," said the judges, "is in our opinion, no smaller, and may even be greater than the liability of him who does the victim to death."

Similarly, the judgment dismissed as "of no avail" Eichmann's plea that he had only acted on orders from his government. This

DEFENDENT EICHMANN
"We never discussed his work."

could not exempt "from their personal criminal responsibility those who gave, and those who carried out the order."

Melting Nerves. Citing legal authorities in six languages, ranging in time from Hugo Grotius in 1625 to the United Nations genocide convention in 1948, the court sought to establish Israel's jurisdiction over Eichmann; although the Israeli state did not exist when the crimes were committed, the judges argued that Israel now represents all Jews.

"The people is one and the crime is one," they said. "To argue that there is no connection is like cutting away a tree root and branch and saying to its trunk: I have not hurt you."

At one point, Eichmann's nerves melted. His face twitched; his tongue flicked his lips and his complexion became sickly pale. But his voice was firm when he made his final statement. "I am not the monster I am made out to be," he said. "This mass slaughter is solely the responsibility of political leaders. My guilt lies in my obedience, my respect for discipline, my allegiance to the colors and the service." He would ask the Jews for pardon, said Eichmann, except that, in view of the verdict, "this would be construed as hypocrisy . . . I must carry the burden imposed on me by fate."

His fate, as decreed by the court: death by hanging. Appeals to the Israeli Supreme Court and to President Izhak Ben-Zvi will postpone the almost certain execution for several months. Until then, Eichmann will be held in a special cell on the top floor of the British-built Teggart Fortress in Ramleh. Meanwhile, a British reporter had sought out Mrs. Veronika Eichmann, now living in seclusion in Germany.

Affirming her husband's innocence, Mrs. Eichmann was "absolutely sure" he would return home. Then, almost as an afterthought, she added: "We never discussed his work."

JACQUELINE KENNEDY

SAMUEL T. RAYBURN

YURI GAGARIN

1962

"Environment" became the watchword, as Rachel Carson's Silent Spring *raised wide concerns about the growing use of pesticides.*

THE SECOND VATICAN COUNCIL OPENED IN ROME ■ THE U.S. COURT OF APPEALS FOUND MISSISSIPPI'S GOVERNOR GUILTY OF CONTEMPT FOR RESISTING UNIVERSITY INTEGRATION ■ WIDESPREAD BIRTH DEFECTS IN EUROPE WERE TRACED TO THE DRUG THALIDOMIDE ■ AND PRESIDENT KENNEDY STOOD UP TO SOVIET AGGRESSION IN CUBA . . .

THE NATION

LT. COL. JOHN GLENN

TENNESSEE WILLIAMS

SEN. EVERETT DIRKSEN

FOREIGN RELATIONS

The Backdown

There was danger in standing still or moving forward. I thought it was the wisest policy to risk that which was incident to the latter course.

— James Monroe
to Thomas Jefferson (1822)

Last week that perilous choice confronted another, younger President of the U.S. Generations to come may well count John Kennedy's resolve as one of the decisive moments of the 20th century. For Kennedy determined to move forward at whatever risk. And when faced by that determination, the bellicose Premier of the Soviet Union first wavered, then weaseled and finally backed down.

To Kennedy, the time of truth arrived when he received sheaves of photographs taken during the preceding few days by U.S. reconnaissance planes over Cuba. They furnished staggering proof of a massive, breakneck buildup of Soviet missile power on Castro's island. Already poised were missiles capable of hurling a megaton each—or roughly 50 times the destructive power of the Hiroshima atomic bomb—at the U.S. Under construction were sites for launching five-megaton missiles.

Into early October, the Soviets proceeded covertly, masking their operations with lies and claims that they were sending only "defensive" weapons to Cuba. Then they threw off stealth, lunging ahead in a frantic, scarcely concealed push to get offensive missiles up and ready to fire. Their aim was devastatingly obvious: they meant to present the U.S. with the accomplished fact of a deadly missile arsenal on Cuba.

If the plan had worked—and it came fearfully close—Nikita Khrushchev would in one mighty stroke have changed the power balance of the cold war. Once again a foreign dictator had seemingly misread the character

of the U.S. and of a U.S. President. At Vienna and later, Khrushchev had sized up Kennedy as a weakling, given to strong talk and timorous action. The U.S. itself, he told Poet Robert Frost, was "too liberal to fight." Now, in the Caribbean, he intended to prove his point. And Berlin would surely come next.

Kennedy shattered those illusions. He did it with a series of dramatic decisions that swiftly brought the U.S. to a showdown not with Fidel Castro but with Khrushchev's own Soviet Union. Basic to those decisions were

KENNEDY PROCLAIMS BLOCKADE
"Too liberal to fight?"

two propositions:

• It would not be enough for the Russians to halt missile shipments to Cuba. Instead, all missiles in Cuba must be dismantled and removed. If necessary, the U.S. would remove them by invasion.

• Any aggressive act from Cuba would be treated by the U.S. as an attack by the Soviet Union itself. And the U.S. would retaliate against Russia with the sudden and full force of its thermonuclear might.

As a first step, and only as a first step, Kennedy decided to impose a partial block-

ade, or quarantine, on Cuba, stopping all shipments of offensive weapons—missiles, warheads, missile launching equipment, bombers and bombs.

Kennedy announced his decisions on television to a somber nation and found that nation overwhelmingly behind him.

Against the surge of feeling, Khrushchev reacted hesitantly. Twelve hours after Kennedy's speech, the Kremlin issued a cautiously worded statement. Then Khrushchev grasped eagerly at a suggestion by U Thant, Acting Secretary-General of the United Nations, for a two or three weeks "suspension," with Russia halting missile shipments to Cuba and Kennedy lifting the blockade. Kennedy politely declined.

But Khrushchev had one more trick up his sleeve. He offered to take his missile bases out of Cuba if the U.S. would dismantle its missile bases in Turkey. With a speed that must have bewildered Khrushchev, the President refused.

That did it. Early Sunday morning came the word from Moscow Radio that Khrushchev had sent a new message to Kennedy. In it, Khrushchev complained about a U-2 flight over Russia on Oct. 28, groused about the continuing "violation" of Cuban airspace. But, he said, he had noted Kennedy's assurances that no invasion of Cuba would take place if all offensive weapons were removed. Hence, wrote Khrushchev, the Soviet Government had "issued a new order for the dismantling of the weapons, which you describe as offensive, their crating and returning to the Soviet Union." Finally, he offered to let United Nations representatives verify the removal of the missiles.

If carried out, it was capitulation. Kennedy said he welcomed Khrushchev's decision. In his stand against Khrushchev, the President had not once missed sight of the central point: that the Soviet missile capability in Cuba was a threat to U.S. survival. By directly challenging Soviet aggression in the hemisphere, Kennedy was acting on the fundamental principle of the Monroe Doctrine. And he had given momentous meaning to the principle of moving forward.

ASTRONOMERS ANNOUNCED THE DISCOVERY OF QUASARS ■ WINSTON CHURCHILL RECEIVED HONORARY U.S. CITIZENSHIP ■ ANDY WARHOL'S PAINTINGS OF SOUP CANS WENT ON DISPLAY AT THE GUGGENHEIM MUSEUM ■ MUHAMMAD ALI WAS STILL KNOWN AS CASSIUS CLAY ■ AND THE REV. DR. MARTIN LUTHER KING DECLARED THAT HE HAD A DREAM . . .

1963

The nation's faith in itself was shaken as President Kennedy was gunned to death while waving to the crowds in a Dallas motorcade.

THE NATION

CIVIL RIGHTS

The March's Meaning

The march on Washington was a triumph. But after everybody agreed on that, the question was: Why?

Hardly in terms of immediate results, since there were none. The battle cry of the march was "Now!" Seas of placards demanded Negro equality—Now! Speakers demanded action—Now! Cried John Lewis, 25, leader of the militant young Student Nonviolent Coordinating Committee (SNICK): "We want our freedom—and we want it NOW!"

But Now! remained a long way off. It would not come today, tomorrow, next month or next year. This was made starkly clear as the leaders of civil rights organizations paid morning calls on Capitol Hill's most powerful citizens. It was made just as starkly clear after the march, when the civil rights leaders went to the White House to see President Kennedy.

To all, the civil rights leaders made specific requests: they demanded passage of the Kennedy Administration's entire civil rights package, including its controversial section banning discrimination in public accommodations. But even the Kennedy package was inadequate: the Negro leaders wanted to add to it sections that would 1) set up a federal fair employment practices commission, and 2) give the Justice Department vast power to intervene in almost all civil rights disputes. From the Capitol Hill leaders, and from the President, the visitors got polite words—and polite refusals.

Wherein, then, lay the triumph of the march? Civil rights leaders themselves had a hard time putting it into words. "We subpoenaed the conscience of the nation," said Martin Luther King Jr. The march was informal, often formless—yet it somehow had great dignity. It had little of the sustained suspense of an astronaut shoot or a national political convention—but it built, despite moments of boredom and restlessness—to an emotion-draining climax. It was in the probable effects on the conscience of millions of previously indifferent Americans that the march might find its true meaning.

Beginning of a Dream

The march from the Washington Monument to the Lincoln Memorial, a distance of about eight-tenths of a mile, had been scheduled to start at 11:30 a.m. But at least 20 minutes before then, a group of Negroes started strolling away from the Monument grounds

MARCHERS IN WASHINGTON
"I have a dream"

on the way to the Memorial. Hundreds, then thousands and tens of thousands, followed. Constitution and Independence Avenues were transformed into oceans of bobbing placards. Some marchers wept as they walked: the faces of many more gleamed with happiness. There were no brass bands. There was little shouting or singing. Instead, for over an hour and a half, there was the sound of thousands of feet shuffling toward the temple erected in the name of Abraham Lincoln.

At the Memorial, the first order of business was a program of professional entertainment. Folk Singers Joan Baez, Josh White, Odetta, Bob Dylan, Peter-Paul-and-Mary rendered hymns and civil right songs.

Now to the platform came Singer Mahalia Jackson. First she sang a slow, sorrowful Gospel song titled *I've Been Buked and I've Been Scorned.* Her voice was marvelous, but her impact was more in her manner. Near tears, she moved her huge audience to tears. But in the very next breath, she would break into an expression of expectant happiness. When that happened, people who had been sobbing a second before began laughing, sharing in her expectancy.

Mahalia was hard to follow—and there probably was only one person in the civil rights world who could have done it quite so successfully. His introduction was drowned out by the roaring cheers of those who saw him heading toward the speakers' platform. He was Atlanta's Rev. Martin Luther King Jr.

"The Negro," he said, "lives on a lonely island of poverty in the midst of a vast ocean of material prosperity and finds himself an exile in his own land." King continued stolidly: "It would be fatal for the nation to overlook the urgency of the moment and to underestimate the determination of the Negro. This sweltering summer of the Negro's legitimate discontent will not pass until there is an invigorating autumn of freedom and equality.

"I have a dream," King cried. The crowd began cheering, but King, never pausing, brought silence as he continued, "I have a dream that one day on the red hills of Georgia the sons of former slaves and the sons of former slaveowners will be able to sit down together at the table of brotherhood."

"I have a dream," King went on, relentlessly shouting down the thunderous swell of the crowd's applause, "that my four little children will one day live in a nation where they will not be judged by the color of their skin but by the content of their character."

Even after King finished, there were some final ceremonies. But to all effective intents and purposes, the day was over. Obeying their leaders' injunctions to leave town as soon as the official ceremonies had ended, the demonstrators made their way back toward their trains, buses, planes and cars. It was a quiet night in Washington—after a day that would never be forgotten.

POPE JOHN XXIII

SARGENT SHRIVER

GEORGE WALLACE

1964

The long, painful process of "escalation" had begun in Viet Nam: U.S. aircraft attacked Northern bases in reprisal for an assault on an American destroyer.

AN EARTHQUAKE IN ALASKA LEFT 114 DEAD ■ INDEPENDENCE WAS DECLARED IN THE FORMER BRITISH COLONIES OF KENYA, NYASALAND, AND NORTHERN RHODESIA ■ NEW YORK'S VERRAZANO-NARROWS, THE WORLD'S LONGEST SUSPENSION BRIDGE, OPENED ■ AND THE WARREN COMMISSION SHARED ITS FINDINGS ON THE KENNEDY ASSASSINATION . . .

W. BUCKMINSTER FULLER

BARRY GOLDWATER

LADY BIRD JOHNSON

NATIONAL NEWS

THE WARREN COMMISSION

The Witnesses

The Warren Commission last week released 26 volumes, totaling 17,741 pages, of the testimony and evidence upon which it based its 888-page report on the assassination of President Kennedy. Included were more than 3,100 exhibits and statements from and interviews with some 550 persons, many of them technical experts, peripheral participants, and even people with some way-out ideas about how and why it happened.

But it was in the sometimes halting, often rambling, stories of those most immediately involved that the testimony had its impact.

Jackie

Chief Justice Warren, Commission Counsel J. Lee Rankin and Bobby Kennedy spent 45 minutes with Jacqueline Kennedy in her Georgetown home when she told of the assassination. She served lemonade, replied softly to Rankin's gentle questioning. Excerpts:

A Quizzical Look. "In the motorcade, you know, I usually would be waving mostly to the left side and he was waving mostly to the right, which is one reason you are not looking at each other very much. It was terribly hot.

"You know there is always noise in a motorcade, and there are always motorcycles beside us, a lot of them backfiring. So I was looking to the left. I guess there was a noise, but it didn't seem like any different noise, really, because there is so much noise, motorcycles and things. But then suddenly Governor Connally was yelling 'Oh, no, no, no!'

"I heard these terrible noises. You know. And my husband never made any sound. So I turned to the right. And all I remember is seeing my husband, he had this sort of quizzical look on his face, and his hand was up, it must have been his left hand. And just as I turned and looked at him, I could see a piece of his skull, and I remember it was flesh-colored. I remember thinking he just looked as if he had a slight headache.

"And then he sort of did this, put his hand to his forehead and fell in my lap. And then I just remember falling on him and saying, 'Oh, no, no, no,' I mean, 'Oh, my God, they have shot my husband.' And 'I love you, Jack,' I remember I was shouting."

The Connallys

At one point during his testimony, Texas' Governor John Connally stripped off his shirt to show the scars on his chest. Repeatedly, his eyes filled with tears as he spoke.

AGENT HILL SCRAMBLING ABOARD KENNEDY CAR
"The whole thing seemed unreal—unbelievable."

Said Connally: "I heard this noise, which I immediately took to be a rifle shot. I instinctively turned to my right because the sound appeared to come from over my right shoulder, so I turned to look back over my right shoulder, and I saw nothing unusual except just people in the crowd, but I did not catch the President in the corner of my eye, and I was interested because, once I heard the shot in my own mind, I identified it as a rifle shot, and I immediately — the only thought that crossed my mind was that this is an assassination attempt."

Hearing It Hit. When Connally himself was hit, his wife pulled him down into her lap.

He was "conscious all the time, and with my eyes open, and then, of course, the third shot sounded, and I heard the shot very clearly. I heard it hit him. I heard the shot hit something, and I assumed again — it never entered my mind that it ever hit anybody but the President.

"Immediately, I could see on my clothes, my clothing, I could see on the interior of the car which, as I recall, was a pale blue, brain tissue, which I immediately recognized, and I recall very well, on my trousers there was one chunk of brain tissue as big almost as my thumbnail, and again I did not see the President at any time either after the first, second or third shots, but I assumed always that it was he who was hit and no one else."

Lady Bird

About a week after the assassination, Lady Bird Johnson dictated her recollections on a tiny tape recorder — "primarily as a form of therapy to help me over the shock and horror of the experience." A transcript was sent to the Warren Commission.

After the shots, the Johnson's car "accelerated terrifically fast — faster and faster. Then suddenly they put on the brakes so hard that I wondered if they were going to make it as we wheeled left and went around the corner. We pulled up to a building. I looked up and saw it said 'Hospital.'

"As we ground to a halt — we were still the third car — Secret Service men began to pull, lead, guide, and hustle us out. I cast one last look over my shoulder and saw, in the President's car, a bundle of pink, just like a drift of blossoms, lying on the back seat. I think it was Mrs. Kennedy lying over the President's body."

Before Lady Bird gave the transcript to the Commission, she had done some editing. On the original, at the point where she discussed Jackie's refusal to change her blood-drenched clothes, Lady Bird had added: "Then with something — if you can say a person that gentle, that dignified, had an element of fierceness — she said, 'I want them to see what they have done to Jack.'"

A SOVIET COSMONAUT FLOATED IN SPACE FOR 10 MINUTES ■ RALPH NADER PUBLISHED *UNSAFE AT ANY SPEED* ■ STUDENT DEMONSTRATIONS BEGAN AGAINST VIET NAM ■ MALCOLM X WAS SHOT IN NEW YORK ■ A POWER BLACKOUT HIT 30 MILLION ■ AND IN ROME, VATICAN II UPDATED THE DOCTRINES OF THE CATHOLIC CHURCH . . .

1965

The nation was stunned by Los Angeles' Watts riots, which claimed 35 lives and tragically focused attention on the despair of inner cities.

TIME ESSAY

VATICAN II: TURNING THE CHURCH TOWARD THE WORLD

"THE whole world expects a step forward," said John XXIII as he opened the Second Vatican Council in October 1962. When Pope Paul VI formally closed it last week, he heralded it as "among the greatest events of the church." Whatever the future's judgment, there can be little doubt that the council indeed represents a momentous step forward in carrying Christendom's oldest, largest body into modern times and bringing it into closer contact with all men—religious or not.

Vatican II was strikingly different from the 20 other ecclesiastical assemblies that Roman Catholicism ranks as ecumenical. It is the first council that did not face, or leave in its wake, heresy or schism. Councils have always been the church's last-resort response to crisis—from the First Council of Nicaea, summoned by Emperor Constantine in 325 to combat the Arian heresy, to the abortive Vatican I (1869-70), which faced the bewildering effects of the ever-widening industrial revolution.

At the time Vatican II convened, there were few obvious threats, few violent complaints among its 560 million members. Yet the church was scarcely facing up to the growing secularization of life, the explosion of science, the bitter claims to social justice in old nations and new. Catholic theology, dominated by a textbook scholasticism, appeared to have stopped in the 13th century. Except by a few pioneer ecumenists, Protestants were unhesitatingly regarded as heretics.

Today this sort of thinking seems almost as remote in the church as the sale of indulgences—and this is perhaps the strongest single measure of the council's achievements. The essentials of Catholic dogma stand, of course, as does Rome's claim of universality. What has changed drastically is atmosphere and attitudes. "Before, the church looked like an immense and immovable colossus, the city set on a hill, the stable bulwark against the revolutionary change," says the English Benedictine

abbot, Dom Christopher Butler. "Now it has become a people on the march—or at least a people which is packing its bags for a pilgrimage."

In all, more than 2,400 patriarchs cardinals, bishops and religious superiors took part in the council's deliberations. For the first time in history, observers from Protestant and

POPE PAUL CELEBRATES MASS
"Packing bags for a pilgrimage"

Orthodox churches not only sat in attendance at the debates but were also consulted.

The 16 promulgated decrees, constitutions and declarations that are the council's legacy divide roughly into two categories. The majority are aimed at the internal renewal and reform of Catholicism, but at least four may profoundly affect the relationship between the church and the non-Catholic world.

One document that has already changed the spiritual life of the church is the constitution *On the Liturgy*, which led to widespread introduction of vernacular languages in the Mass. Another constitution, *On the Church*, asserting that bishops collectively share ruling

power over the church with the Pope, is the charter for what many theologians feel will be a slow but unstoppable democratization.

Of more concern to non-Catholics are the documents that clearly define the end of the church's Counter Reformation hostility to other faiths. One is the much rewritten constitution *On the Church in the Modern World*, which attempts to express the mind of Catholicism on such matters of common concern as peace and war, world poverty, industrialism, social and economic justice. A decree *On Ecumenism*, committing Catholicism to work for Christian unity, for the first time acknowledges Protestant bodies as churches that share God's grace and favor.

Many bishops readily admit that these and other documents of Vatican II show some omissions and outright failures. The ecclesiastical legislation had to be shaped and sometimes compromised to gain the approval of disparate men—Italian country bishops who have seldom seen Protestants, and Dutch prelates who pray with them almost daily; U.S. cardinals whose most pressing concern is a multimillion-dollar building fund, and Asian missionaries whose church is a Quonset hut. Methodist Observer Albert C. Outler of Texas says that "several of the declarations are substandard; several are no better than mediocre."

The success or failure of Vatican II cannot be judged merely by the bulk of written documents. More important is the spirit that brought the council together and inspired its discussions. In general, the council indicates a new attitude toward a complex, pluralistic world. Without denying its own belief that it has a special divine mission, Catholicism now acknowledges that it is but one of many spiritual voices with something to tell perplexed modern man. The more the church returns in spirit to the unfettered simplicity of the Gospel from which it sprang, the more likely it is that its voice will be heeded again by the world.

SEN. WILLIAM FULBRIGHT

"PEANUTS"

GEMINI RENDEZVOUS

1966

A "cultural revolution" raged in China, as Red Guards brandished copies of Mao's quotations and violently demonstrated against foreign influences.

DE GAULLE REQUESTED THE REMOVAL OF NATO FORCES FROM FRENCH SOIL ■ THE NEW METROPOLITAN OPERA HOUSE OPENED AT NEW YORK'S LINCOLN CENTER ■ LUCI BAINES JOHNSON MARRIED PATRICK NUGENT ■ AND TRUMAN CAPOTE PLANNED A "BLACK AND WHITE PARTY" AT THE PLAZA HOTEL IN NEW YORK . . .

ARTUR RUBENSTEIN

ROBERT S. MCNAMARA

WALTER CRONKITE

MODERN LIVING

PARTIES

Truman's Compote

"They just don't understand," said Novelist Truman Capote, not deigning to identify "they." "This is purely and simply a party for my friends." The trouble was that no one could quite believe that Truman's 540 most intimate friends could be composed of the likes of Averell Harriman and Sammy Davis Jr., Walter Lippmann and Frankie Sinatra, William Baldwin, James Baldwin, Tallulah Bankhead and the Marquis and Marchioness of Dufferin and Ava. Yet the fact is that he possesses an almost endless entrée into the world of the great and the glamorous; as he modestly puts it: "I have an awful lot of friends all over the world."

A Mess of Piranhas. Capote's friends are nothing if not loyal — in fact, some of them feel he has changed their lives forever by opening new vistas. When his latest book came out, Kay Graham threw a big party for him in Washington and he promised her last spring, "I'm going to give a party for you because you gave one for me." The place would just have to be the Plaza Hotel, "because it has the only truly beautiful ballroom left in New York." And the decor would be straight out of Cecil Beaton's Ascot scene in *My Fair Lady;* everyone must come in black and white.

Most fun of all for Capote, who has played at giving fantasy parties since childhood, was to decree that everyone should wear a mask. The whole point of a *bal masqué,* he explained, "is to ask anyone you want to dance and sit wherever you want, and then, when the masks come off at midnight, you can find out who your new chums are, or join your old chums." In October the invitations went off, and suddenly Capote was swamped with pleading messages from those whom he had left out. "I feel like I fell into a whole mess of piranha fish," he moaned to *Women's Wear Daily.*

Came the Deluge. For days preceding the party last week, jets from London, Paris, Rome, Washington, Los Angeles and Garden City,

BUSSED BY BACALL, OUTMUGGED BY RYAN
Like an international Who's Who for the guillotine

Kans., flew in the guests. [Capote invited eleven Kansans with whom he became friends while researching and writing *In Cold Blood.*] All day before the ball, fashionable East Side hairdressers fought off nervous breakdowns, and the 16 hosts and hostesses who had volunteered to give pre-ball dinners simmered on the verge of hysteria. Capote and Kay Graham had a quiet little "bird and bottle" picnic supper in his Plaza suite. Shortly after 10 p.m., the deluge came. By the droves, masked figures ducked in out of the rain, past the reporters and TV lights in the lobby, pushed their way into elevators, and passed the two check-in tables on their way to greet Truman and Kay at the ballroom door.

"The guest book reads like an international list for the guillotine," muttered Leo Lerman from *Mademoiselle.* In swarmed the jet-setters (Gloria Guinness, Lee Radziwill, Count and Countess Rudolfo Crespi, Mr. John Barry Ryan III), the intellectuals (Arthur Schlesinger Jr., McGeorge Bundy, William Buckley), show-biz folk (Henry Fonda, Lauren Bacall, Jerome Robbins), the writers (Edward Albee, Marianne Moore, Norman Mailer) and official Washington (Nicholas Katzenbach, John Sherman Cooper, Jacob Javits).

Slow-Motion Passes. For himself, Capote

had selected a 39¢ domino mask from F.A.O. Schwarz; it was bested for economy by Alice Roosevelt Longworth, 82-year-old daughter of Theodore Roosevelt. She had shopped around and got a similar mask for 4¢ less. But few of the other ladies tried to pare expenses; some spent $600 and more for their extravaganzas. Rose Kennedy picked out several masks in case she changed her mind, finally settled on an elaborate domino with towering egret plumes. Mrs. Henry Ford II came wearing a white organdy butterfly.

Most men tucked their masks in their pockets as soon as they arrived. Explained Alfred Gwynne Vanderbilt: "It itches and I can't see." Soon the women followed suit, long before the magical hour of midnight. While the bands alternated rock 'n' roll and pop tunes, the favorite sport became people watching, until the question arose, what next? With no climax in sight and no single star to shine, part of the answer was 450 bottles of nonvintage Taittinger champagne. *Paris Review* Editor George Plimpton began throwing slow-motion forward passes with a napkin to Receiver John Kenneth Galbraith, Lynda Bird danced on and on with Actor Roddy McDowall, and Frank Sinatra and Mia drifted out to his favorite West Side bar.

SYNTHETIC DNA WAS PRODUCED AT STANFORD ■ DR. CHRISTIAAN BARNARD PERFORMED THE FIRST HEART TRANSPLANT ■ MICKEY MANTLE HIT HIS 500TH HOME RUN ■ BONNIE AND CLYDE HIGHTAILED IT ON THE SCREEN ■ AND THE BEATLES' "SGT. PEPPER" ALBUM CONFIRMED THE GROUP'S POP MUSIC GENIUS . . .

1967

Following the Six-Day War with Arab powers, Israel occupied Sinai, the West Bank, the Golan Heights and proclaimed a united Jerusalem.

MUSIC

POP MUSIC
The Messengers

The cover on a new LP album called *Sgt. Pepper's Lonely Hearts Club Band* is a photomontage of a crowd gathered round a grave. And a curious crowd it is: Marilyn Monroe is there, so are Karl Marx, Edgar Allan Poe, Albert Einstein, Lawrence of Arabia, Mae West, Sonny Liston and eight Beatles.

Eight? Well, four of them, standing around looking like wax dummies, are indeed wax models of the Beatles as most people remember them: nicely brushed long hair, dark suits, faces like sassy choirboys. The other four Beatles are very much alive: thin, hippie-looking, mustachioed, bedecked in bright, bizarre uniforms. Though their expressions seem subdued, their eyes glint with a new awareness tinged with a little of the old mischief. As for the grave in the foreground, it has THE BEATLES spelled out in flowers trimmed with marijuana plants. With characteristic self-mockery, the Beatles are proclaiming that they have snuffed out their old selves to make room for the new Beatles incarnate.

Rich and secure enough to go on repeating themselves—or to do nothing at all—they have exercised a compulsion for growth, change and experimentation. Messengers from beyond rock 'n' roll, they are creating the most original, expressive and musically interesting sounds being heard in pop music. They are leading an evolution in which the best of current post-rock sounds are becoming something that pop music has never been before: an art form. "Serious musicians" are listening to them and marking their work as a historic departure in the progress of music—any music.

Ned Rorem, composer of some of the best of today's art songs, says: "They are colleagues of mine, speaking the same language with different accents." In fact, he adds, the Beatles' haunting composition, *She's Leaving Home*—one of twelve songs in the *Sgt. Pepper* album—"is equal to any song that Schubert ever wrote." Conductor Leonard Bernstein's appreciation is just as high; he cites Schumann. As Musicologist Henry Pleasants says: "The Beatles are where music is right now."

Like all good popular artists, the Beatles have a talent for distilling the moods of their time. Gilbert and Sullivan's frolics limned the pomposities of the Victorian British Empah; Cole Porter's urbanities were wonderful tonics for the hung-over '30s; Rodgers and Hammerstein's ballads reflected the sentiment and seriousness of the World War II era. Today the Beatles' cunning collages piece

THE BEATLES
"I'd love to turn you on."

together scraps of tension between the generations, the loneliness of the dislocated '60s, and the bitter sweets of young love in any age. At the same time, their sensitivity to the absurd is sharper than ever.

By contrast, their early music had exuberance and an occasional oasis of unexpected harmony, but otherwise blended monotonously into the parched badlands of rock. *I Want to Hold Your Hand*, the Beatles' biggest hit single, was a cliché boy-girl lyric and a simple tune hammered onto the regulation pop-song structure. But the boys found their conventional sound and juvenile verses stultifying. Thus it was that the group's chief lyricist, John Lennon, began tuning in on U.S. Folk Singer Bob Dylan (*The Times They Are A-Changin'*); it wasn't Dylan's sullen anger about life that Lennon found appealing so much as the striving to "tell it like it is." Gradually, the Beatles' work began to tell it too. Their 1965 song, *Nowhere Man* ("Doesn't have a point of view, knows not where he's going to") asked: "Isn't he a bit like you and me?"

Fantasy took flight in their songs, from *Yellow Submarine's* childlike picture of a carefree existence beneath the waves to the vastly more complex and ominous vision in *Strawberry Fields Forever* of a retreat from uncertainty into a psychedelic cop-out. Its four separate meters, free-wheeling modulations and titillating tonal trappings, showed that the Beatles had flowered as musicians. They learned to bend and stretch the pop-song mold, enriched their harmonic palette with modal colors, mixed in cross-rhythms, and pinched the classical devices of composers from Bach to Stockhausen. They supplemented their guitar sound with strings, baroque trumpets, even a calliope. With the help of their engineer, arranger and record producer, George Martin, they plugged into a galaxy of space-age electronic effects, achieved partly through a mixture of tapes run backward and at various speeds.

All the successes of the past two years were a foreshadowing of *Sgt. Pepper*, which more than anything else dramatizes, note for note, word for word, the brilliance of the new Beatles. In three months, it has sold a staggering 2,500,000 copies—each a guaranteed package of psychic shivers. Loosely strung together on a scheme that plays the younger and older generations off against each other, it sizzles with musical montage, tricky electronics and sleight-of-hand lyrics that range between 1920s ricky-tick and 1960s raga. *A Day in the Life* is by all odds the most disturbingly beautiful song the group has ever produced. At the end, the refrain, "I'd love to turn you on," leads to a hair-raising chromatic crescendo by a full orchestra and a final blurred chord that is sustained for 40 seconds, like a trance of escape, or perhaps resignation.

THE PILL

MAO TSE-TUNG

KING HUSSEIN

1968

In an attempt to humanize Communist rule, Czech leader Alexander Dubçek announced reforms and was arrested following invasion by East Bloc troops.

112 OLYMPIC TEAMS COMPETED IN MEXICO CITY ■ THREE ASTRONAUTS ORBITED THE MOON IN *APOLLO 8* ■ THE NAVY INTELLIGENCE SHIP *PUEBLO* WAS SEIZED BY NORTH KOREA ■ MARTIN LUTHER KING WAS ASSASSINATED IN A MEMPHIS MOTEL ■ AND A BLOODY, INCREASINGLY CONTROVERSIAL WAR RAGED IN VIET NAM . . .

SEN. EUGENE MCCARTHY

ROBERT F. KENNEDY

MAYOR JOHN LINDSAY

THE WORLD

THE WAR

The General's Gamble

Though ominous harbingers of trouble had been in the air for days, most of South Viet Nam lazed in uneasy truce, savoring the happiest and holiest holiday of the Vietnamese year. All but a few Americans retired to their compounds to leave the feast of Tet to the Vietnamese celebrators filling the streets. Thousands of firecrackers popped and fizzed in the moonless night. The Year of the Monkey had begun, and every Vietnamese knew that it was wise to make merry while there was yet time; in the twelve-year Buddhist lunar cycle, 1968 is a grimly inauspicious year.

Through the streets of Saigon, and in the dark approaches to dozens of towns and military installations throughout South Viet Nam, other Vietnamese made their furtive way, intent on celebrating only death. After the merrymakers had retired and the last firecrackers had sputtered out, they struck with a fierceness and bloody destructiveness that Viet Nam has not seen even in three decades of nearly continuous warfare. Up and down the narrow length of South Viet Nam, more than 36,000 North Vietnamese and Viet Cong soldiers joined in a widespread, general offensive against airfields and military bases, government buildings, population centers and just plain civilians.

The Communists hit in a hundred places, from Quang Tri near the DMZ in the north all the way to Duong Dong on the tiny island of Phu Quoc off the Delta coast some 500 miles to the south. No target was too big or too impossible, including Saigon itself and General William Westmoreland's MACV headquarters. South Viet Nam's capital, which even in the worst days of the Indo-China war had never been hit so hard, was turned into a city besieged and sundered by house-to-house fighting.

In Hue, the ancient imperial city of Viet Nam, the Communists seized large parts of the city—and only grudgingly yielded them block by block under heavy allied counterattacks at week's end.

Allied intelligence had predicted that there would be some attempted city attacks during Tet, but the size, the scale and, above all, the careful planning and coordination of the actual assaults took the U.S. and South Vietnamese military by surprise. In that sense, and because they continued after five days of fighting to hang on to some of their targets, the Communists undeniably won a victory of sorts. They succeeded in demonstrating that, despite nearly three years of steady allied progress in the war, Communist commandos

G.I. AIDS WOUNDED BUDDY IN SAIGON
The Year of the Monkey had begun

can still strike at will virtually anywhere in the country.

The Battle of Bunker's Bunker

The most daring attack of the week—and certainly one of the most embarrassing—occurred when 19 Viet Cong commandos of the C-10 Sapper Battalion made the U.S. embassy their target. When Ambassador Ellsworth Bunker opened the white reinforced-concrete complex last September, few American missions ever settled into more seemingly impregnable quarters. Looming behind a 10-ft.-high wall, the six-story symbol of U.S. power and prestige is encased in a massive concrete sunscreen that overlaps shatterproof Plexiglas windows. Saigon wags soon dubbed it "Bunker's Bunker."

At 3:03 a.m., supporting V.C. troops positioned around the embassy began lobbing mortar fire onto the grounds. Then the 19 commandos appeared, wearing civilian clothes (with identifying red armbands) and carrying automatic weapons, rockets and enough high explosives to demolish the building. Attacking simultaneously, some of the guerrillas blasted a hole in the concrete wall with an antitank gun and swarmed through it; others quickly scaled a rear fence. Though allied intelligence had predicted the attack, the embassy's defense consisted of only five U.S. military guards—just one more than normal. They fought back so fiercely that only their courage denied the enemy complete success. Sergeant Ronald W. Harper, 20, a Marine Guard, managed to heave shut the embassy's massive teakwood front doors just seconds before the guerrillas battered at them with rockets and machine guns, thus denying the V.C. entry to the main building.

Unable to penetrate the main chancery, the V.C. commandos ran aimlessly through the compound, firing on everything they saw. Meanwhile, small groups of Marines and MPs began arriving outside the walls of the embattled embassy. The Viet Cong burst into the embassy's consular building and various other buildings in the compound, but the Americans in the scene threw such heavy fire at them that the guerrillas were kept too busy to set off their explosives. Finally, just before 8 a.m., Pfc. Paul Healey, 20, led a counterattack through the front gate, personally killing five V.C. with grenades and his M-16 rifle.

As the troopers advanced, a wounded guerrilla staggered into Mission Coordinator George Jacobson's white villa behind the embassy. He started upstairs, spotted the 56-year-old retired Army colonel there, and fired three shots. He missed, and Jacobson got him with a .45. When the 6 ½-hour battle ended, five Americans lay dead, as did two Vietnamese chauffeurs for the embassy who were apparently caught in the crossfire.

SIRHAN SIRHAN WAS CONVICTED OF MURDERING ROBERT KENNEDY ■ THE WOODSTOCK FESTIVAL ATTRACTED MORE THAN 300,000 ENTHUSIASTS ■ THE U.S. AGREED TO RETURN OKINAWA TO JAPAN ■ BRITISH TROOPS ENTERED BELFAST ■ AND FROM THE MOON, EARTH RECEIVED WORD THAT "THE *EAGLE* HAS LANDED" . . .

1969

As public dissatisfaction against the Viet Nam War intensified, Nixon announced the first American troop withdrawals.

THE MOON

A GIANT LEAP FOR MANKIND

THE ghostly, white-clad figure slowly descended the ladder. Having reached the bottom rung, he lowered himself into the bowl-shaped footpad of *Eagle*, the spindly lunar module of Apollo 11. Then he extended his left foot, cautiously, tentatively, as if testing water in a pool. That groping foot, encased in a heavy multilayered boot (size 9½ B), would remain indelible in the minds of millions who watched it on TV, and a symbol of man's determination to step — and forever keep stepping — toward the unknown.

After a few short but interminable seconds, U.S. Astronaut Neil Armstrong placed his foot firmly on the fine-grained surface of the moon. The time was 10:56 p.m., E.D.T., July 20, 1969. Pausing briefly, the first man on the moon spoke the first words on lunar soil:

"That's one small step for a man, one giant leap for mankind."

With a cautious, almost shuffling gait, the astronaut began moving about in the harsh light of the lunar morning. "The surface is fine and powdery, it adheres in fine layers, like powdered charcoal, to the soles and sides of my foot," he said. "I can see the footprints of my boots and the treads in the fine, sandy particles." Minutes later, Armstrong was joined by Edwin Aldrin. Then, gaining confidence with every step, the two jumped and loped across the barren landscape for 2 hrs. 14 min., while the TV camera they had set up some 50 ft. from *Eagle* transmitted their movements with remarkable clarity to enthralled audiences on earth, a quarter of a million miles away. Sometimes moving in surrealistic slow motion, sometimes bounding around in the weak lunar gravity like exuberant kangaroos, they set up experiments and scooped up rocks, snapped pictures and probed the soil, apparently enjoying every moment of their stay in the moon's alien environment.

After centuries of dreams and prophecies, the moment had come. Man had broken his

NEIL ARMSTRONG BEFORE TAKEOFF

terrestrial shackles and set foot on another world. Standing on the lifeless, rock-studded surface he could see the earth, a lovely blue and white hemisphere suspended in the velvety black sky. The spectacular view might well help him place his problems, as well as his world, in a new perspective.

Although the Apollo 11 astronauts planted an American flag on the moon their feat was far more than a national triumph. It was a stunning scientific and intellectual accomplishment for a creature who, in the space of a few million years — an instant in evolutionary chronology — emerged from primeval forests to hurl himself at the stars. Its eventual effect on human civilization is a matter of conjecture. But it was in any event a shining reaffirmation of the premise that whatever man imagines he can bring to pass.

For those who watched, the whole period that began with *Eagle's* undocking from *Columbia*, the command module, and its descent

to the moon seemed difficult to believe.

As the orbiting command module and the lunar module emerged from behind the moon, having undocked while they were out of radio communication, an anxious capsule commentator in Houston inquired: "How does it look?" Replied Armstrong: "The *Eagle* has wings." The lunar module was on its own, ready for its landing on the moon.

Its twelve-minute burn was scheduled to end only when the craft was within two yards of the lunar surface. One of the most dangerous parts of Apollo 11's long journey had begun. Just 160 ft. from the surface Aldrin reported: "Quantity light." The light signaled that only 114 seconds of fuel remained. Armstrong and Aldrin had 40 seconds to decide if they could land within the next 20 seconds. If they could not, they would have to abort.

At that critical point, Armstrong, a 39-year-old civilian with 23 years of experience at flying everything from Ford tri-motors to experimental X-15 rocket planes, took decisive action. The automatic landing system was taking *Eagle* down into a football-field-size crater littered with rocks and boulders. Armstrong explained: "It required a manual takeover to find a reasonably good area." Had *Eagle* continued on its computer-guided course, it might well have crashed.

Now the craft was close to the surface. "Forty feet," called Aldrin, rattling off attitudes and rates of descent with crackling precision. "Things look good. Picking up some dust. O.K. Engine stop." Armstrong quickly recited a ten-second check list of switches to turn off. Then came the word that the world had been waiting for.

"Houston," Armstrong called. "Tranquility Base here. The *Eagle* has landed." The time: 4:17:41 p.m.. E.D.T., just about 1½ minutes earlier than the landing time scheduled months before. There were cheers, tears and frantic applause at Mission Control in Houston.

CESAR CHAVEZ

LT. WILLIAM CALLEY, JR.

RALPH NADER

THE ARTISTS

WALT DISNEY AN ARTIST? OF COURSE, AND A PIONEERING ARTIST AT THAT, WHO MERGED DRAWING AND FILM TECHNOLOGY TO CREATE — MAGIC. LIKE THE OTHER GREAT ARTISTS OF OUR CENTURY, DISNEY'S AIM WAS NOT SIMPLY TO CREATE OBJECTS TO BE LOOKED AT, BUT TO REDEFINE THE WAY WE *SEE*. PICASSO SURPRISED US BY SPLINTERING IMAGES, MATISSE BY CUTTING PAPER INTO PURE COLORS, EDWARD HOPPER BY DISTILLING MOOD ONTO CANVAS. BY THE 1960S, ARTISTS HAD TAUGHT US THAT THERE WAS AMPLE FOOD FOR THE EYE AND MIND EVEN IN THE LABEL OF A SOUP CAN.

HOMER ST. GAUDENS
1924

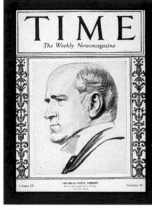

CHARLES DANA GIBSON
1927

WALT DISNEY
1937

MILTON CANIFF
1947

EDWARD HOPPER
1956

HENRY MOORE
1959

AUGUSTUS EDWIN JOHN
1928

HENRI MATISSE
1930

THOMAS HART BENTON
1934

SALVADOR DALI
1936

DIEGO RIVERA
1949

PABLO PICASSO
1950

AL CAPP
1950

GRANDMA MOSES
1953

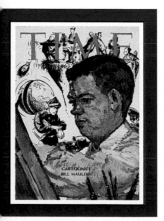

BILL MAULDIN
1961

ANDREW WYETH
1963

ROBERT RAUSCHENBERG
1976

ART AND MONEY
1989

1970s

The President's Odyssey

It is a lonely arrival. One probably will never know if Richard Nixon expected such a soundless, emotionless affair. After the storm of publicity in the U.S., all the smells and sounds of power that have gone with the presidency to produce this event, the few minutes in the weak sun of a clear China morning are — well, perhaps they are pure Chinese.

About ten minutes before touchdown, the silence of the sky is broken. The presidential plane drops into view. Soon the plane is on the ground. Just then Chou En-lai and a corporal's guard of officials come casually out. It is an understatement. Not in memory has a host not been in place when the presidential jet came to rest. The President and Pat Nixon appear in the doorway to a ripple of applause from Chou's thin line down below.

The huge, roaring, dazzling spectacle of the presidency that has mesmerized whole nations is simply swallowed up in China. It is muffled, shrouded, forced into surrealism.
March 6, 1972

Kent State Martyrs

When the compact formation reached the top of the hill, some National Guardsmen knelt quickly and aimed at the students who were hurling rocks from below. A handful of demonstrators kept moving toward the troops. Other Guardsmen stood behind the kneeling troops, pointing their rifles down the hill. A few aimed over the students' heads. Several witnesses later claimed that an officer brought his baton down in a sweeping signal. Within seconds, a sickening staccato of rifle fire signaled the transformation of a once-placid campus into the site of an historic American tragedy.

Minutes later, the Guardsmen assumed parade-rest positions, apparently to signal the crowd that the fusillade would not be resumed unless the Guardsmen were threatened again. The campus was suddenly still. Horrified students flung themselves to the ground, ran for cover behind buildings and parked cars, or just stood stunned. Then screams broke out. "My God, they're killing us!" one girl cried. They were.
May 18, 1970

DAVID RUBINGER

Breakthrough

All day Sunday, the U.S. pressed hard. At 3 p.m. they turned to the Sinai settlements, and Carter's aides waiting outside the President's pine-paneled study grew more and more worried. Then, at 4:30, Carter looked out the window and flashed the thumbs-up sign. They had a deal. Outside, the rain was torrential. Begin told Sadat he would come over to his cabin, Dogwood, as soon as the rain stopped. For 25 minutes Begin visited Sadat. A half-hour later, Sadat suddenly appeared, without warning, at the door of Begin's cabin to return the call. Begin suggested, "Let's both go tomorrow night to hear President Carter address the Congress." Sadat agreed. Already, Carter's aides were making the arrangements for the trip down from the mountain to tell the world what the three leaders had wrought.
September 25, 1978

RAYMOND DEPARDON — CAMERA LIAISON

Horror at the Olympics

Munich Police Chief Manfred Schreiber boldly walked up to the besieged apartment house, and was met by a terrorist in a white tennis hat and sunglasses. He was apparently the leader of the group — and, as it turned out, the most fanatical. "It occurred to me," the police chief said later, "that I might try to take him hostage. He must have sensed what I was thinking. 'Do you want to take me?' he asked, opening his hand. I saw a hand grenade. He had his thumb on the pin."

At 9 a.m. the Arabs tossed out of a window a message in English that listed 200 Arab prisoners presently held in Israeli jails and demanded their release. As the police read the list, the Olympic Games continued only 400 yards away, and 2,000 cheering fans — many of them still unaware of the drama — watched a volleyball game between West Germany and Japan.
September 18, 1972

BETTMANN ARCHIVE

1970s

DOUGLAS KIRKLAND / SYGMA

High Steppin' to Stardom

Saturday Night Fever has started John Travolta along a yellow-brick show-biz road that reaches out of sight, raised discomania to a national craze and made superstars of a likable rock group called the Bee Gees for the second, or maybe it's the third time.

When Travolta first appears in *Saturday Night Fever*, there's an instant charge — a shock of recognition, of excitement, of acceptance. He has the moves, the presence, the princely mystique. No one can fully define star quality, but you can find illustration enough. And in 1978, that walk is the best one around.
April 3, 1978

Burger Country

Statistics alone cannot adequately measure the impact of McDonald's on U.S. life. The company's relentless advertising campaign ($50 million budgeted this year) has made the McDonald's jingle *You Deserve a Break Today* almost as familiar as *The Star Spangled Banner*. But the chain's managers have wrought their proudest achievement by taking a familiar American institution, the greasy-spoon hamburger joint, and transforming it into a totally different though no less quintessentially American operation: a computerized, standardized, premeasured super-clean production machine. No one has ever surpassed McDonald's in automating the ancient art of cooking and serving food.

McDonald's has expanded overseas with all the zeal of missionaries bringing hamburgers to the heathen. One American girl, stopping at the Paris McDonald's on the Champs-Elysees, explains: "Over here, you're supposed to try new things, so I tried the Big Mac."
September 17, 1973

Summer of the Shark

Jaws, which opens in 490 theaters this week, is part of a bracing revival of high-adventure films and thrillers

over the past few months. It is expensive ($8 million), elaborate, technically intricate and wonderfully crafted, a movie whose every shock is a devastating surprise. *Jaws* promises to hit right in the old collective unconscious and to draw millions irresistibly to the box office. If the great white shark that terrorizes the beaches of an island summer colony is one of nature's most efficient killing machines, *Jaws* is an efficient entertainment machine.

By the time the final scenes were shot last October, the movie was 100% over budget and over schedule. After the last day of *Jaws* shooting on Martha's Vineyard, Director Steven Spielberg, 27, climbed into a boat and headed for the mainland, shouting to cast and crew like a still bold but newly wise commander, "I shall not return!"
June 23, 1975

Opera's Golden Tenor

No other tenor in modern times has hit the opera world with such seismic force. At 6 ft. and nearly 300 lbs., "Big P," as Soprano Joan Sutherland calls him, is more than life-size, as is everything about him — his clarion high Cs, his fees of $8,000 per night for an opera and $20,000 for a recital, his Rabelaisian zest for food and fun. Luciano Pavarotti is one of those magnetic performers, like Nureyev in dance and Olivier in theater, who not only please the *cognoscenti* but also wow the masses.

Nobody knows Pavarotti's precise poundage. He keeps his own scales and his own counsel. When asked how much he weighs, he replies: "Less than before." How much did he weigh before? "More than now." Hence reports of his fluctuations spread through the opera world like a runaway Dow Jones average: up 25, down 80, up 60.
September 24, 1979

1970

Antiwar protests peaked with tragic consequences: four students were killed by the National Guard during a Kent State University demonstration.

THE CIVIL WAR ENDED IN NIGERIA AS BIAFRA CAPITULATED TO THE CENTRAL GOVERNMENT ■ KHRUSHCHEV'S MEMOIRS WERE PUBLISHED IN THE WEST ■ POPE PAUL VI REAFFIRMED "PRIESTLY CELIBACY" ■ MARXIST SALVADOR ALLENDE WAS ELECTED PRESIDENT OF CHILE ■ AND MASTERS AND JOHNSON POPULARIZED "SEX THERAPY" . . .

SALVADOR ALLENDE

MARTHA MITCHELL

AMERICAN POW'S

BEHAVIOR

REPAIRING THE CONJUGAL BED

Harry Miller is not his true name, but his problem is genuine enough. He is a failure in bed. Years have passed since Harry and his wife, who are in their late 30s, have given or taken any pleasure in sex. With considerable hesitation and embarrassment, they confided their difficulty to their minister, who was sympathetic but unable to help. He referred them to the Reproductive Biology Research Foundation in St. Louis. On arrival, the Millers checked into a red brick residential building where the foundation leases apartments at $100 a week for out-of-town patients. At 9 the next morning, they called for their first appointment.

Ultimate Communication

There they met Dr. William Howell Masters, the director, an owlish, stern-looking man of 54, and Mrs. Virginia Johnson, 45, his research associate, whose manner is as outgoing as Masters' is reserved. The Millers were told that this first interview, and all others, would be taped — a measure designed to protect the patients by eliminating stenographers from the necessary history-taking. They were reminded of the foundation's credo as worded by Masters: "There is no such thing as an uninvolved partner in a sexually distressed marriage." Indeed, had the Millers not entered treatment together, they could not have entered at all. Finally, they were asked to refrain from any sexual activity whatsoever until otherwise directed.

The message, in short, was that the Millers were not there to perform or be judged. They were there to rediscover, under guidance but not observation, the ultimate form of human communication that takes place in the marriage bed.

The Millers are a hypothetical though representative example of the 790 cases of sexual incompatibility that have been treated in St. Louis over the past eleven years. In a new book called *Human Sexual Inadequacy* (Little,

MASTERS AND JOHNSON INTERVIEWING PATIENTS AT ST. LOUIS CLINIC

Brown; $12.50), Dr. Masters and Mrs. Johnson summarize their therapeutic approach to the problem of what they call sexual "dysfunction." Written in less than six weeks, the book is poorly organized and clotted with jargon that makes it almost unreadable for all but the doctors, psychologists, marriage counselors and other professionals for whom it was intended. Nonetheless, the work is already a bestseller, and with some reason. In the underdeveloped field of sex research, the authors are pioneers; they are the most important explorers since Alfred Kinsey into the most mysterious, misunderstood and rewarding of human functions.

Sex as Salvation

In an era of pop sex, which fictionally and visually glorifies coition and accepts the idea of honeymoon-before-marriage, it might seem strange that there are any sexual hang-ups left to be treated. Whatever the "sexual revolution" may mean, it certainly has freed modern woman of the Victorian notion that females do not enjoy sex; the modern woman knows what she is missing, erotically speaking. On the other hand, the American male has succumbed to the widely advertised notion the he should

be the super-performer in what has been called the decade of orgasmic preoccupation — a preoccupation that could be enhanced by Masters' and Johnson's emphasis on sex as a form of salvation.

Behind this new (or old) morality lurk many of the same fears of inadequacy, the same sexual myths and mistakes, that disturbed earlier generations. Dr. Eugene Schoenfeld ("Dr. HIPpocrates"), whose free-wheeling column of medical advice runs in 15 underground newspapers, reports that a surprising number of his supposedly liberated young male readers worry about penis length. He also gets letters from men with hang-ups about masturbation: "They're worried that it will grow hair on the palms of their hands or rot their brains out or something." And Virginia Johnson has known women who thought that men, like Priapus, have permanent erections.

In their treatment of sexually myth-ridden patients, Masters and Johnson use an eclectic and considerate approach. One example: the use of therapeutic teams composed of one man and one woman relieves the couple entering treatment from having to discuss, at first, humiliating shortcomings with someone of the opposite sex.

CIGARETTE COMMERCIALS WERE BANNED FROM U.S. TELEVISION ■ A FIVE-DAY UPRISING AT NEW YORK'S ATTICA PRISON LEFT 42 DEAD ■ AMTRAK BEGAN PASSENGER RAIL SERVICE ■ GEORGE C. SCOTT GARNERED AN OSCAR FOR "PATTON" ■ BEVERLY SILLS WAS AMERICA'S QUEEN OF OPERA ■ AND COMPOSER IGOR STRAVINSKY DIED IN NEW YORK AT AGE 88 . . .

1971

U.S.-China relations began to thaw, as China hosted the U.S. table tennis team, followed by a secret trip by Henry Kissinger to arrange President Nixon's visit.

MUSIC

THE RIGHTNESS OF HIS WRONGS

"Mark him well," Diaghilev said of the 27-year-old Igor Stravinsky. "He is a man on the eve of celebrity." When celebrity came, Stravinsky had a long day of it: a stormy dawn of controversy, a high blaze of creative influence, a waning afternoon of waspish polemics and high-priced memorabilia. Last week the night finally fell, as Stravinsky died in Manhattan at 88. It was the end of six decades of dominance, in which he had incalculably shaped the musical thought of generations to come. It was the end, too, of what Conductor Colin Davis called "a chain of great composers left us by the 19th century, and a line of music that began with the early church music of the 14th century." With his passing, the music world lost its most vital link with both the future and the past.

The young Stravinsky's artistic calling card was a bombshell: *The Rite of Spring*, a sophisticated evocation of primitive myths and energies completed in 1913. Conductor Pierre Monteux recalled that when he first heard the composer run through it on the piano, bobbing up and down to accentuate its jagged rhythms, "I was convinced that he was raving mad." Later, when the work had its Paris première at the Théâtre des Champs Elysées, many members of the audience thought so too. They erupted in perhaps the most notorious riot of music history, booing, fighting one another, pelting Monteux and the players with programs and hats.

No Repeats. Polytonal, polymodal, polyrhythmic, *The Rite* took some getting used to. It did not so much reject conventional harmony, as did the twelve-tone works of Arnold Schoenberg. Rather it brought contrasting tonalities crashing dangerously into one another. With its unexpected clustered stresses and pile-driving climaxes, it raised rhythm to an unprecedented pre-eminence. Jarring the 20th century out of its lingering romanticism, it was more than "the cornerstone of modern music," as Pierre Boulez calls it. It was one of those works, like Joyce's *Ulysses* and Picasso's *Les Demoiselles d'Avignon*, that announced a new consciousness. *The Rite* influenced nearly every composer who followed except the serialists—and Stravinsky himself, whose genius never repeated itself.

Bisexual Hairdo. Despite

THE BETTMANN ARCHIVE

AS DRAWN BY PICASSO, 1920

Stravinsky's fragile, birdlike appearance (in his prime, 5 ft. 3 in., 120 lbs.), he had indomitable physical zest. Repeated onslaughts of lung congestion, blood clotting and surgery reduced his body to "a ruin," according to his doctor. Yet until the end, which was attributed to arteriosclerotic heart disease, every one of his maladies seemed somewhat curable, save for his hypochondria. The remarkable features that had been caricatured by such friends as Cocteau and Picasso — bull-fiddle nose, guitar-like ears, pince-nez, natty mustache — remained mobile and alert. Stravinsky carried on with the conver-

sational crowds he loved so well, often speaking to one guest in French, another in English, or in Russian to his wife Vera, a former costume designer for Diaghilev. And always there was plenty of good food and wine.

Nor did the 30-year-old Ballantine's Scotch that he consumed in moderate rations (down from the half quart a day of former times) ever dull his tart, epigrammatic wit. Conductors, critics and colleagues regularly felt its sting. Stravinsky once said of Leopold Stokowski that "he must have spent an hour a day trying to find the perfect bisexual hairdo." He called *New Yorker* Music Critic Winthrop Sergeant "W.S. Deaf." Of a new Gian Carlo Menotti opera, he said, "It is 'farther out' than anything I've seen in a decade; in the wrong direction, of course." He also took on broader targets. The technology of today's recording engineers, he complained, removed natural sound and human errors, producing "a super-glossy, chem-fab music substitute that was never heard on sea or land, including Philadelphia."

Jaunty Note. Not surprisingly for a composer who lived to such a ripe age, Stravinsky wrote his own requiem. This week his body was to be flown to Venice for burial in the Russian corner of the cemetery of San Michele. His *Requiem Canticles* (1966) were to be sung at a final service in the church of Santi Giovanni e Paolo. All this is in accordance with the composer's own devout wishes. Still, even Stravinsky himself might have liked the additional jaunty note of the epitaph he tossed off nine years ago, before leaving for an African conducting tour: "If a lion eats me, you will hear the news from him. He will say, 'The old man was tough, but a tasty meal.'"

DICK CAVETT

ANWAR SADAT

THE PENTAGON PAPERS

1972

Five men were arrested burglarizing the Democratic National Headquarters at the Watergate complex. But, seemingly unaffected, Nixon won a second term in a landslide.

GOVERNOR GEORGE WALLACE OF ALABAMA WAS SHOT AND PARTIALLY PARALYZED ■ IN THE PHILIPPINES, THE TASADAY TRIBE WAS DISCOVERED LIVING IN STONE-AGE CONDITIONS ■ LIZA MINNELLI INVITED MOVIE AUDIENCES TO "COME TO THE CABARET" ■ AND OLYMPIAN MARK SPITZ SLICED THROUGH THE WATER IN MUNICH . . .

LEONID BREZHNEV

VIET NAM

SEN. GEORGE MCGOVERN

SPORTS

COVER STORY

Spitz über Alles in Deutschland

Scene I: Mexico City, 1968. A gawky youngster of 18, who looks as if he could be Jerry Lewis' younger brother, perfunctorily addresses a putt. On the course beside him is his coach and constant companion, Sherman Chavoor. Since the boy had recently boasted that he would become the first Olympian to win six gold medals, he needs all the relaxing he can get. Not today. A passerby happens to spot him on the green and shouts, "Hey, Jew boy, you aren't going to win any gold medals!" The brutal slur is delivered by one of the youth's comrades on the U.S. men's swimming team.

Scene II: Munich, 1972. A sinewy young man of 22, who looks as if he could be Omar Sharif's younger brother, confidently strides through the Olympic Village. Surrounding him is a retinue of coaches and teammates —the entourage of an athletic eminence. At the village entrance, dozens of jock groupies strain to touch him, plead for his autograph. Inside, competitors from other countries seek his signature. "Oh, look!" cries a delighted U.S. mermaid. "There he is!" Journalists pursue him into the shower before practice. People persistently ask: Can he win seven gold medals? Yes, he answers with quiet confidence.

The Mexico City *schlemiel* and the Munich superstar are the same person: Mark Andrew Spitz of Carmichael, Calif. The sullen, abrasively cocky kid with the sunken visage has matured into a smooth, adroitly confident young man with modish locks and mustache. More important, he has developed into a talent without peer in the world of competitive swimming. In the four years since his personal disaster in Mexico City, where he won only two gold medals (and those in relay events), Spitz has grown up, graduated from college and at one time or another, broken 28 world freestyle and butterfly records. That spectacular string of victories continued as the XX Olympiad got

under way last week. Spitz led a green but able young American team into the competition with an incandescent performance that ranks with the legendary triumphs of Jim Thorpe, Paavo Nurmi and Jesse Owens.

Spitz and the other 11,999 athletes from 124 nations opened the Olympiad under the bright Bavarian sunlight in Munich's vast acrylic-domed stadium. The national teams paraded by the grandstand in a panoply of colors as massed bands played modern dance tunes instead of the traditional martial anthems. The Olympic flame, carried some 3,500 miles by an international team of 5,976 runners, was borne to the torch by Gunter Zahn, 18, a West German runner. West German President Gustav Heinemann officially initiated the games with the prescribed 14-word pronunciamento: "I declare open the Olympic Games celebrating the XX Olympiad of the modern era." The mountain horns flourished, and 80,000 enthusiastic spectators and hundreds of millions of TV viewers settled back to watch the drama begin.

The first act belonged mainly to Mark Spitz and his American teammates. Plowing out of the water like Poseidon, Spitz with his high-chested motion churned up the *Schwimmhalle* pool in the 200-m. butterfly. There may have been butterflies in Spitz's stomach too: "I remembered what happened in Mexico City," he admitted. Nonetheless, Mark knocked 2.6 seconds off his own world record of 2:3.3 to win the first of his 1972 pendants of Olympic gold. Finishing in second and third place, respectively, were Gary Hall, Spitz's teammate at Indiana University and roommate in Munich, and Robin Backhaus of Redlands, Calif.

The Americans considered Spitz's opening triumph as little short of a sign from Neptune. Said Peter Daland, head coach of the U.S. men's swimming team: "If Mark had lost his first race, he could have been discouraged. But the Mark Spitz of '72 is a

tough person." Tough enough, in fact, to anchor another victory in the 400-meter freestyle relay later that night, giving him two gold medals and two world records on his first day of Olympian work. The next evening he came to the blocks in the finals of the 200-meter freestyle. His toughest competition, as it turned out, came from gritty Teammate Steve Genter, 21, of Lakewood, Calif., who only the day before was released from a hospital following chest surgery for a partially collapsed lung. Genter led at the 100- and 150-meter turns, but Spitz, slicing through the water with his simian arms and immense hands, surged ahead of Genter to clip .72 sec. from his own world record and gain another gold medal.

Harpooning. Two days later Spitz splashed his way to more gold and more records in the 100-meter butterfly (54.27 sec.) and 800-meter freestyle relay, thereby tying the record for gold medals (five) set in 1920 by an Italian fencer, Nedo Nadi. At week's end it seemed that nothing short of harpooning Spitz in mid-stroke would prevent him from garnering medals Nos. 6 and 7 in the 100-meter freestyle and 400-meter medley relay.

About one Olympic fact, however, there can be little controversy: Mark Spitz is in as complete command of his sport as any other athlete in history. There are many reasons for his proficiency, but his physical attributes alone would seem to give him a pool-length advantage over a greased porpoise. He carries 170 lbs. easily on a tightly compacted 6-ft. frame. Hanging from his wide shoulders are a pair of long supple arms terminating in a pair of scoop-shovel hands than can pull him cleanly through the water with scarcely a ripple. He also has the curious ability to flex his lower legs slightly forward at the knee, which allows him to kick 6 to 12 in. deeper in the water than his opponents. Says his father Arnold, a production engineer in Oakland, Calif.: "Mark's whole body is so flexible that the water just seems to slip by him."

EAST AND WEST GERMANY ESTABLISHED DIPLOMATIC RELATIONS ■ NIXON AND SOVIET LEADER BREZHNEV SIGNED AN ARMS LIMITATION PACT ■ THE FILM "DEEP THROAT" WAS DECLARED "IRREDEEMABLY OBSCENE" BY A NEW YORK CRIMINAL COURT ■ VICE PRESIDENT SPIRO AGNEW RESIGNED ■ AND AMERICANS FACED GAS SHORTAGES AS "THE OIL CRISIS" BEGAN . . .

1973

In a landmark decision, the U.S. Supreme Court ruled that states could not prohibit abortions during the first six months of pregnancy.

THE WORLD

MIDDLE EAST

Black October: Old Enemies at War Again

The sirens began to wail while all Israel was observing Yom Kippur, the holiest and also the quietest day of the Jewish year.

By tradition, tens of thousands of servicemen were home on leave; Israel Broadcasting had shut down for the day. As crowds of worshipers emerged from synagogues at the end of the five-hour long morning services of atonement, they found the streets filled with speeding trucks, buses and Jeeps. By late afternoon virtually every Israeli — and much of the rest of the world as well — knew that what Defense Minister Moshe Dayan defiantly called "all-out war" had begun again.

The fighting erupted when Egyptian troops surged across the Suez Canal and Syrian soldiers struck in the north on the Golan Heights. Both forces swept through Israel's front lines and punched their way into Israeli-held territory under the glare of an afternoon sun.

The Political Weapon

After muttering vaguely about using their abundant oil as a "political weapon," the newly unified Arab leaders finally unsheathed it last week. They vowed to cut the oil production on which the fuel-short West depends and to raise prices sharply. That oil squeeze could easily lead to cold homes, hospitals and schools, shuttered factories, slower travel, brownouts, consumer rationing, aggravated inflation and even worsened air pollution in the U.S., Europe and Japan.

The Arabs took three steps:

1) Ten Arab countries meeting in Kuwait decided that each month from now on they will reduce oil output at least 5% below the preceding month. The cutback will continue, they said, "until an Israel withdrawal is completed, and until the restoration of the legal rights of the Palestinian people."

2) King Faisal of Saudi Arabia, the biggest Mideast producer, at first decreed a 10% cut in output. But by week's end, as the war seemed to be going against the Arabs, he announced a total ban on oil shipments to

GASLESS SUNDAY ARRIVES IN NEW JERSEY.
And schools are closing down to save oil.

the U.S. Presently, 3.4% of the crude oil consumed daily by the U.S. comes from Saudi Arabia. Libya, Algeria and Abu Dhabi also announced new embargos.

3) Six Persian Gulf oil countries lifted the posted price of crude oil (a theoretical figure on which royalties and taxes are based) by a stunning 70% to $5.11 per bbl. It will keep Arab oil revenues rising — helping to pay for the war against Israel — even as fewer barrels are shipped out.

Dimouts and Slowdowns

Rushing to work last week, John Doe, American, swung his car onto the freeway — only to discover that the posted speed limit had been reduced from 60 m.p.h. to 50 m.p.h. When he stopped at a gas station for a refill, *he learned that overnight the price had gone up 2¢ per gal. At his office he felt unusually cool because the thermostats had been pushed down a couple of degrees, to a brisk 68°.*

As the voracious demand for oil increasingly outstripped new sources of supply in recent years, an energy crisis crept up on the world with fateful inevitability. Yet, despite spreading signs of scarcity, most government leaders in the U.S., Europe and Japan paid little heed to calls from oilmen for urgent measures to expand energy resources and curb waste. Instead, they chose to believe that there was time to formulate some painless strategy to avert a genuine global emergency.

Now time has abruptly run out. The Arabs, who control nearly 60% of the world's proven deposits, are slowing down the flow. Through this strategy of squeeze, they hope to pressure the industrial nations into forcing Israel to make peace on terms favorable to the Arabs. Moreover, they are steadily intensifying their oil shakedown. Originally they planned to reduce production by at least 5% each month. Later they embargoed all oil shipments to the U.S. and The Netherlands, in punishment for their support of Israel. Last week, showing new unity and clout, ten Arab countries announced that production for November will be slashed a minimum of 25% below the September total of 20.5 million bbl. per day.

The implications of the oil warfare reach far beyond the Arab-Israeli dispute. Not since World War II has any event carried more potential for global change. Even if the Arabs were to reopen their taps tomorrow, the world would never again be the same. The sudden shortage of fuel has finally jolted governments into a realization that the era of cheap and ample energy is dead and that people will have to learn to live permanently with less heating, lighting and transport and pay more for each of them.

SEN. SAM ERVIN

"SECRETARIAT"

GERALD FORD

1974

Lifestyle issues were gaining prominence in America: in a significant move, the nation's largest private employer, AT&T, banned anti-gay discrimination.

ALEXANDER SOLZHENITSYN WAS STRIPPED OF SOVIET CITIZENSHIP AND EXILED ■ INDIA EXPLODED A NUCLEAR DEVICE ■ THE *MARINER 10* SATELLITE TRANSMITTED PICTURES OF VENUS AND MERCURY ■ "STREAKERS" WORE SNEAKERS AND LITTLE ELSE ■ AND THE WATERGATE AFFAIR CAME TO A CLOSE WITH NIXON'S RESIGNATION . . .

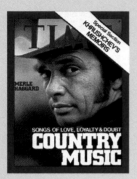

MERLE HAGGARD

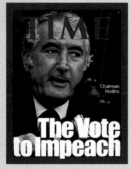

PETER RODINO

YASSER ARAFAT

THE NATION

STATE OF THE UNION

At Last, Time for Healing the Wounds

It was over. At last, after so many months of poisonous suspicion, a kind of undeclared civil war that finally engaged all three branches of the American Government, the ordeal had ended. As the *Spirit of '76* in one last errand arced across central Missouri carrying Richard Nixon to his retirement, Gerald Rudolph Ford stood in the East Room of the White House, placed his hand upon his eldest son's Bible, and repeated the presidential oath "to preserve, protect and defend the Constitution of the United States." By the time the 37th President of the U.S. arrived at the Pacific, the 38th President had taken command.

It was the first time in American history that a President had resigned his office. The precedent was melancholy, but it was hardly traumatic. All of the damage had been done before in the seemingly interminable spectacle of high officials marched through courtrooms, in the recitation of burglaries, crooked campaign contributions and bribes, enemies lists, powers abused, subpoenas ignored, and above all, in the ugly but mesmerizing suspense as the investigations drew closer and closer to the Oval Office. Now the dominant emotion throughout the nation was one of sheer relief.

A few of Nixon's last supporters still summoned up bitterness. Not a few Americans cracked open bottles of champagne. Mostly, the nation was massively grateful to have it ended. As Ford said at his swearing-in, "Our long national nightmare is over." By his leaving, Nixon seemed at last to redeem the 1968 pledge he took from a girl holding up a campaign sign in Ohio: BRING US TOGETHER.

The denouement was jarring in its swift resolution and therefore a bit surreal. Nearly 800 days after the Watergate break-in, 289 days after the Saturday Night Massacre, 97 days after the White House transcripts were released, twelve days after the Supreme

NIXON TELLING DAUGHTER JULIE HIS DECISION
Redeeming pledge to bring us together

Court voted, 8 to 0, that the President must surrender 6 more tapes, five days after the House Judiciary Committee voted out articles of impeachment, Nixon's defenses finally vanished. On Monday he issued the June 23, 1972, transcript that amounted to a confession to obstruction of justice and to lying to the American people. With that his clock had run out.

His televised resignation speech was a peculiar performance. In some ways, it sounded like a State of the Union address, a recitation of his achievements. He admitted no guilt, only casually did he mention mistakes made "in the best interests of the nation." If some expected a bitter, angry valedictory, Nixon was controlled and ultimately conciliatory. Nixon once said that the test of a people is the way it handles the transition of power, and last week — in his resignation speech if not in his mawkish,

self-pitying White House goodbye — he deserved credit for helping to bring off the transition with dignity in what must have been the most painful moment of his life.

The departure of Nixon was, above all, an extraordinary triumph of the American system. There were, of course, useful accidents of fate and generous helpings of blind luck. A night watchman named Frank Wills came upon the Watergate burglars one night when they taped some door locks with an almost ostentatious incompetence. The system was fortunate that Judge John Sirica pursued the case. And above all that Richard Nixon was surreptitiously taping his own conversations, and that he somehow never thought, or considered it necessary, or perhaps just did not dare, to heave all the tapes into the White House incinerator after their existence became known. Had it not been for the tapes, Richard Nixon would quite possibly have remained in the White House until January 1977. No presidency in the nation's history has ever been so well documented, and it is safe to predict that none will be again.

But it was, at last, Richard Nixon who destroyed his own presidency. His White House, as revealed in the transcripts, was saturated with pettiness and hatred, a siege mentality, Us against Them. It was an unhappy and self-defeating spirit in which to govern a democracy.

Nixon is gone — not a martyred figure as he may believe but tragic at least in his fall from a great height. He is gone because, with all its luck in this case, the American system, the Congress and the Judiciary, with the eventual overwhelming support of public opinion, slowly and carefully excised him from the body politic. If there is a certain "the-king-is-dead-long-live-the-king" spirit in the American mood, the nation feels also that it deserves something better in its leadership and is going to get it.

Photo credit: OLLIE ATKINS — THE WHITE HOUSE

MARGARET THATCHER BECAME THE LEADER OF BRITAIN'S CONSERVATIVES ■ DISSIDENT SOVIET PHYSICIST ANDREI SAKHAROV RECEIVED THE NOBEL PEACE PRIZE ■ AS THE LAST MAJOR COLONIAL POWER, PORTUGAL GAVE INDEPENDENCE TO VAST AFRICAN TERRITORIES ■ STALLONE SLUGGED AWAY IN "ROCKY" ■ AND AN HEIRESS BECAME A FUGITIVE . . .

1975

Two decades of American military involvement ended in Viet Nam; Communists seized Saigon and the U.S. hastily evacuated its embassy.

THE NATION

RADICALS/COVER STORY

PATTY'S TWISTED JOURNEY

The evidence was fragmentary and scattered and painfully hard to gather, but slowly it accumulated—a red Volkswagen camper, a fingerprint discovered at a farmhouse in Pennsylvania, a post office box in San Francisco. Suddenly last week the bits fitted into a pattern. When they did, an FBI agent and a policeman climbed stealthily up the back stairs to the top-floor apartment of the modest house on the edge of San Francisco. They knocked, and the door swung open. Standing in the room was the thin, pale young woman. "Don't shoot," said Patty Hearst. "I'll go with you."

That quiet drama ended a 19-½-month chase — one of the longest and most intensive in U.S. history — and climaxed a bizarre odyssey that had a special and disturbing fascination for Americans. They had been appalled by the violence of the whole affair: the strong-arm kidnaping near a college campus, then the bank robbery in which Patty herself wielded a gun, then the surrealistic, nationally televised shootout that left six of her companions dead. With some apprehension, parents debated just why Patty, the heiress to a celebrated fortune, had become a self-proclaimed revolutionary. Many people claimed to have spotted her in various parts of the world, yet she managed to elude the great chase — until last Thursday.

Captured along with Patty was her close companion, Wendy Yoshimura, 32. An hour earlier, outside an old white two-story house three miles away, the FBI had arrested two of Patty's other friends: robust William Harris, 30, and his wan and tired wife, Emily, 28. All four were comrades-in-arms in the explosive and tiny cult of revolutionaries who grandiosely called themselves the Symbionese Liberation Army. With the arrests, said the FBI, the S.L.A. had ceased to exist. All dozen members of the group, which had first shown willingness to kill in the ambush-slaying of Oakland School Superintendent Marcus Foster in 1973, were either jailed or dead.

Some of the mysteries of the Patty Hearst case began to lift when the four were arraigned two hours later in a crowded San Francisco federal court. The first to be handled was Wendy Yoshimura, a Japanese-American artist who disappeared in 1972 after being charged with taking part in a plan to bomb the naval-architecture building on the Berkeley campus of the University of California. Federal authorities believe that she and Patty Hearst have been together since at least the summer of 1974. Magistrate Owen Woodruff dismissed federal fugitive charges against Yoshimura, and remanded her to the custody of Alameda County authorities to face arraignment for her part in the Berkeley incident. As she was taken from the courtroom, she paused at the defense table and touched the outstretched hand of Patty Hearst.

Then it was Patty's turn. Newsmen and spectators in the crowded chamber strained to get a good look at the defendant in Case No. 74-364, *The United States of America v. Patricia Campbell Hearst*. Sitting near her at the witness table was her cousin, William Randolph Hearst III, 26, the first member of her family she saw after her capture. They had been close friends, and he seemed on the verge of tears. They avoided each other's eyes.

Patty had changed. Not only had her long dark-blonde hair been cut shorter and dyed red but she had lost her healthy, cover-girl looks. Her face was noticeably drawn. But she did not look or act like a victim who had been forced by her abductors to rob a bank and denounce her grieving parents and her fiancé as "pigs" and "clowns." She was as casual as if she had dropped by to answer a traffic summons. She was wearing stained rubber clogs and dark brown cotton pants, and beneath her striped, long-sleeved jersey she was braless. Throughout the proceedings, she

A DEFIANT PATTY HEARST

nonchalantly smiled and chewed gum.

Standing before Woodruff, Patty lowered her voice to almost a whisper as she gave her age — 21 — and acknowledged her name, not mentioning the revolutionary name of Tania that she had adopted while on the run. She was then arraigned on charges of armed bank robbery and violation of the Federal Firearms Act. Armed bank robbery carries a maximum 25-year sentence and is only one of 22 federal and state charges that she faces; they could jail her for life. Her bail was set at $1.5 million. At one point Patty Hearst stood erect, tightly clenched her small right fist and flourished it aloft remorselessly in the salute of the social revolutionary.

Next, Patty's friends Bill and Emily Harris went before Woodruff. As Harris entered the courtroom, he scanned the expectant audience and cried out, "What do you say, comrades? Keep on trucking!" Then he lifted his left hand in a clenched-fist salute. The Harrises were arraigned on charges of illegal possession of arms; bail was set at $550,000 for each.

The Harrises and Patty Hearst were sent to the San Mateo jail, 30 miles to the south. As they were being driven away, Emily Harris raised her own clenched fist to newsmen, and Patty grinned broadly.

CHOU EN-LAI

CHER

THE BUSING BATTLE

1976

The year saw a marked improvement in U.S.-Soviet relations; for the first time, on-site inspection of nuclear facilities was agreed upon.

THE PRO-INDEPENDENCE PARTY GAINED A MAJORITY IN QUEBEC ■ SUPERSONIC PASSENGER SERVICE WAS INITIATED BETWEEN EUROPE AND THE U.S. ■ FRENCH ARCHBISHOP LEFEBVRE WAS SUSPENDED FOR REJECTING VATICAN II REFORMS ■ SAIGON WAS RENAMED HO CHI MINH CITY ■ AND AMERICA'S SHORES TEEMED WITH WAVES OF NEW IMMIGRANTS . . .

DANIEL P. MOYNIHAN

"CHARLIE'S ANGELS"

THE ECONOMY AND THE ELECTION

THE NATION

COVER STORY

The New Immigrants:
Still the Promised Land

We are not a narrow tribe of men . . . No: our blood is as the flood of the Amazon, made up of a thousand noble currents all pouring into one. We are not a nation so much as a world. — Herman Melville

It is hard. It is hard to turn the key and lock the door, hard to leave, probably forever, the little white stucco house in the Peloponnesian town of Argos. The little house was Niki Kaffas' dowry when she married Theodosios twelve years ago, and the tears start to her eyes as she speaks of "the wonderful garden and the cage of canaries that sing all day. Now we must leave it all behind. But they tell me America is a nice place." Theodosios Kaffas is determined to make it so. A barber who had to go out of business, a restaurant cook who couldn't earn more than $300 a month, he has dreamed of going to America ever since he was a boy. Now he is 36. "Argos is a good place for those who own fields and orange groves," says Kaffas, "but the workers are better paid in America. I want a better life for my family. I want to educate my children."

Victor Vallés Solán, too, feels passionately about his children. He has five of them, and in Cuba, where he once ran a small steel foundry, he began to feel that they were becoming hostages to the fortunes of the state. "We were allowed a ration of only one liter of fresh milk every other day," says Vallés , 46, "but what is more important is that every day the children learned Communist doctrine in the schools, and going to church was never talked about. I realize that I am going to the United States with many illusions, but for

WEEKLY FLIGHTS BRING CUBANS FROM SPAIN TO NEW YORK

"I am going with many illusions," said one

me your country is the place on earth where democracy is purest."

Dr. Brian Pethica already knows the U.S. well and he has no problems political or financial. Now 49, a research chemist at the Unilever Corp. in Port Sunlight, near Liverpool, Pethica has been crossing the Atlantic at least once a year since 1958, and he likes what he calls "the entrepreneurial attitude." But he wants to teach. Says he: "The university system in Britain seems somehow less open, more rigid, more hierarchical. In the U.S. there is a broad diversity of systems, which allows you to educate everyone as far as he can go."

Last week, these voyagers all took off for America, just in time to celebrate their first July 4 holidays. The Kaffases, with their two children of 11 and 8, headed for Philadelphia, where Niki's brother hopes to find Theodosios work in a restaurant. Victor Vallés Solán took his family to Melrose Park, Ill., where he has a job making engine blocks. Dr. Pethica was bound for Potsdam, N.Y., where he will become dean of the faculty of arts and sciences at Clarkson College of Technology.

Changing Styles. These are just a few of the new immigrants who today are changing the face of America. Though many people think of mass immigration as a closed chapter in the nation's history, more than 1,000 newcomers now arrive in the U.S. every day. Since American birth rates are

declining, that influx from abroad represents about one-fifth of the nation's annual increase in population. The new immigrants are changing local styles, too. Miami's Eighth Street is now Calle Ocho, the main thoroughfare of bustling Little Havana (pop. 450,000), alive to the *pachanga* beat and the rich aroma of *sofrito* seasoning. San Francisco's Chinatown is rivaled by Los Angeles' Koreatown (pop. 65,000), the fastest-growing settlement in the city, where Korean dance studios and karate schools have sprouted along Olympic Boulevard.

All in all, the 400,000 new immigrants arriving every year represent, after decades of discriminatory national quotas, a comparatively enlightened policy that admits more people from poorer countries, particularly more Orientals. Though the new policy is more evenhanded toward foreign nations, it does explicitly favor professionals and the middle classes, not those huddled masses and wretched refuse once hymned by Emma Lazarus.

Their goals have changed somewhat over the years. Political conflict is still a major cause of immigration, as demonstrated by last year's sudden swirl of refugees from Viet Nam; but religious persecution, which once sprinkled the land with Shakers and Huguenots and Hutterian Brethren, is hardly an element any more. The new immigrants do occasionally talk of getting rich, but they know that this is no longer a land of gold rushes and oil strikes. Yet they do see on the distant shoreline of America something that many Americans take for granted or even forget they possess—freedom. That means not simply freedom from oppression and hunger but also from unbreakable caste systems and generations of inherited ignorance.

Truisms really are true, as George Orwell once wrote, and America remains that cliché of clichés, the promised land, the land of opportunity. The newcomers find out soon enough that the U.S. is not without its share of poverty and prejudice; but to their eyes it nonetheless gleams with the light of Utopia.

NOVELIST ALEX HALEY'S *ROOTS* WAS A MEGA-HIT ■ PRESIDENT CARTER PARDONED NEARLY ALL U.S. DRAFT EVADERS ■ THE DISCO CRAZE HIT AND MILLIONS CAUGHT "SATURDAY NIGHT FEVER" ■ "SEATTLE SLEW" WON THE TRIPLE CROWN ■ AND A LANDMARK U.S. GATHERING OUTLINED AN AGENDA FOR WOMEN . . .

1977

Opposition to Communist human rights abuses escalated; 241 Czech intellectuals signed a manifesto, while prominent Soviet dissidents were arrested.

Nation

What Next for U.S. Women?

Houston produces new alliances and a drive for grass-roots power

The battle was over — and to the curators went the spoils. The blue-and-white lectern emblem proclaiming NATIONAL WOMAN'S CONFERENCE 1977, which had hung for three hectic, fractious, exhilarating days in Houston, last week was headed for Washington's Smithsonian Institution. It will repose with such other memorabilia as the star-spangled banner that flew over Fort McHenry and Charles Lindbergh's *Spirit of St. Louis*. And well it might. Over a weekend, American women had reached some kind of watershed in their own history, and in that of the nation.

Declared Eleanor Smeal of Pittsburgh, housewife and president of the 65,000-member National Organization for Women: "Houston was a rite of passage." Ruth Clusen of Green Bay, Wis., president of the League of Women Voters, struck the same theme: "Even for women who are outside organizational life, who don't see themselves as part of the women's movement, something has happened in their lives as a result of this meeting, whether they realize it or not."

What happened, particularly for the 14,000 who attended the Houston meeting, was an end to the psychological isolation that had constrained their activities and ambitions. They learned that many other middle-of-the-road, American-as-Mom's-apple-pie women shared with them a sense of second-class citizenship and a craving for greater social and economic equality. Said Ida Castro, an alternate delegate from New Jersey: "It was a total high to get together and discover so many people who agree on so many issues, and finding that I am not alone."

Over and over, the convention was described as "a rainbow of women." No previous women's gathering could begin to match its diversity of age, income, race, occupation or opinion. There were 1,442 delegates who had been elected at 56 state and territorial meetings that were open to the public; 400 more had been appointed at large by an

Bella Abzug chairs Houston conference
"In the second stage, action and power"

overseeing national commission. They were white, black, yellow, Hispanic and Indian — and four were Eskimo. They were rich, poor, radical, conservative, Democratic, Republican and politically noninvolved. Three Presidents' wives were guests: Rosalynn Carter, Betty Ford and Lady Bird Johnson. (Jackie Onassis turned down an invitation; Pat Nixon was ill.)

By the end of the Houston conference, the women's movement had armed itself with a 25-point, revised National Plan of Action. By convincing majorities, the delegates called for passage of the Equal Rights Amendment; free choice on abortion, along with federal and state funds for those who cannot afford it; a national health insurance plan with special provisions for women; extension of Social Security benefits to housewives; elimination of job, housing and credit discrimination against lesbians,

and their right to have custody of their children; federally and state-funded programs for victims of child abuse and for education in rape prevention; state-supported shelters for wives who are abused by their husbands.

The cost of the programs in the National Plan of Action might well run into billions of dollars. On other grounds as well, women can expect great difficulty in getting some of them past legislators.

About 20% of the convention delegates, mostly from the South and the West, were "pro-family" conservatives who opposed some of the more controversial proposals. There were three "hot button" resolutions — those covering the ERA, abortion and lesbian rights — on which the delegates were sharply divided. With other resolutions, even the conservatives were more inclined to agree.

On few issues was that unity more convincingly displayed than the minority rights resolution that was drafted by conference organizers but later rewritten and toughened by the one-third of delegates who were black, Hispanic, Indian or Oriental. The revised version was carried with virtual unanimity by delegates who had split bitterly on other issues. Exulted Liz Carpenter, leader of ERAmerica, the group spearheading the amendment ratification drive: "We can no longer be accused of being a middle class white women's cause." Now the women's movement faces the much more complex, challenging and drawn-out task of turning at least some of its propositions into reality. Said Bella Abzug, presiding officer of the conference: "We are in the second stage, of action and political power." As delegates streamed home from the conference, they seemed to reinforce Abzug's message. Confirmed in their confidence, women vowed to place their interests on the political stage as never before.

RUPERT MURDOCH

IDI AMIN

HIGH SCHOOLS IN TROUBLE

1978

Martial law was declared in Iran and Moslem leader Khomeini called for agitation to end the Shah's rule; labor strife halted Iran's oil production.

MAJOR NEW YORK DAILY NEWSPAPERS WERE SHUT BY STRIKING UNIONS ■ CHERYL TIEGS WAS THE ALL-AMERICAN MODEL ■ THE U.S. DOLLAR PLUNGED TO RECORD LOWS AGAINST FOREIGN CURRENCIES ■ THE FIRST NON-ITALIAN IN FIVE CENTURIES WAS ELECTED POPE ■ AND "PROPOSITION 13" LED TO AN UNPRECEDENTED AMERICAN TAX REVOLT . . .

PRINCE CHARLES

SHAH OF IRAN

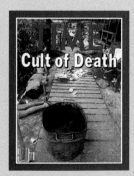

JONESTOWN DEATHS

Nation

Sound and Fury over Taxes

Howard Jarvis and the voters send a message: "We're mad as hell"

That sound roaring out of the West — what was it? A California earthquake? A Pacific tidal wave threatening to sweep across the country? Literally, it was neither; figuratively, it was both. That angry noise was the sound of a middle class tax revolt erupting, and its tremors are shaking public officials from Sacramento to Washington, D.C. Suddenly all kinds of candidates in election year 1978 are joining the chorus of seductive antitax sentiment, assailing high taxes, inflation and government spending.

The full significance of the revolt — and it is nothing less than that — was made plain by the magnitude of the victory won by proponents of California's now famous, or infamous, Proposition 13: 4.2 million voters supported the measure, overwhelming by nearly 2 to 1 the 2.3 million who refused to go along. It was as though millions of the state's taxpayers had thrown open their windows like the fed-up characters in the movie *Network* and shouted in thunderous unison: "I'm mad as hell — and I'm not going to take it any more!"

What the nation's most populous state last week refused to accept was the soaring, inflation-fueled rise in its property taxes. In the most radical slash in property taxes since Depression days, Californians voted themselves a 57% cut — more than $7 billion — in the levy that hurts them most, the tax on the rising value of their homes. Ignoring warnings that schools may not be able to educate, libraries may close and crime rates may climb, the voters further decreed that any local tax hereafter may increase no more than 2% a year — substantially less than the anticipated hikes in the cost of living.

California was the epicenter of the tax-quake, but there were Richter Scale readings nearly everywhere. On the same Tuesday that Proposition 13 swept to victory,

taxpayers in Ohio turned down 86 of 139 school tax levies, including emergency outlays designed to save public schools in Cleveland and Columbus from bankruptcy. Conservative candidates for the U.S. Senate won victories in Iowa and New Jersey by campaigning hard for tax cuts. Twenty-

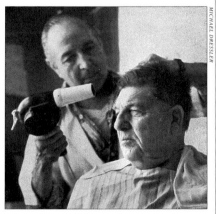

After a 16-year fight, Jarvis prepares for victory night

A war of machetes, and some heads might be cut off

three state legislatures have called for an unprecedented constitutional convention to weigh an amendment requiring the Federal Government to operate on a balanced budget. Limits on state and local spending have been enacted in three states (Colorado, New Jersey and Tennessee), and efforts to clamp on similar lids are under way in 19 others. And Howard Jarvis, the crusty curmudgeon who spearheaded the California tax revolt, has already been asked to carry his crusade to 40 states.

He will get a warm welcome. Tax foes elsewhere are smoldering in anger and frustration — not only at the ever bigger bites being taken out of their pocketbooks but

also at what they see as more waste and fewer services from government. Commenting on Proposition 13, Florida's Democratic Congressman Sam Gibbons declared: "It's one of the healthiest things that's happened in a long time. I thought California was the most overbloated state government I'd ever seen, and the Federal Government is overstuffed and can stand a lot of trimming down too."

The fact that Californians wielded a meat ax as they cut into taxes bothered many advocates of more moderate efforts to put limitations on government spending. Liberal Economist Walter Heller, chairman of the Council of Economic Advisers under both John F. Kennedy and Lyndon Johnson, noted in the *Wall Street Journal* last week: "Clearly, governments the country over need to be brought to book, they need to deliver more per dollar of tax, and they need to deliver excess tax dollars back to the taxpayer. But all of that can be readily granted without committing fiscal *hara-kiri*." To John Petersen, an official of the Municipal Finance Officers Association, a group that views virtually any tax cut as a form of *hara-kiri*, Proposition 13 is "a Frankenstein, a green hulk emerging from the swamps of the West."

The 75-year-old father of Proposition 13, basking in his first victory in a lifetime of attacking free-spending public officials, is no Frankenstein, but is a self-defined "pain in the ass. You gotta be to get these people to listen to you." On election evening, Howard Jarvis denied that he was vengeful. "Tonight was a victory against money, the politicians, the government," said the gruff, tireless campaigner as he sagged into an easy chair in an eleventh-floor suite at Los Angeles' Biltmore Hotel. "Government simply must be limited. Excessive taxation leads to either bankruptcy or dictatorship."

SOVIET TROOPS INVADED AFGHANISTAN ■ MARGARET THATCHER WAS NAMED PRIME MINISTER, THE FIRST WOMAN TO LEAD THE BRITISH GOVERNMENT ■ RAMPANT INFLATION DROVE INVESTORS FROM BANKS AND INTO GOLD, SILVER, ANTIQUES, AND ART ■ AND THE THREE MILE ISLAND NUCLEAR FACILITY HAD AN "EVENT" . . .

1979

In a humanitarian gesture, President Carter allowed the deposed Iranian Shah to seek medical treatment in the U.S.; a rioting mob seized the U.S. embassy in Tehran, holding occupants hostage.

Nation

A Nuclear Nightmare

Confusion and fear spew from a damaged reactor in Pennsylvania

In the dead of night, the hulks of four 372-ft. cooling towers and two high-domed nuclear reactor container buildings were scarcely discernible above the gentle waters of the Susquehanna River, eleven miles southeast of Harrisburg, Pa. Inside the brightly lit control room of Metropolitan Edison's Unit 2, technicians on the lobster shift one night last week faced a tranquil, even boring watch. Suddenly, at 4 a.m., alarm lights blinked red on their instrument panels. A siren whooped a warning. In the understated jargon of the nuclear power industry, an "event" had occurred. In plain English, it was the beginning of the worst accident in the history of U.S. nuclear power production, and of a long, often confused nightmare that threw the future of the nuclear industry into question.

There was no panic at the plant, situated on a stretch of muddy soil called Three Mile Island in an otherwise scenic bend in the river. The men in the control room had heard those sirens before. They went about their task of meeting what looked at first like just another "transient," a minor glitch somewhere in the complex system like so many they had dealt with in the past. Unit 2's huge turbine, which generates 880 megawatts of electricity, had "tripped," shut down automatically, as it should when the steam that turns it has somehow been cut off. The technicians assumed that the cause would be easy to find and correct.

They could hardly have been more wrong. For the next several days, radioactive steam and gas seeped sporadically into the atmosphere from the plant. Pennsylvania Governor Richard Thornburgh advised the evacuation of all pregnant women and preschool children living within five miles of Three Mile Island, and thousands of people fled the area. As tension mounted, engineers struggled to cool the reactor's core. There was a genuine danger of a "meltdown," in which the core could drop into the water coolant at the bottom of its chamber, causing a steam explosion that could rupture the 4-ft.-thick concrete walls of the containment building; or the molten core could burn through the even thicker concrete base and deep into the earth. In either case, lethally radioactive gases would be released, causing a nuclear catastrophe.

At week's end officials insisted that while the danger of a meltdown had not vanished, it was receding. Nevertheless, suspense as to the eventual outcome buttressed the claims of nuclear power's foes that all the wondrous fail-safe gadgets of modern technology had turned out to be just as fallible as the men who had designed and built them. Declared Nuclear Power Critic Ralph Nader: "This is the beginning of the end of nuclear power in this country."

That, of course, was a considerable rush to judgment. But the already beleaguered nuclear power industry had clearly suffered a crippling setback. Not only are its plans for expansion now in grave doubt, but the Three Mile Island accident came at a time when President Carter was about to propose a new approach to the nation's energy problems. He had already urged a speedup in putting new nuclear power plants into operation by reducing the years it takes to pass through all of the regulatory challenges. While a case could still be made that bureaucratic indecision and delay ought to be minimized, even tougher safety standards would almost inevitably be one result of the Pennsylvania breakdown. Whatever the final report, months from now, on what went wrong and how at Three Mile Island, the way in which federal and plant officials seemed to handle the breakdown will not help the industry's image. The trouble was dismissed at first by Jack Herbein, Metropoli-

Anti-nuclear protesters marching up Sixth Avenue in New York City

tan Edison's vice president for power generation, in a memorable engineer's euphemism as merely "a normal aberration." Reassuring statements spewed from the plant's press spokesmen, sounding as if they were taken right out of the script for the film *The China Syndrome,* a thriller that depicts nuclear plant officials as placing greed for profits far above their concern for public safety. But if the movie, starring real-life Antinuclear Activist Jane Fonda, is unfair in its villainous caricature of power-and construction-industry officials, its basic premise will no longer seem so farfetched to those moviegoers until now unattuned to the nation's debate over nuclear power. The premise: that a nuclear power plant is not nearly as accident-proof as its builders proclaim and that "the China Syndrome," a total meltdown that causes the core to sink lethally into the earth (hence, fancifully, toward China), is not a totally outlandish possibility.

Ironically, though the film's fictional plant is located in California, the example that is offered of the devastation a meltdown could cause is an area the size of Pennsylvania. Even more ironically, given the bias of the film makers, what actually happened at Three Mile Island is far more serious than the "event" portrayed at the fictional plant.

AYATULLAH KHOMEINI

MARGARET THATCHER

OPEC'S SQUEEZE

THE
WRITERS

JAMES JOYCE, A TIME COVER SUBJECT IN THE 1930S, SET FORTH THE WRITER'S MANIFESTO: "TO FORGE IN THE SMITHY OF MY SOUL THE UNCREATED CONSCIENCE OF MY RACE." THIS IS THE GREAT VISION OF LITERATURE, THE VISION OF WILLIAM FAULKNER OR THOMAS MANN. OTHER WRITERS REPORT FROM THE FRONT, SKETCHING INDELIBLE PORTRAITS OF THEIR TIMES, WHETHER IT IS NOEL COWARD CHOREOGRAPHING A BATTLE OF THE SEXES— OR JOHN UPDIKE REVEALING THAT SUBURBANITES *HAVE* SEX. AND SOME WRITERS, LIKE SCOTT TUROW, OFFER ENTERTAINMENT WITHOUT APOLOGY, QUITE CONTENT SIMPLY TO CREATE A YARN THAT KEEPS US GUESSING.

JOSEPH CONRAD
1923

H. G. WELLS
1926

JOHN DOS PASSOS
1936

VIRGINIA WOOLF
1937

ROBERT FROST
1950

WILLIAM SHAKESPEARE
1960

WILLA CATHER
1931

NOEL COWARD
1933

THOMAS MANN
1934

JAMES JOYCE
1934

CLIFFORD ODETS
1938

WILLIAM FAULKNER
1939

EUGENE O'NEILL
1946

REBECCA WEST
1947

ROBERT LOWELL
1967

JOHN UPDIKE
1968

WOODY ALLEN
1979

SCOTT TUROW
1990

An End to the Long Ordeal

Joy at the restoration of pride to a nation that had been humbled for too long by a puny tormentor was but one of the many reactions of Americans to Iran's final release of the 52 U.S. hostages last week. There was a sense of relief too. And scorn for Iran. But above all the initial dominant mood was one of continuing celebration, from the moment the first plane rolled down the runway in Tehran at 12:33 p.m. Washington time — just eleven minutes after the Inauguration ceremony of Ronald Reagan had ended on the Capitol's West Front.

At Weisbaden, West Germany, the returnees assembled in a bril-

A Nation Mourns

The eye accepted what the mind could not: a sudden burst of white and yellow fire, then white trails streaming up and out from the fireball to form a twisted Y against a pure heaven, and the metal turning to rags, dragging white ribbons into the ocean. A terrible beauty exploded like a primal event of physics — the birth of a universe; the death of a star; a fierce, enigmatic violence out of the blue. The mind recoiled in sheer surprise. Then it filled with horror.

The loss of the *Challenger* inflicted upon Americans the purest pain that they have collectively felt in years. It was a pain uncontaminated by the anger and hatred and hungering for revenge that come in the aftermath of terrorist killings, for example. It was a pain uncomplicated by the divisions, political, racial, moral, that usually beset American tragedies (Viet Nam and Watergate, to name two). The shuttle crew, spectacularly democratic, was the best of us, Americans thought, doing the best of things Americans do. The mission seemed symbolically immaculate, the farthest reach of the perfectly American ambition to create new frontiers. And it simply vanished into the air.
February 10, 1986

antly lighted community room on
ie hospital's third floor to meet
mmy Carter. The former President
eld up three newspapers, which
annered the release of the hostages
nd gave the Inauguration secondary
lay. "As you can see," said Carter,
we've had a change of presidency,
ut even that was second in people's
iinds."
ebruary 2, 1981

"He Gave Us Hope"

Six months ago, Lech Walesa
was an unemployed electrician. Today, as leader of Solidarity, the Communist world's only independent
labor union, he is one of the most
powerful men in Poland, a folk hero
not only to millions of his countrymen but to much of the world. His
achievement all but defies descrip-
tion; in effect, he single-handed ral-
lied his fellow workers to stand up
against the will and the might of the
Soviet Union.

Walesa looks ill-suited for such
eminence. He is 5 ft. 7 in. tall and a
trifle overweight. His face is an elfin
caricature, the pale cheeks almost
submerged under a wide mustache,
the profile dominated by a prominent
nose and an outthrust jaw. Yet he
radiates an unmistakable air of authority, along with an infectious good
humor. Working a crowd, he displays the charisma of a natural
leader. Said a Gdansk woman
worker after hearing him speak last
week: "He is the right man at the right
time. He was able to give us hope."
December 29, 1980

low-up

"Vancouver, Vancouver, this is
!" The frantic warning was radioed
precisely 8:31 a.m. on that fateful
unday by Volcano Expert David
ihnston, 30, who had climbed to a
onitoring site five miles from
ashington State's Mount St.
elens. He wanted to peer through
noculars at an enormous bulge
uilding up below the crater, which
d been rumbling and steaming for
ght weeks, and report his observa-
ons to the U.S. Geological Survey
nter in Vancouver, Wash.

Seconds after his shouted message, a stupendous explosion of
trapped gases, generating about 500
times the force of the atomic bomb
dropped on Hiroshima, blew the
entire top off Mount St. Helens. In a
single burst St. Helens was transformed from a postcard-symmetrical
cone 9,677 ft. high to an ugly flattop
1,300 ft. lower. Clouds of hot ash
made up of pulverized rock were
belched twelve miles into the sky.
Giant mud slides, composed of
melted snow mixed with ash and
propelled by waves of superheated

gas erupting out of the crater,
rumbled down the slopes and crashed
through valleys, leaving millions of
trees knocked down in rows, as
though a giant had been playing pickup sticks.

David Johnston was never heard
from again. His campsite was
strewn with boulders, broken tree
trunks and ash with the consistency
of wet cement.
June 2, 1980

Magic in the Daylight

In plan and in prospect, the marrying of H.R.H. the Prince of Wales, 32, to Lady Diana Spencer, 20, the well-born and distinctively dishy commoner, is a fairy tale of present pomp and past glory, a last page from the tattered book of empire with the

Why He's a Thriller

Today Michael Jackson is in the air everywhere. The pulse of America and much of the rest of the world moves irregularly, beating in time to the tough strut of *Billie Jean*, the asphalt aria of *Beat It*, the supremely cool chills of *Thriller*. Jackson's high-flying tenor makes him sound like the lead in some funked-up boys choir, even as the sexual dynamism irradiating from the arch of his dancing body challenges Government standards for a nuclear meltdown. His lithe frame, five-fathom eyes, long lashes might be threatening if Jackson gave, even for a second, the impression that he is obtainable. But the audience's sense of his sensuality becomes quite deliberately tangled with the mirror image of his life: the good boy, the God-fearing Jehovah's Witness, the adamant vegetarian, the resolute non-indulger in smoke, strong drink or dope of any kind, the impossibly insulated innocent.
March 19, 1984

The Day the Music Died

Just a voice out of the American night. "Mr. Lennon." He started to turn around. There is no knowing whether John Lennon saw, for what would have been the second time that day, the young man in the black raincoat stepping out of the shadows. The first shot hit him that fast, through the chest. There were at least three others.

Not just for his wife or son but for more people than anyone could even begin to number, the killing of John Lennon was a death in the family. For all the official records, the death would be called murder. For everyone who cherished the sustaining myth of the Beatles — which is to say, for much of an entire generation that is passing, as Lennon was, at age 40, into middle age, and coming suddenly up against its own mortality —

the murder was something else. It was an assassination, a ritual slaying of something that could hardly be named. Hope, perhaps; or idealism. Or time. Not only lost, but suddenly dislocated, fractured. The last *Day in the Life*. "I read the news today, oh boy..."
December 22, 1980

gold leaf still intact. It is by Rudyard Kipling out of Walter Bagehot, a ceremony intended to refurbish and reaffirm tradition. "The monarchy's mystery," Bagehot wrote in 1867, "is its life. We must not let in daylight upon magic." This wedding on the cusp of high noon, in front of a world short on ritual and parched for romance, is in fact one grand pass of the royal wand, a masterly and pricey piece of prestidigitation in which, at once, the old values are upheld, the future is assured, and everyone can be queen for a day.
August 3, 1981

DOUGLAS KIRKLAND/SYGMA

WAYNE SORCE

America Shapes Up

As recently as 20 years ago for most people, the body was hardly more than an interesting mass somewhere down there below the head. It could be barricaded in gray flannel and wantonly pleased in steak houses and French restaurants. If the body belonged to Clint Eastwood or Sophia Loren, it was interesting. Otherwise, except in bed, it was ignored in favor of more important pursuits like winning the space race or building the New Society.

By the early 70s, however, a sweeping change was literally afoot; the sport of mass running had begun. Suburbanites jogged like herds of oestrous gazelles down side streets. Marriages were threatened when one spouse trained for a marathon and never arrived home for an evening meal. Dinner itself became a lean affair, of *crudités* and boiled fish. Executives could be seen pumping iron like buttoned-down Schwarzeneggers. For a while it seemed to be a fad, one more instantaneous American fixation like the twist or the Hula-Hoop. "It'll never last," said the wise guys over the second martini at the bar.

Surprise, fellas. The fitness boom has grown for a decade, and improving the body has become an enduring, and perhaps historically significant, national obsession. These days, even the wise guys order a second Perrier.
November 2, 1981

AP

1980

The troubled Carter presidency gave way to the Republican challenger, the beginning of what followers billed "The Reagan Revolution" in Washington.

JOHN LENNON WAS KILLED ON A NEW YORK STREET CORNER ■ TELEVISION AUDIENCES WONDERED "WHO SHOT J.R.?" ■ IRAN AND IRAQ BECAME LOCKED IN A MERCILESS BLOODBATH ■ *VOYAGER I* TRANSMITTED THE FIRST CLOSE-UP PHOTOS OF SATURN'S RINGS ■ AND NEW YORK'S MUSEUM OF MODERN ART TURNED THE SPOTLIGHT ON PICASSO . . .

RONALD REAGAN

JOHN LENNON

MT. ST. HELENS

Art

The Show of Shows

Picasso, modernism's father, comes home to MOMA

In imaginative force and outright *terribilità*, it is quite possibly the most crushing and exhilarating exhibition of work by a 20th century artist ever held in the U.S. Beginning this week, over the next four months nearly a million people will queue outside New York City's Museum of Modern Art to get a glimpse of it. Pablo Picasso, who died in 1973, is being honored in a show of nearly 1,000 of his works, some never exhibited before, drawn from collections the world over.

What gives the exhibit its overwhelming character is the range and fecundity of Picasso's talent—the flashes of demonic restlessness, the heights of confidence and depths of insecurity, the relationships (alternately loving and cannibalistic) to the art of the past, but above all the sustained intensity of feeling. "Pablo Picasso: A Retrospective" contains good paintings and bad, some so weak that they look like forgeries (but are not), as well as a great many works of art for which the word masterpiece — exiled for the crime of elitism over the past decade—must now be reinstated. It is the largest exhibition of one artist's work that MOMA has ever held, or probably ever will. It contains pieces ranging in size from *Guernica*, Picasso's 26-ft.-wide mural of protest against the fascist bombing of a Basque town during the Spanish Civil War, to a cluster of peg dolls he painted for his daughter Paloma. Paintings, drawings, collages, prints of every kind, sculpture in bronze, wood, wire, tin, paper and clay; there was virtually no medium the Spaniard did not use.

Picasso never painted an abstract picture in his life. His instinct for the real world was so strong that he probably would have produced something woman-shaped every time he took brush in hand. Nevertheless,

CAMERA PRESS

Pablo Picasso

He tried to embody child and savage

some of his cubist still lifes of 1911 run close to total abstraction. Objects were sunk in a twinkling field of vectors and shadows, solid lapping into transparency, things penetrating and turning away, leaving behind the merest signs for themselves — a letter or two, the bowl of a pipe, the sound hole of a guitar. This sense of multiple relationships was the core of cubism's modernity. It declared that all visual experience could be set forth as a shifting field that included the onlooker. It was painting's unconscious answer to the theory of relativity.

After World War I, Picasso would depend wholly on himself and his feelings. The corollary was that Picasso gave feeling itself an extraordinary, self-regarding intensity, so that the most vivid images of braggadocio and rage, castration fear and sexual appetite in modern art still belong to the Spaniard. This frankness — allied with Picasso's power of metamorphosis, which linked every image together in a ravenous, animistic vitality — is with-

out parallel among other artists.

Basically, Picasso cared nothing about civilization or its discontents. He admired, and tried to embody, the child and the savage, both prodigies of appetite. To feel, to seize, to penetrate, to abandon: these were the verbs of his art, as they were of his cruelly narcissistic relationships with the "goddesses or doormats," as he categorized the women in his life. Hence, the energy of *The Embrace*, 1925, its lovers grappling on a sofa in their orifice-laden knot of apoplectic randiness. Hence, too, the fear (amounting sometimes to holy terror, but more often to a witch-killing misogyny) that emanates from creatures like the bony mantis woman of *Seated Bather*, 1930. Such images are cathartic. One needs colossal self-confidence to expose such insecurities.

Picasso's climactic work of the '30s was *Guernica*, 1937. In its way it is a classicizing painting, not only in its friezelike effect, but also in its details. The only modern image in it is a light bulb; but for its presence, the mural would scarcely seem to belong in this world of Heinkel bombers and incendiary bombs. Yet its black, white and gray palette also suggests the documentary photo, while the texture of strokes on the horse's body is more like collaged newsprint than hair.

Picasso was the most influential artist of his own time; for many lesser figures a catastrophic influence, and for those who could deal with him — from Braque, through Giacometti, to de Kooning and Arshile Gorky — an almost indescribably fruitful one. Today such a career seems inconceivable. No one even shows signs of assuming the empty mantle. If ever a man created his own historical role and was not the pawn of circumstances, it was that Nietzschean monster from Malaga.

THE HOSTAGE CRISIS ENDED AS REAGAN ASSUMED OFFICE AND MILITANTS ALMOST SIMULTANEOUSLY RELEASED CAPTIVES ■ ANWAR SADAT WAS KILLED BY A FUNDAMENTALIST FANATIC ■ THE SPACE SHUTTLE *COLUMBIA* MADE ITS FIRST FLIGHT ■ PRINCE CHARLES AND LADY DIANA SPENCER TIED THE ROYAL KNOT ■ AND THE HOSTAGES IN IRAN NEARED FREEDOM . . .

1981

As fears emerged of Third World nuclear capabilities, Israeli bombers destroyed an Iraqi reactor in what was described as a preemptive strike.

Nation

Hostage Breakthrough

In his final days as President, Carter reaches agreement with Iran

Finally, after more than 14 months of false starts and faded hopes, the breakthrough that could end America's agonizing — and humiliating — hostage crisis came, as a dramatic climax to a pressure-packed week of high-level international bargaining. The evidence that the end was at hand could not have been more tangible: at Tehran's Mehrabad Airport, which was suddenly closed to routine air traffic, sat a Boeing 707 Algerian airliner, poised to fly the 52 Americans to freedom.

To be sure, a final agreement on the terms for release had not yet been signed by the U.S. and Iran. But the Iranians announced publicly that all of the major differences between the negotiators had been resolved. On Sunday morning U.S. time, Behzad Nabavi, Iran's chief hostage negotiator, declared: "The government of the Islamic Republic of Iran and the United States finally reached agreement on resolving the issue of the hostages today." In Washington, Vice President Walter Mondale declined to go quite that far. Said he: "We're very, very close, but we do not yet have an agreement." President Carter, who had been spending his last weekend in office at Camp David, helicoptered to the White House, where his speechwriters were at work on a major announcement. Carter went directly from the helicopter to his Oval Office. He first summoned Secretary of State Edmund Muskie to the White House. Then they called U.S. diplomats in Algiers for a briefing on the negotiations.

Everything seemed in place for an imminent end to America's most humbling experience since its withdrawal from Viet Nam. A team of Algerian doctors had flown to Tehran to examine the hostages. Some $2.2 billion in Iranian gold and currency had been transferred from New York to London so that it could be turned over to

Iran within minutes of the Americans' departure from Tehran. A 30-member U.S. hostage recovery team, including former Secretary of State Cyrus Vance, was ready in Washington to fly to West Germany to meet the released hostages at a U.S. military hospital. Carter also considered going to West Germany to welcome the Americans.

Still it would take an intricate series of specific actions to set the actual release into

Speaker of the Iranian Parliament Rafsanjani, in turban, at news conference

motion. English, French and Farsi versions of the final text of the complex agreements would have to be compared. Carter would have to sign certain papers and order certain actions for the U.S. Beyond the $2.2 billion positioned for delivery, European and American bankers apparently would have to transfer other funds before that Algerian airliner could take off. Once it was in the air with the Americans, Iran's leverage over any further cash deliveries would evaporate.

Despite all the evidence of a deal, some nagging specifics had to be worked out at the last moment. Iran's Nabavi termed them "trivial details." A U.S. State Department official said that the precise time at which both sides would begin to carry out the release terms still had to be decided, but he

added: "For all practical purposes, there is agreement." U.S. officials expected the Americans to be out of Iran before Ronald Reagan was inaugurated. On a top-secret document in Tehran, Iranian Prime Minister Muhammed Ali Raja'i wrote: "Transfer scheduled for Tuesday morning Tehran time." That would be Monday night in the U.S.

If so that would be a fitting consolation for Jimmy Carter, whose presidency became haunted by the hostage issue. His early restraint in handling Iran's affront to America's pride had at first earned him widespread praise for coolness under fire. But as months passed, public patience in the U.S. ebbed. The fiery failure in an Iranian desert of a U.S. military rescue mission symbolized the nation's frustration. In the end, the lingering hostage affair did much to ensure Carter's election defeat in November.

For the hostages, the confinement had been akin to an emotional sweatbox of unrelieved uncertainty over their ultimate fate. Would they be freed? Tried as spies? Executed? For their families at home, the months of recurring rumors of imminent release, fed by Iranian propagandists, had been painful too. Even on the verge of the actual release, noted Dorothea Morefield of San Diego, whose husband is consul general of the captive U.S. embassy: "Everybody's walking around with their fingers crossed." Said Susan Cooke of Memphis about her hostage son Donald: "I just want to grab him and hang on for dear life."

Her chance of delivering that hug was made possible by the patience and persistence this week of the outgoing President and his tireless diplomats, who labored through marathon meetings in Washington and Algiers, as other key actors in the drama, including turbaned Iranian clerics and pin-striped international bankers, continued to meet in London, New York, and Tehran.

MAYOR ED KOCH

COCAINE

VIET NAM VETS

1982

Lebanon became a worldwide metaphor for tragedy, as Beirut was virtually destroyed in fighting and hundreds of Palestinians died in refugee camp massacres.

BREZHNEV'S DEATH WAS ANNOUNCED BY MOSCOW ■ BRITAIN AND ARGENTINA WENT TO WAR OVER POSSESSION OF THE FALKLAND ISLANDS ■ AUTOMAKER JOHN DELOREAN WAS ARRESTED FOR DRUG POSSESSION ■ MILLIONS OF MOVIEGOERS BEFRIENDED "E.T." ■ AND THE PERSONAL COMPUTER REVOLUTION WAS IN FULL SWING . . .

FALKLANDS WAR

GIORGIO ARMANI

MASSACRE IN LEBANON

MACHINE OF THE YEAR

The Computer Moves In

By the millions, it is beeping its way into offices, schools and homes

WILL SOMEONE PLEASE TELL ME, the bright red advertisement asks in mock irritation, WHAT A PERSONAL COMPUTER CAN DO? The ad provides not merely an answer, but 100 of them. A personal computer, it says, can send letters at the speed of light, diagnose a sick poodle, custom-tailor an insurance program in minutes, test recipes for beer.

As the Apple Computer advertisement indicates, the enduring American love affairs with the automobile and the television set are now being transformed into a giddy passion for the personal computer. This passion is partly fad, partly a sense of how life could be made better, partly a gigantic sales campaign.

The sales figures are awesome and will become more so. In 1980 some two dozen firms sold 724,000 personal computers for $1.8 billion. When the final figures are in for 1982, according to Dataquest, a California research firm, more than 100 companies will probably have sold 2.8 million units for $4.9 billion. Estimates for the number of personal computers in use by the end of the century run as high as 80 million. The "information revolution" that futurists have long predicted has arrived, bringing with it the promise of dramatic changes in the way people live and work, perhaps even in the way they think. America will never be the same.

The most visible aspect of the computer revolution, the video game, is its least significant. But even if the buzz and clang of the arcades is largely a teenage fad, doomed to go the way of Rubik's Cube and the Hula Hoop, it is nonetheless a remarkable phenomenon. About 20 corporations are selling some 250 different game cassettes for roughly $2 billion this year. According to some estimates, more than half of all the personal computers bought for home use are devoted mainly to games.

More than half of all employed Americans now earn their living not by producing things, but as "knowledge workers," exchanging various kinds of information, and the personal computer stands ready to change how all of them do their jobs.

Elaine Ng, 5, of Dallas, likes computer class

By itself, the personal computer is a machine with formidable capabilities for tabulating, modeling or recording. The capabilities can be multiplied almost indefinitely by plugging it into a network of other computers. This is generally done by attaching a desktop model to a telephone line (two-way cables and earth satellites are coming increasingly into use). One can then dial an electronic data base, which not only provides all manner of information but also collects and transmits messages: electronic mail.

The 1,450 databases that now exist in the U.S. range from general information services like *The Source*, a *Reader's Digest* subsidiary in McLean, Va., which can provide stock prices, airline schedules or movie reviews, to more specialized services like the American Medical Association's AMA/NET, to real esoterica like the Hughes Ro-

tary Rig Report. Fees vary from $300 an hour to less than $10.

Just as the term personal computer can apply to both a home machine and an office machine (and indeed blurs the distinction between the two places) many of the first enthusiastic users of these devices have been people who do much of their work at home: doctors, lawyers, small businessmen, writers, engineers. Such people also have special needs for the networks of specialized data. Just as the computer is changing the way work is done in home offices, so it is revolutionizing the office. Routine tasks like managing payrolls and checking inventories have long since been turned over to computers, but now the typewriter is giving way to the word processor, and every office thus becomes part of a network. In one survey of corporations, 55% said they were planning to acquire the latest equipment. This technology involves not just word processors but computerized electronic message systems that could eventually make paper obsolete, and wall-size, two-way TV teleconference screens that will obviate traveling to meetings.

So the revolution has begun, and as usually happens with revolutions, nobody can agree on where it is going. Nils Nilson, director of the Artificial Intelligence Center at SRI International, believes the personal computer, like television, can "greatly increase the forces of both good and evil." Marvin Minsky, one of M.I.T.'s computer experts, believes the key significance of the personal computer is not the establishment of an intellectual ruling class, as some fear, but rather a kind of democratization of the new technology. Says he: "The desktop revolution has brought the tools that only professionals have had into the hands of the public. God knows what will happen now."

U.S. MARINES DIED WHEN A SUICIDE ATTACK DESTROYED BEIRUT BARRACKS ■ SALLY RIDE BECAME THE FIRST AMERICAN WOMAN TO TRAVEL IN SPACE ■ VIDEO AND ROCK JOINED FORCES ON MTV ■ PHILIPPINE OPPOSITION LEADER BENIGNO AQUINO WAS ASSASSINATED ■ AND BLACK INVOLVEMENT IN POLITICS WAS EPITOMIZED BY JESSE JACKSON . . .

1983

The détente in East-West relations was severely tried: MIGS shot down a Korean airliner, claiming airspace violations, while Soviet negotiators walked out of Geneva arms talks.

Nation

Seeking Votes and Clout

Jesse Jackson spearheads a new black drive for political power

Run, Jesse, run! Run, Jesse, run! The chants roll toward him, rumbling like a pent-up storm, rising to the rafters and the stained-glass portrait of the Rev. Martin Luther King Jr. With the practiced rhythms of preacher and pitchman, he launches his sermon on power. "There's a freedom train acoming," he intones. "But you got to be registered to ride." *Amen!* "Get on board! Get on board!" There is fire in his eyes, a pin in his starched collar, a finger in the air. "We can move from the slave ship to the championship! From the guttermost to the uppermost! From the outhouse to the courthouse! From the statehouse to the White House!" The well-dressed congregation of the First African Methodist Episcopal Church in Los Angeles erupts with the same chant that has resounded in the Delta country of Mississippi, in Chicago, in Atlanta. It is a rising cry that the self-styled country preacher seems less and less likely to resist. *Run, Jesse run! Run, Jesse, run!*

Jesse Louis Jackson, 41, the illegitimate son of a South Carolina high school student has for 15 years sought to don the mantle of his mentor Martin Luther King Jr. By turns he can be fascinating and frightening, inspiring and irritating, charismatic and controversial. And so too is the crusade he has been considering. On one level it would be the ultimate embodiment of the American political ideal, an affirmation that every child of the nation, yes even a black one, can some day seek the presidency. Yet on another level, it would be as far removed from conventional politics as Jackson is removed from conventional politicians.

For the past few months, Jackson has been crisscrossing the country conducting voter-registration revival meetings to bring blacks into the political process. He will cry: "We need 10,000 blacks running for office from Virginia around to Texas — county clerks, supervisors, sheriffs, judges, legislators, Governors — Just run! Run! Run!" His audience will interrupt: *Run, Jesse, run! Run, Jesse, run!* "When You run, the masses register and vote. When you run, you put your program on the front

Preaching in Los Angeles: "We can move from the statehouse to the White House"

burner. If you run, you might lose. If you don't run, you're guaranteed to lose." And the chant for him to run sounds again. In creating such fervor, raising such grassroots expectations, he leaves himself little choice but to take their advice. But perhaps more important, they are taking his. Blacks are registering to vote and running for office in a groundswell of activism that promises to alter permanently the political balance on local, state and national levels.

The significance of a potential Jackson candidacy comes not from whatever chance he would have of being a broker at a deadlocked convention (probably very little) or the possibility that he might actually win (virtually none at all). On the contrary, he could even injure the black cause, as many leaders have been quick to point out, by

drawing support away from liberal candidates like Walter Mondale. His crusade also threatens to cause deep divisions within the ranks of black leadership, and it could strain the relationship between blacks and the Democratic Party.

But in the view of Jackson's supporters, a candidacy could significantly reshape the 1984 political landscape for the better and help the Democratic Party oust Ronald Reagan. If black voter participation increased 25% by the time of the general election, Reagan could lose eight states that he won in 1980 even if he should get the same percentage of white votes he did then. In Alabama, for example, there were 272,390 unregistered blacks. Even in New York there are 900,000 unregistered blacks (55% of those eligible), more than five times as many as Reagan's 1980 margin of victory there.

The excitement generated by Jackson's potential campaign reflects, and contributes to, a resurgence of black political activism not seen since the 1960s.

This political reawakening was spurred in part by Reagan's domestic budget cuts and perceived insensitivity to civil rights. "Reagan has been a stimulant, no question about it," says Joseph Lowery, president of the Southern Christian Leadership Conference (S.C.L.C.). The surprise victory of Harold Washington in the Chicago mayoral race last April showed blacks anew that the voting booth could be a path to power. So did W. Wilson Goode's triumph in the Democratic primary race for mayor of Philadelphia.

"We've spent at least ten years being mostly dormant," says Robert Starks, a professor of inner-city studies at Northeastern Illinois University. "The only people that were busy were the Jesse Helms types. Now we're going to do them one better."

THE DEATH PENALTY

LEE IACOCCA

SPLITTING AT&T

1984

Tragedy in Bhopal, India underscored growing concerns about environmental hazards; thousands were killed when poison gas leaked from a pesticide plant.

LOS ANGELES HOSTED THE OLYMPIC GAMES, BOYCOTTED BY SOVIET-BLOC TEAMS ■ DEMOCRATS NOMINATED GERALDINE FERRARO FOR THE VICE PRESIDENCY, THE FIRST WOMAN CHOSEN BY A MAJOR U.S. PARTY ■ FILM DIRECTOR DAVID LEAN MADE THE SWEEPING "A PASSAGE TO INDIA" ■ AND MILLIONS LAUGHED ALONG WITH A CERTAIN HOUSEWIFE-HUMORIST . . .

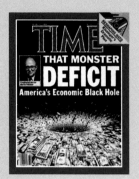

THE DEFICIT

MICHAEL JACKSON

WALTER MONDALE

Living

Erma in Bomburbia

For a survivor of housework and motherhood, laughter is still the best revenge

Notice: Car-pool moms entered in the U-Haul Mother-of-the-Year brake-off should complete the following literary quiz. Answers must be written in eyebrow pencil, and nuttiness counts.

1) For ten points, and a year's supply of mental floss, what American philosopher, whose latest book has been ensconced on the New York Times best seller list for 40 weeks, described the stance of a pregnant woman as "like a kangaroo wearing Earth Shoes"?

2) Who first defined the contribution of American mothers to the psychological well-being of their children as "guilt: the gift that keeps on giving"?

3) From whom did Tocqueville, while touring American suburbs, steal his famous one-liner that "the grass is always greener over the septic tank"? Hint: Henry David Thoreau is a good guess, but wrong.

4) What noted existentialist and television celebrity, when asked in supermarket parking lots whether she is the legendary Erma Bombeck, blushes prettily, lowers her gaze and says, "No, I'm Ann-Margret, but thank you anyway"?

"I'll be honest," says Bombeck (for it is indeed she, the syndicated star humorist of 900 papers in the U.S. and Canada, and the baggy-toreador-pants clown of ABC's *Good Morning America*), "when I started, I thought I was squirrelly. I thought it was just me. After the first columns, everyone on the block confessed it was them too." Those early columns, written in Centerville, Ohio, back in the early '60s, were not quite Corinthian, but they sure were Ermaic. Their message was that housework, if it is done right, can kill you. It was that the women who kept house in the happy hunting ground called suburbia were so lonely that they held meaningful conver-

sations with their tropical fish. It was that "you become about as exciting as your food blender. The kids come in, look you in the eye, and ask you if anybody's home."

With raw material: Betsy, Andrew, Matthew, and Bill

The message has not changed in substance, although many of the women she wrote about 20 years ago have gone on to divorces, master's degrees and careers, and Bombeck and her husband are now the wealthy proprietors not of an $18,000 tract house near Dayton but of a lavish hacienda on a hilltop near Phoenix. "Women around the world are coming to the point where they are looking at their domestic situations and saying, 'My God, I'm going crazy, it's climbing-the-wall time,'" says Bombeck. She is 57 now ("somewhere between estrogen and death," she mutters); her three children are grown and flown, and the elegant white walls of her fine house do not have crayon marks or grape jelly on them. But motherhood is a sentence without parole — have some guilt with your chicken soup; eat, eat!

— and Bombeck and her fans have no trouble understanding each other. "I could move up to Alaska," she says, "where the nearest neighbor is 300 miles away, get there by dog sled, walk into the cabin, pour a cup of coffee and then hear her say, 'These kids are driving me crazy.'"

Dropping in is what Bombeck does. Three times a week in the newspapers, and twice more on television, she plays the nation's dingbatty neighbor, who comes in the back door without knocking and cheers everyone up by saying, "Never mind the mess here, honey, let me tell you about world-class squalidness." And then yarns away, maybe, about babies so wet that their diapers give off rainbows (a Phyllis Diller line she loves to steal).

Or about her husband, the football watcher, who sits in front of the tube "like a dead sponge surrounded by bottle caps" until "the sound of his deep, labored breathing puts the cork on another confetti-filled evening." About her schoolboy son who flunked lunch. About her washing machine which eats one sock in every pair; her kids ask where the lost ones go, and she tells them that they go to live with Jesus. And about how, when one kid ate an unknown quantity of fruit on a supermarket expedition, she offered to weigh him and pay for everything over 53 lbs. About why it is all right to store useless leftovers in the refrigerator: "Garbage, if it's made right, takes a full week." About how young mothers want desperately to talk to someone who isn't teething, and the woeful results when they try to generate conversation with those lumps, their husbands, by asking, "What kind of a day did you have dear?" One husband reportedly answered by kicking the dog. Another went pale and couldn't find words. Another bit his necktie in half.

PRESIDENT REAGAN AROUSED ANGER FOR LAYING A WREATH AT A GERMAN WAR CEMETERY ■ BERNHARD GOETZ WAS TRIED FOR NEW YORK SUBWAY SHOOTINGS ■ TERRORISTS SEIZED THE CRUISE SHIP *ACHILLE LAURO* ■ A KILLER EARTHQUAKE REDUCED MUCH OF MEXICO CITY TO RUBBLE ■ AND REAGAN AND GORBACHEV MET FACE-TO-FACE FOR THE FIRST TIME . . .

1985

With the postwar rivalry between the U.S. and the Soviet Union poised to enter its fifth decade, Moscow installed a new leader — unknown Mikhail Gorbachev.

Nation

Fencing at the Fireside Summit

With candor and civility, Reagan and Gorbachev grapple for answers to the arms-race riddle

The President of the United States offered his vision of a safer world, and the General Secretary of the Soviet Union's Communist Party did not believe a word of it. As the two superpower leaders sat across from each other last week at the bargaining table in an elegant salon in Geneva, Ronald Reagan implored Mikhail Gorbachev to join him in his dream of "rendering nuclear weapons obsolete" with a space-based missile defense system. Coldly fixing Reagan in his gaze, Gorbachev would have none of it. "It's not convincing. It's emotional. It's a dream. Who can control it? Who can monitor it? It opens up an arms race in space."

In a purposely calm voice, Reagan responded, "As I said to you, I have a right to think you want to use your missiles against us. With mere words we cannot abolish the threat."

Frustrated, Gorbachev exclaimed, "Why don't you believe us when we say we will not use weapons against you?"

As Reagan tried to speak, Gorbachev interrupted, "Please answer me, Mr. President. What is your answer?" Again Reagan began to reply; again Gorbachev angrily insisted, "Answer my simple question!"

Finally, Reagan was able to utter a reply: "I cannot say to the American people that I could take you at your word if *you* don't believe *us.*"

Rarely have the inexorable forces of history been so starkly revealed by an exchange between two world leaders. Despite all the public handshakes and smiles, and despite the apparent rapport that emerged between two confident and forceful men last week, they were caught by a stark axiom of the Soviet-American rivalry: neither side can afford to base the security of a nation on trust alone. For 40 years, ever since the earliest days of the cold war, each American

President, each Kremlin leader, has felt compelled to counter every move by a counter-move, every new weapon with a newer weapon, every show of strength with a greater show of strength. The two hands that con-

Conferring after dinner at Reagan's summit residence

FACKELMAN-MINER — THE WHITE HOUSE

trol the planet's survival may clasp in a show of summit cordiality, but measurable progress to curtail their nuclear arsenals requires far, far more than ceremonial displays of goodwill.

And yet, as Reagan and Gorbachev met at the summit last week, the eleventh such meeting between the U.S. and Soviet leaders in the past three decades, they knew, and reminded each other, that there can be no winners in a nuclear war. For two days, as the world warily watched, the two men groped for some kind of human understanding, some way to master the nuclear riddle. Meeting face to face for the first time, Reagan and Gorbachev tried to set some rules to contain the arms race, some guidelines to rein in their rivalries.

That they failed in the brief time allowed was perhaps inevitable. That they tried, and agreed to keep on trying, was good news after six years of stonewalling and invective at long range. Equally important,

the frank but earnest exchange between the two leaders may have served to shore up support back home, without which neither leader can deliver on any good intentions.

The "fireside summit," as Reagan described his meeting with Gorbachev, was not, in the lexicon of diplomacy, "precooked." The principles had no orchestrated script to follow, no important, let alone prearranged, accords to proclaim. For almost five of the eight hours allotted to the sessions, the two men surprised their aides by closeting themselves alone, each trying to probe the other's mind and test his will.

Reagan's advisers were delighted with the boss's performance. Said Donald Regan, the President's chief of staff, in reply to those who had doubted the President's ability to stand up to the Soviet: "This movie actor, this President who had to have his staff prop him up, the man who couldn't do anything without a script, was able to take on this dynamic personality and hold his own, not give away the shop, not eat crow."

In terms of substance, Reagan and Gorbachev did not achieve much. A 4-1/2-page joint statement pledged to "accelerate" arms-control negotiations and called for a 50% reduction in nuclear arms by each side. But it offered no instructions on how to break the impasse over what to count in the 50%, which stymies the ongoing Geneva arms talks. Reagan refused to back off from his Strategic Defense Initiative (SDI), known as Star Wars, and Gorbachev refused to back away from his insistence that the arms race be barred from outer space. Though the summit served to give diplomacy between the two powers some much needed impetus, the fruits are unknowable. As Reagan candidly conceded at the end, "The real report card on Geneva will not come in for months or even years."

AIDS

T. BOONE PICKENS

MADONNA

1986

In the first of many scandals that were to rock Wall Street, financier Ivan Boesky was arrested for insider trading.

AMERICANS WATCHED IN HORROR AS THE SPACE SHUTTLE *CHALLENGER* EXPLODED ON TAKEOFF ■ THE DUVALIER REIGN OF TERROR ENDED IN HAITI ■ THE CHERNOBYL MELTDOWN GAVE THE WORLD ITS WORST NUCLEAR ACCIDENT ■ AND TENSIONS INCREASED IN THE PHILIPPINES WITH THE RISE OF CORAZON AQUINO . . .

DANIEL ORTEGA

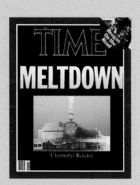

CHERNOBYL REACTOR

RALPH LAUREN

World

A Test for Democracy

For the Philippines and the U.S., stakes are high as Marcos faces the voters

Never in the long and turbulent history of the Philippines has there been an election campaign quite like it. In the muddy streets and squares of provincial cities and villages on the island of Mindanao last week, tens of thousands of farmers and plantation workers waited for a glimpse of an unusual political heroine, a retiring, bespectacled housewife with only nine weeks of political experience. Sometimes that vigil lasted for hours, under glaring sunshine and the occasional tropical downpour, but the crowds were quiet and uncomplaining. Finally, when the long-awaited political caravan straggled into view, the throngs invariably exploded into ecstasy. As small children ran alongside the open jeep that bore Opposition Candidate Corazon ("Cory") Aquino, 53, supporters threw yellow and white confetti and shouted a welcome: "Cory! Cory! Cory!"

Back in Manila, the capital, a different kind of spectacle was unfolding. President Ferdinand Marcos, 68, an ailing autocrat possessed of formidable political powers, made an election foray of his own from Malacañang Palace to address 7,000 long-shoremen on the city's South Pier. Everything was carefully choreographed: a stream of local entertainers kept the crowd's attention until Marcos, looking drawn, tired and weak, was escorted to the podium. The President joked about rumors that he had suffered a physical collapse, and dismissed reports of his obvious ill health as so much "black propaganda." Wife Imelda by his side, Marcos then made a fervent pitch for support as a bulwark against the growing Communist-led insurgency that is stalking the country. Said he defiantly: "Once a champion, always a champion."

For the first time in 20 years, many Filipinos were not so sure. Less than two weeks before some 30 million voters are expected to go to the polls on Feb. 7, the strange election exercise that has mesmerized the Philippines since November had blossomed into something unexpected: a real race. As city and rural folk thronged in astonishing numbers to Aquino rallies, her campaign organizers extolled the local outpouring as "people power," an antidote for the highly organized and often unscrupu-

In pursuit of power: an Aquino rally on Luzon

lous campaign machine that has kept Marcos in office since 1965. Members of the President's ruling New Society Movement, who had heard their leader predict an 80-20 victory for himself, were shading that estimate back to 60-40. At least two senior members of Marcos' Cabinet were even more cautious, predicting only a 55-45 win for the President. Exulted Linggoy Alcuaz, an official of one of the country's myriad splinter opposition parties: "There are times in history when things come to a boil, and this is one of them."

Few of his countrymen would argue with that assessment. The mood in Manila, thick with political tension ever since Marcos issued his surprise election call, grew even more claustrophobic last week with the latest campaign soundings. The rumor mills that grind endlessly in the city's crowded coffeehouses increased their outpourings of speculation. Fears flew that Marcos might

try to cancel the balloting, a possibility that he has never quite rejected. Opponents of the President were worried that he intended to rig the election contest even more blatantly than other votes have been altered in the past. If that happened, they warned darkly, Aquino supporters by the tens of thousands would take to the streets. The Philippines, said Jose ("Peping") Cojuangco, Aquino's campaign manager, was "a powder keg." Agreed Jaime Ongpin, a wealthy businessman and key Aquino campaign adviser: "I have never felt more uncertain about the future than I do now."

That sentiment is widely shared in the Philippines and in Washington. In both places, there is a near overwhelming sense that a chapter of history is almost over: the Marcos era. Over the two decades since his first democratic election in 1965, the President has run the gamut of transformation, changing from a populist reformer to a modernizing strongman to, in recent years, a fading and often grotesque shadow of his former authoritarian self. In the process, he has profoundly changed his country, at times in the past for the better, but of late decidedly for the worse.

Now events in the sprawling Pacific archipelago appear to be moving rapidly beyond Marcos' fading ability to control them with anything like the skill and ruthlessness that he so often displayed in the past. While the President continues to hold sway in the Spanish colonial-style Malacañang Palace, the vacuum of authority outside the palace has reached alarming proportions. Among other things, it has led U.S. Assistant Secretary of State Paul Wolfowitz to warn that the Philippines is heading toward "civil war on a massive scale" within three to five years if the insurgency spearheaded by the communist New People's Army continues to grow.

GARY HART SURRENDERED HIS PRESIDENTIAL BID WHEN HIS EXTRAMARITAL AFFAIR HIT THE HEADLINES ■ THE NATION WAS RIVETED BY OLIVER NORTH'S CONGRESSIONAL TESTIMONY ON HIS ROLE IN THE IRAN-CONTRA SCANDAL ■ LILLIAN GISH CAPPED A 72-YEAR CAREER AS A SCREEN STAR IN "THE WHALES OF AUGUST" ■ AND AMERICAN TELEVANGELISM WAS EXPOSED . . .

1987

The free-spending days of the 1980s abruptly halted when October's Black Monday sent the Dow Jones Industrial Average plummeting 23%.

Nation

God and Money

PTL, facing bankruptcy, fights for survival

By turns angry, bewildered and curious, an anxious crowd descended on the Jefferson Square Theater in Columbia S.C., last week. Their aim: to play a role in the next installment of a long-running American serial of sex, cash and power — a show resembling some lurid made-for-TV mini-series that might be called *God and Money*. For six hours, harassed officials of the embattled PTL (for Praise the Lord or People That Love) ministry were confronted at a public bankruptcy hearing by members of the flock that had supported the $203 million religious empire created by its ousted leaders, Jim and Tammy Bakker. The officials struggled to assure PTL donors that the foundering television-and-theme-park ministry, now about $68 million in debt, might soon turn a profit. Asserted the new PTL chief operating officer, Harry Hargrave: "We will be able to pay our debts. We are very confident of that."

Someone apparently less confident, though, was Televangelist Jerry Falwell. The Lynchburg, Va., preacher, who took control of PTL after Jim Bakker's March 19 resignation, looked grim as he faced studio cameras later in the week on PTL's regular morning television show. Falwell told viewers that donations had taken a nosedive since PTL formally filed for bankruptcy on June 12. If $1.75 million is not raised by July 31, he announced, PTL might be forced to stop broadcasting on some of the 161 stations that, for a fee, carry the ministry's born-again message. Said Falwell: "There's no more postponing. We've come down to D-day."

But as Falwell spoke, the PTL scandal continued to cast a pall across the entire secretive big business of televangelism. As never before, "skeptics have fuel for their fires," said David Hubbard, president of Fuller Theological Seminary in Pasadena, Calif. "They may see this as reflecting on the excesses of the whole evangelical movement."

Aside from his cash flow, one urgent problem facing Falwell is what to do about

"A dream to build something very special."

the claims of 120,000 PTL "Lifetime Partners" who each gave at least $1,000 to the organization, with the promise of free lodging for three nights a year at the ministry's theme-park hotel. The organization, though, has little hope of fulfilling those pledges because the number of donors exceeds the number of hotel rooms available by 5 to 1. Falwell noted last week that if the court declares those donations, which total $180 million, as debt, PTL will have to close down.

Days of reckoning have seemed to come and go with nightmarish frequency for PTL since Jim Bakker's admission that he had had a sexual tryst with Jessica Hahn, a church secretary from Long Island, N.Y., and had paid out $265,000 in hush money. Last week Hahn's lawyer announced that she would cash in further on the incident by telling her story in *Playboy* for an undisclosed sum.

As last week's bankruptcy hearing wore on — in anticipation of PTL's corporate-reorganization plan due in October — no fewer than 18 investigators from the Justice Department, the U.S. Postal Service and the Internal Revenue Service pored over mountains of the ministry's financial records at its headquarters in Fort Mill, S.C. The officials were readying material for a federal grand jury hearing scheduled to begin in Charlotte, N.C., on Aug. 17. The focus, according to sources close to the investigation: the possibility of criminal tax fraud, wire fraud and mail fraud by Jim Bakker and other PTL leaders who have left the ministry since Falwell took over.

Increasingly, a growing number of Americans are focusing on the doings of the huge, semisecret gospel business empires like PTL that have sprung up in little more than a decade of fervent television preaching. Many are not happy with what they see. A Gallup poll survey this spring showed that since 1980 there has been a sharp decline in American public esteem for four of the country's most important TV preachers: Oklahoma-based Oral Roberts (whose approval rating dropped from 66% to 28%), Swaggart (76% to 44%), Virginia's Pat Robertson (65% to 50%) and California's Robert Schuller (78% to 61%).

The televangelists are also suffering where it hurts the most — among viewers. Says Fred Vierra, president of United Cable, the nation's eighth largest operator: "We do not see their audiences growing." One evangelist cracks, "I was in West Irian on the island of New Guinea, and even some of the Stone Age people are familiar with the PTL scandal. That's how far it has gone."

LT. COL. OLIVER NORTH

MIKHAIL GORBACHEV

BILL COSBY

1988

Gorbachev's program of liberalization in the Soviet Union had an unintended consequence, as nationalist groups agitated for increased autonomy and outright independence.

GEORGE BUSH SWEPT TO VICTORY AGAINST MASSACHUSETTS GOVERNOR MICHAEL DUKAKIS ■ SOVIET TROOPS ABANDONED AFGHANISTAN AFTER A NINE-YEAR INVOLVEMENT THERE ■ BROADWAY WAS UNDER THE SPELL OF A MYSTERIOUS "PHANTOM" ■ AND THE REAGANS WERE EMBARRASSED BY DONALD REGAN'S REVELATIONS . . .

MANUEL NORIEGA

MICHAEL DUKAKIS

RAISA GORBACHEV

Nation

Good Heavens!

An astrologer dictating the President's schedule? So says former White House Chief of Staff Donald Regan in an explosive book

In his memoir, *For the Record*, former White House Chief of Staff Donald T. Regan wasted no time before dropping his biggest bombshell. "Because actions that would otherwise bewilder the reader cannot be understood in its absence," writes Regan in a foreword, "I have revealed in this book what was probably the most closely guarded domestic secret of the Reagan White House."

The secret: First Lady Nancy Reagan's reliance on a San Francisco astrologer to determine the timing of the President's every public move. This was more than a charming eccentricity shared with the 50 million or so other Americans who, casually or in dead earnest, look to the alignment of the stars for guidance. As White House chief of staff for two years, before he was forced to resign in February, 1987, Regan was in a position to see how the First Lady's faith in the astrologer's pronouncements wreaked havoc with her husband's schedule. At times, he writes, the most powerful man on earth was a virtual prisoner in the White House.

Donald Regan never knew the name of the "Friend," as Nancy Reagan referred to her astrologer. But TIME learned last week that she is Nob Hill Socialite Joan Quigley, sixtyish, a Vassar graduate who has written three books on astrology.

As the sensational tip of Regan's revelatory iceberg broke into the headlines last week, it evoked titillation among Washington insiders and an angry response from Ronald Reagan. "I would have preferred it if he decided to attack me," he said on Friday. "From what I hear, he's chosen to attack my wife, and I don't look kindly on that at all."

Nor is he likely to look kindly on his former aide's portrayal of the Reagan White

House. Regan shows the President as immensely likable but disturbingly passive and vulnerable to manipulation. And

A friend in need: Quigley in a 1971 publicity photo

he paints a surprisingly dark, mean-spirited First Lady, whose meddling became the "random factor in the Reagan presidency." Regan, who served the Administration for six years, the first four as Secretary of the Treasury, details how Nancy, and not her husband, stage-managed his ouster. His profile of her in *For the Record,* which Harcourt Brace Jovanovich is publishing this month, constitutes Exhibit 1 in the defense of Donald T. Regan.

The First Lady dabbled in astrology as far back as 1967. In 1981 Quigley made Nancy a believer by showing how the astrologer's charts could have foretold that the period on or around March 30, 1981, would be extremely dangerous for the President. On that day a bullet from John Hinckley Jr.'s handgun gravely wounded the President. From then on, Nancy, obsessed with her husband's safety, was convinced of her

Friend's power to protect him. And from then on, no presidential public appearance was slated without the Friend's say-so.

To this day, Nancy's Friend continues to influence the President's schedule. For the Reagan-Gorbachev Washington summit, she cast the charts of both men and determined that 2 p.m. on Dec. 8, 1987, was the most propitious moment for them to sign the intermediate-range nuclear forces treaty. At Nancy's behest, the entire summit was built around that hour. For the upcoming Moscow summit, Gorbachev's chart (he is a Pisces) has been recast alongside Reagan's (Aquarius).

Both Reagans have always been superstitious, observing such harmless rituals as knocking on wood and walking around, never under, ladders. The President puts a certain coin and gold lucky charm in his pocket each morning, and routinely tosses salt over his left shoulder not just when he spills some but before all his meals. Ronald Reagan freely admits his superstition, but in a manner that allays concern. In his 1965 autobiography, *Where's the Rest of Me?*, he breezily describes his and Nancy's attention to syndicated horoscopes. And Nancy Reagan is far from the first First Lady to seek guidance from the extrascientific sources. Mary Todd Lincoln attended séances trying to contact her dead son Willie, and Edith Wilson and Florence Harding consulted the same clairvoyant.

Regan ends his book by emphasizing that "my admiration for Reagan as President remains very great." But the contempt Regan holds for those "frivolous gossips and sycophants" who helped force him out under a cloud is equally great. If revenge is a dish best savored cold, then Don Regan, 14 months after " the bitterest event of my life," should be in for quite a feast.

U.S. TROOPS INVADED PANAMA AND ARRESTED STRONGMAN MANUEL NORIEGA ■ AUTHOR SALMAN RUSHDIE WAS FORCED INTO HIDING WHEN "SENTENCED" TO DEATH BY MOSLEM FUNDAMENTALISTS ■ BRAVING TANKS IN TIANANMEN SQUARE, CHINESE STUDENTS DEMONSTRATED FOR DEMOCRACY ■ AND THE BERLIN WALL CAME TUMBLING DOWN . . .

1989

Preserving the resources of the Amazon's rainforests became a major issue among environmentalists.

World

Freedom!

The Wall crumbles overnight, Berliners embrace in disbelieving joy, and a stunned world ponders the consequences

For 28 years it had stood as the symbol of the division of Europe and the world, of Communist suppression, of the xenophobia of a regime that had to lock its people in lest they be tempted by another, freer life — the Berlin Wall, that hideous, 28-mile-long scar through the heart of a once proud European capital, not to mention the soul of a people. And then — poof! — it was gone. Not physically, at least yet, but gone as an effective barrier between East and West, opened in one unthinkable, stunning stroke to a people it had kept apart for more than a generation. It was one of those rare times when the tectonic plates of history shift beneath men's feet, and nothing after is quite the same.

What happened in Berlin last week was a combination of the fall of the Bastille and a New Year's Eve blowout, of revolution and celebration. At the stroke of midnight on Nov. 9, a date that not only Germans would remember, thousands who had gathered on both sides of the Wall let out a roar and started going through it, as well as up and over. West Berliners pulled East Berliners to the top of the barrier along which in years past many an East German had been shot while trying to escape; at times the Wall almost disappeared beneath the waves of humanity. They tooted trumpets and danced on the top. They brought out hammers and chisels and whacked away at the hated symbol of imprisonment, knocking loose chunks of concrete and waving them triumphantly before television cameras. They spilled out into the streets of West Berlin for a champagne-spraying, horn-honking bash that continued well past dawn, into the following day and then another dawn.

Nor was the Wall the only thing to come tumbling down. Many who served the regime that had built the barrier dropped from power last week. Both East Germany's Cabinet and the Communist Party Politburo resigned *en masse*, to be replaced by bodies in which reformers mingled with hard-liners. And that, supposedly, was only the start. On the same day that East Germany threw open its borders, Egon Drenz, 52, President and party leader, promised "free,

At one checkpoint, tears were the only proper response

general, democratic and secret elections," though there was no official word as to when. Could the Socialist Unity Party, as the Communists call themselves in East Germany, lose in such balloting? "Theoretically," replied Günter Schabowski, the East Berlin party boss and Politburo member.

Thus East Germany probably can be added, along with Poland and Hungary, to the list of East European states that are trying to abandon orthodox Communism for some as-yet-nebulous form of social democracy. The next to be engulfed by the tides of change appears to be Bulgaria; Todor Zhivkov, 78, its longtime, hard-line boss, unexpectedly resigned at week's end. Outlining the urgent need for " restructuring," his successor, Petar Mladenov, said, "This implies complex and far from foreseeable processes. But there is no alternative." In all of what used to be called the Soviet bloc, Zhivkov's departure leaves in

power only Nicolae Ceausescu in Rumania and Milos Jakes in Czechoslovakia, both old-style Communist dictators. Their fate? Who knows? Only a few weeks ago, East Germany seemed one of the most stolidly Stalinist of all Moscow's allies and the one least likely to undergo swift, dramatic change.

The collapse of the old regimes and the astonishing changes under way in the Soviet Union open prospects for a Europe of cooperation in which the Iron Curtain disappears, people and goods move freely across frontiers, NATO and the Warsaw Pact evolve from military powerhouses into merely formal alliances, and the threat of war steadily fades. They also raise the question of German reunification, an issue for which politicians in the West or, for that matter, Moscow have yet to formulate strategies. Finally, should protest get out of hand, there is the risk of dissolution into chaos, sooner or later neccessitating a crackdown and, possibly, a painful turn back to authoritarianism.

The Wall, of course, was built in August 1961 for the very purpose of stanching an earlier exodus of historic dimensions, and for more than a generation it performed the task with brutal efficiency. Opening it up would have seemed the least likely way to stem the current outflow. Ronald Reagan in 1987, standing at the Brandenburg Gate with his back to the barrier, was the most recent in a long line of visiting Western leaders who challenged the Communists to level the Wall if they wanted to prove that they were serious about liberalizing their societies. "Mr. Gorbachev, open this gate!" cried the President. "Mr. Gorbachev, tear down this wall!" There was no answer from Moscow at the time; only nine months ago, Honecker vowed that the Wall would remain for 100 years.

THE ROLLING STONES

DONALD TRUMP

BARBARA BUSH

QUESTIONS WE'VE ASKED

IT WAS PERHAPS THE MOST FAMOUS SINGLE COVER IN THE HISTORY OF TIME MAGAZINE. YET IT DID NOT FEATURE A WAR, A TRAGEDY, A MAN OF THE YEAR, OR A GREAT PICTURE; AGAINST A BLACK BACKGROUND, IT SIMPLY DISPLAYED NINE LETTERS OF THE ALPHABET AND A QUESTION MARK: IS GOD DEAD? THE 1966 COVER QUERY REVERBERATED FOR YEARS, UNTIL THE EDITORS REVIVED THE QUESTION (IF NOT THE DEITY) IN 1969. THOUGH CRITICS HAVE OCCASIONALLY CHARGED TIME WITH BELIEVING IT HAS ALL THE ANSWERS, THE EDITORS WILL GLADLY SETTLE FOR ASKING THE RIGHT QUESTIONS.

IS GOD DEAD?
1966

IS GOD COMING BACK
TO LIFE?
1969

HOW FAR DOES IT GO?
(ARMS SALES TO IRAN)
1986

WHY IS SERVICE SO BAD?
1987

DO WE CARE ABOUT
OUR KIDS?
1990

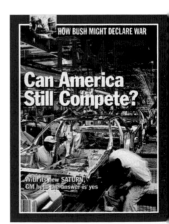

CAN AMERICA STILL
COMPETE?
1990

How Much Did He Know? (Nixon)
1973

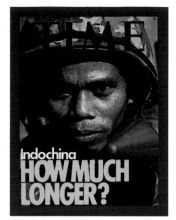

How Much Longer? (Viet Nam)
1975

How Safe?
1977

Who Will Fight For America?
1980

Should Drugs Be Made Legal?
1988

Who's Teaching Our Children?
1988

Is Government Dead?
1989

Is Anything Safe?
1989

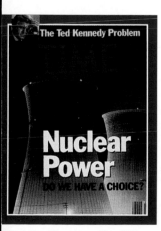

Nuclear Power: Do We Have A Choice?
1991

How Bad Is It?
1992

Can We All Get Along?
1992

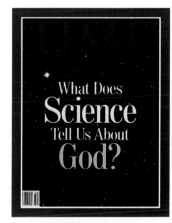

What Does Science Tell Us About God?
1992

1990s

Sex, Lies and Politics

The United States Senate is not a circus that children should attend. It is far too dangerous. Last week, as the lawmakers presided over the public evisceration of Clarence Thomas and Anita Hill, it became clear that this was a circus with an ancient history stretching back to the days when people were fed to lions. This was the kind with real victims, and no nets.

Hour after hour, an intensely personal drama was played out under achingly bright lights and devoured by tens of millions around the world. The questions came from a group of Senators who had been disfigured by a failure of both intellect and empathy. When the circus tent opened, there sat a row of white men, some of great stature, who made every effort to disappear behind the thin silhouette of their microphones. The actual spectacle left the watcher feeling demeaned and humiliated and terribly sad. So much substance was at stake, and so many symbols, that it almost seemed preferable to call it all off and go home before any more damage was done. In the end, of course, there would be no winners, only scars.
October 21, 1991

The Fire This Time

For more than a year he had been a writhing body twisting on the ground under kicks and nightstick blows in what may be the most endlessly replayed videotape ever made. Then on Friday afternoon TV finally gave Rodney King a face and a voice — a hesitant, almost sobbing voice that yet was more eloquent than any other that spoke during the terrible week. "Stop making it horrible," King pleaded with the rioters who had been doing just that in Los Angeles. He sounded almost dazed by the violence that followed a jury's acquittal of the cops who had beaten him: the killing, burning and looting, he muttered, were "just not right ...just not right." As to black-white relations: "Can we all get along?"

Would that the nation's leaders, of both races, could find such plain but heartfelt words.
May 11, 1992

JOHN T. BARR — GAMMA LIAISON

White Flags in the Desert

Suddenly, there he was, the only major participant in this most televised war in history who had remained off-camera. For weeks, the world had watched the nightly pyrotechnics over Baghdad, the battered allied pilots on Iraqi TV, Patriots rising to meet Scuds, the nose-camera view of smart bombs at work, the artificial twilight above the burning oil fields, top guns catapulting into the mist, even Saddam Hussein presiding over his Revolutionary Command Council. Only the frontline Iraqi soldier had stayed out of sight. But he was never out of mind. As long as he was invisible, he was easy to imagine as one of half a million clones of Saddam himself, smug, defiant and murderous.

Tragedy in Waco

The sun didn't blacken, nor the moon turn red, but the world did come to an end, just as their prophet had promised. The End drove up to their doorstep in a tank, spitting gas, fulfilling prophecies. *And if anyone wants to harm them*, says the Book of Revelations, *fire pours from their mouth and consumes their foes*.

Buzzards circled overhead and the wind blew hard the day the Branch Davidians died. A few minutes past noon, FBI snipers say they saw a man in a gas mask cupping his hands, as though lighting something. An explosion rocked the compound, then another and another as ammunition stores blew up. The building shuddered, like the earthquake Koresh had foretold.

By now 30-m.p.h. prairie winds had sent the flames gulping through the compound. The fire raced through the big parlor, feeding on the wooden benches and the stacks of Bibles kept by the door. The chapel crackled as flames consumed hundreds of thousands of dollars' worth of equipment from the messiah's rock-'n'-roll band and the wooden pew-like bleachers for his audience. Table after table in the cafeteria burned, and rows of children's bunk beds upstairs, as the flames spread faster, through the attic that ran the length of the building like a wind tunnel. It burned fast because it was built on the cheap, a tar-paper, yellow-pine and plasterboard crematorium.
May 3, 1993

So it came as something of a shock when he scrambled out of his hole in the ground. He was thin, pitiable, and quivering with the fear that his captors were going to shoot him on the spot. When he realized he was going to be fed and cared for, he fell to his knees and kissed the hands of a U.S. Marine.

They surrendered all along what was supposed to be the mighty "Saddam line," in squads, then platoons. Many waved tattered pieces of white cloth. Some held aloft the Koran. Several groups of prisoners even began chanting the name of George Bush. It was as though they sensed that their defeat was a necessary step toward the liberation not only of Kuwait but of Iraq as well.
March 11, 1991

1990

In a move that galvanized the U.S. and allies, Saddam Hussein's troops seized Kuwait; preparations for armed intervention began following fruitless economic sanctions.

GERMANY WAS UNITED FOR THE FIRST TIME SINCE 1945 ■ NELSON MANDELA WON RELEASE FROM A 27-YEAR IMPRISONMENT, AND RECEIVED A HERO'S WELCOME IN THE U.S. ■ MARGARET THATCHER LOST HER IRON GRIP ON BRITAIN'S CONSERVATIVE PARTY, AND WAS REPLACED BY JOHN MAJOR ■ AND "THE GREED DECADE" WAS OFFICIALLY OVER . . .

NELSON MANDELA

DAN QUAYLE

HELMUT KOHL

Business

Predator's Fall

The collapse of Drexel Burnham marks the end of a money-mad era of hostile takeovers, lavish living and heedless disregard for debt

"Are the vultures still out there?"
— Drexel staffer, sneering at reporters as she walked out the door
"Vultures? Look who's talking."
— Security guard

The final plunge of the most powerful and dreaded firm on Wall Street in the Roaring Eighties came with astonishing speed. Like the abrupt fall of the Berlin Wall thousands of miles away, the collapse suddenly confirmed what everyone in the financial world could already feel in the wind: a new era had arrived. After a desperate three-day search for cash in which it was spurned by its bankers, Drexel Burnham Lambert Group filed bankruptcy papers an hour before midnight last Tuesday.

While only the parent company sought protection under Chapter 11, no one expected the investment firm to rise from the ashes. In an industry that operates on trust and good faith, Drexel had exhausted its reserves. The move meant that Drexel, whose financial wizardry reshaped corporate America and ushered in an age of runaway debt and excess, will swiftly liquidate its business. The 152-year-old titan — with 6,300 employees and $3.6 billion in assets — will vanish almost overnight in the biggest failure in Wall Street history.

Drexel's staff got the word in a terse statement from chief executive Frederick Joseph over the firm's intercom. Joseph refused to take questions and quickly signed off, leaving stunned employees to hunt for scarce jobs in an already depressed Wall Street market. Drexel's layoffs, which began Friday, will add thousands more workers to the 37,000 already dismissed by investment firms in the past two years, almost 10% of Wall Street's work force. In a final

A Drexel worker leaves with her belongings

bitter send-off, the firm's employees, who owned 54% of Drexel's stock, saw the value of their holdings evaporate with the bankruptcy filing.

In the firm's lobby at 60 Broad Street in New York City, security guards searched bags to prevent workers from carting away computers and company records. "People are in a state of shock. They're laughing and crying," said bond salesman Taylor Greene. Retorted a young broker as he stepped into a limousine with one last show of '80s bravado: "I'll enjoy reading about all this from Hawaii."

The echo carried that far and beyond. Drexel's notorious junk bonds — debt instruments that pay high rates of interest because of the relative shakiness of the ventures they fund — turned the financial world topsy-turvy and helped set the tone for the money lust that gripped America in the '80s. Armed with the bonds, corporate

raiders swiftly raised the money they needed to attack even the largest companies. At the same time, investment bankers raked in billions of dollars by advising the raiders and selling junk bonds to eager borrowers. In what corporate America saw as a glorified protection racket, Drexel and its imitators sold services to targets as well, to help them keep raiders at bay.

On Wall Street the debt-propelled takeover binge gave rise to the era's get-rich-quick mentality. Michael Milken, the deposed Drexel guru who pioneered junk bonds and nurtured them into a $200 billion market, was paid $550 million in 1987 for his unrivaled expertise. In a perverse version of the trickle-down theory, lower echelon bankers raked in multimillion-dollar salaries, and new recruits with two years' experience earned six-figure sums. The fantastic payoff created a brain drain as the best and the brightest from top colleges and business schools across the U.S. flocked to Wall Street. In 1986 nearly half the senior class at Yale applied for jobs at First Boston, a leading Wall Street investment banker.

But now Wall Street's boom has run out of gas, largely because corporate America has loaded up with all the debt it cares — or dares — to take on. Wall Street is suffering a dearth of deals, but no one is shedding tears for it. The flashy wealth displayed by investment firms has created a backlash on Main Street, which watched with mounting fury as Wall Street got rich through paper-shuffling deals that manipulated companies at the expense of the workers and communities. Says Samuel Hayes, an investment-banking professor at Harvard, "There is a lot of pent up anger and disgust with behavior on Wall Street."

THE NATION WAS MESMERIZED BY THE PALM BEACH RAPE TRIAL OF WILLIAM KENNEDY SMITH ■ YELLOW RIBBONS, IN SUPPORT OF DESERT STORM TROOPS, APPEARED EVERYWHERE ■ GENTLE-SOUNDING "THE SILENCE OF THE LAMBS" WAS ANYTHING BUT, AND WON FOUR MAJOR OSCARS ■ AND THE TELEVISING OF THE GULF WAR BROUGHT NEW DIMENSIONS TO THE NEWS . . .

1991

The Russian government was threatened by a reactionary coup; the plot failed, but Gorbachev was forced to cede power to Boris Yeltsin.

The Gulf War

Live from the Middle East!

CNN scores a reporting coup as TV dramatically captures the first major war in the era of instant worldwide communication

It was a war that television had spent five months preparing to cover, and the start of hostilities was almost bizarrely well timed: smack in the middle of the networks' evening newscasts. ABC anchorman Peter Jennings had just finished a live phone conversation with correspondent Gary Shepard in Baghdad, who said that all was quiet in the Iraqi capital. A couple of minutes later, however, Shepard was back on the air, reporting that bright flashes and tracer fire were lighting up the sky west of the city. "An attack is under way," he said. So was the TV drama.

For the ensuing hours and days, TV held the nation riveted. Not, for the most part, with pictures; those were meager, slow in coming and tightly restricted by tough Pentagon rules limiting press coverage of the conflict. Not with the sort of gripping combat footage that had brought the Vietnam War so painfully into America's living rooms. Not (at least, not yet) with heart-wrenching scenes of body bags and grieving families. Mostly, TV conveyed the story in the simple words of reporters: ordinary people caught up in the extraordinary events, describing the sights and sounds and feelings of war.

Those words and images had an instant, indelible impact. Across the nation, in homes and offices and bars, people stopped in their tracks, gathered around the TV set and held their collective breath. Like the Kennedy assassination or the space-shuttle disaster, the outbreak of war in the Gulf was one of these historic events destined to be remembered forever in the terms by which television defined it.

The undisputed star of the initial coverage was CNN, the 24-hour-news channel, which affirmed its credibility and worldwide clout with new authority. Though ABC, NBC, and CNN managed to air telephone reports with their correspondents in Baghdad during the initial shelling (CBS, unluckily, could not get its phone line working), ABC and NBC lost contact after a few minutes. Only CNN was able to keep its line

"No city has come under chemical attack before. It could be under way."

open and broadcast continuously throughout the attack. Three reporters on the ninth floor of the Al Rasheed Hotel — anchorman Bernard Shaw, veteran combat correspondent Peter Arnett and reporter John Holliman — provided an exceptional, and perhaps unprecedented, live account of the start of war from inside an enemy capital.

Their reports were a low-tech throwback to Edward R. Murrow's famous radio broadcasts from London during the blitz. As viewers watched a still screen, disembodied voices described what was happening in graphic, excited, sometimes overwrought language. Holliman: "We just heard—whoa! Holy cow! That was a large airburst that we saw." Arnett: "We're crouched behind a window in here. . . The antiaircraft is erupting again." Shaw: "This feels like we're in the center of hell." The dramatic scene was punctuated by interludes of awkward comedy, as the reporters scurried around the room on hands and knees and exchanged nervous banter. "It occurs to me that I didn't get dinner tonight," said Shaw at one point. "There's tuna fish, Bernie," replied Holliman, "plenty of tuna fish."

CNN finally lost contact with its Baghdad team 16 hours later, when Iraqi military officials shut down its phone line for what they said were security reasons. Shaw, Holliman and most other U.S. TV reporters left Baghdad the next day. (Arnett remained there until Saturday, when Iraqi officials ordered all Western journalists to leave the city "temporarily.") ABC's Shepard, hitching a ride with a CBS producer, reached Amman, Jordan, on Friday afternoon after being stalled for four hours near an air base in western Iraq that was being shelled by U.S. warplanes. "It sure brought back a lot of memories," said Shepard, a former Vietnam correspondent. "But this is the first time I have ever reported from behind enemy lines."

In a quirk of timing oddly fitting or the TV age, the drama often heated up just as the prime-time hours approached. On Thursday viewers watched in apprehension as network correspondents in Tel Aviv and Jerusalem relayed tense accounts of Iraqi missiles striking Israel. There were confusing and conflicting reports about whether the missiles were carrying chemical weapons, and scary, surrealistic scenes of correspondents being urged by anchormen back home to take precautions — and calmly resuming their reports after donning gas masks. When NBC's Brokaw told his Tel Aviv correspondent Martin Fletcher to "put on your mask," Fletcher replied, "I think I will. This is no time for heroics."

"CRACK KIDS"

BORIS YELTSIN

ANITA HILL AND CLARENCE THOMAS

1992

The end of Communist hegemony in Eastern Europe revealed a dark side: rival factions unleashed civil war on former Yugoslavia, and a siege of Sarajevo began.

EL SALVADOR ANNOUNCED SETTLEMENT OF A 12-YEAR-OLD CIVIL WAR ■ HOTEL QUEEN LEONA HELMSLEY STARTED SERVING A SENTENCE FOR INCOME TAX EVASION ■ THE U.S. SENT TROOPS TO STARVING SOMALIA TO RESTORE ORDER AND PROTECT RELIEF SHIPMENTS ■ AND A CRACK CAMPAIGN EFFORT PROPELLED ARKANSAS GOV. BILL CLINTON TO VICTORY . . .

GARTH BROOKS

ROSS PEROT

THE EARTH SUMMIT

U.S CAMPAIGN

THE TEAM BEHIND THE CLINTONS

Though Clinton and his wife have the last word on how the campaign is run, they rely on an unlikely cadre of strategists who deserve the credit for getting the candidate's act together

FOR BILL CLINTON AND AL GORE, Iowa last week became their own Field of Dreams. A shimmering summer's day was just beginning its slow fade into dusk as the eight-bus caravan pulled into Manchester for a carefully orchestrated "unscheduled" stop. The local Democrats had done their part — a crowd of nearly 1,000 had been waiting for several hours to gambol in the limelight. Gore, fast becoming the Ed McMahon of political warm-up acts, gave his patter-perfect introduction. Then Clinton clambered up onto the small outdoor podium for a quick rendition of his stump speech.

A good deal of the credit for the success of appearances like these — and for the success, to date, of Clinton's campaign efforts — goes to the unlikely trio that now holds day-to-day responsibility for directing the campaign — James Carville, George Stephanopoulos and Betsey Wright. Each represents a different facet of the totality that is Clinton. Top strategist Carville is the grit, the guts and the unyielding determination. Stephanopoulos, like the candidate a Rhodes Scholar, mirrors Clinton's thinking and intuits his likely responses. Wright, Clinton's chief of staff during most of his years as Arkansas Governor, is the keeper and the ardent defender of his record. To understand the dramatic summer transformation of Clinton's candidacy from junker to juggernaut, take a closer look at the triumphant trio in Little Rock.

THE RAGIN' CAJUN: Carville, 47, is a constant study in coiled tension; he holds his body Marine-style rigid; his brooding brow and his closely cropped, sparse hair all convey the same message as the T-shirts and pressed jeans that he favors: This is not a man to be messed with. As Carville describes himself: "I walk the edge between being colorful and controversial."

Carville was a late bloomer — a Vietnam-era Marine (who was never sent to Vietnam); a Louisiana lawyer reluctant to practice; a political hired gun who moved into the front rank of Democratic consultants only by masterminding last year's upset Pennsylvania Senate victory of Harris

Clinton's triumphant strategist James Carville

Wofford. Carville first met Clinton last summer through another client, Georgia Governor Zell Miller, and joined the campaign in November. Carville's first impression of Clinton: "So this is what major league pitching looks like."

If Carville is motivated by one principle, it is "Hit 'em back hard." Nothing better reflects his combative personality than the inspirational slogans he posts in the war room. On the central issue of the campaign: THE ECONOMY, STUPID.

THE ALTER EGO: Stephanopoulos' influence in the campaign is no secret — he is handed over 100 telephone-message slips a day. But still, as a campaign insider puts it, "Everybody underestimates him. He looks like he's 14 years old." With a shock of dark brown hair, a boyish face and an imperturbable, almost brusque manner, Stephanopoulos, 31, is the ultimate quick study. Joining the campaign last summer, after being heavily wooed by Bob Kerrey,

Stephanopoulos became Clinton's constant traveling companion throughout the primaries. His mastery of Clinton's ideas and his ability to anticipate the candidate's reactions to any situation is uncanny. Stephanopoulous's explanation: "He's a great teacher."

A pivotal moment in the campaign came in May, when Stephanopoulos was detached from Clinton's side to manage the nerve center in Little Rock as communications director. Suddenly, good ideas that had been kicking around the campaign were carried out. Media advisor Mandy Grunwald had been arguing for months that Clinton should do *The Arsenio Hall Show.* In fact, Clinton's comeback may well have begun on *Arsenio,* when the image of Slick Willie gave way to Saxophone Bill.

THE SECRETARY OF DEFENSE: Wright, 48, first met Clinton when both were young liberal idealists working in her native Texas on the 1972 George McGovern campaign.

Her rapid rise in the campaign hierarchy — symbolized by her new title of deputy campaign chairman — was not without political infighting and moments of drama. But her position is secure because of her deep allegiance to both Clinton and Hillary. During much of the 1980s, Wright spent half her life at the Governor's mansion with the Clintons and their daughter Chelsea.

In the mid-1970s, she gravitated to Washington, where she ran the Women's National Education Fund, recruiting women candidates for office. After Clinton was defeated for re-election as Governor in 1980, he called upon Wright to run his comeback crusade. She accepted instantly because, as she recalls, "it was always important to me that strong political feminists have relationships with strong male politicians. And Bill Clinton has no problem with strong women."

AMERICANS HEEDED A CALL FOR CHANGE AND ENTERED "THE CLINTON ERA" ■ JAPAN'S ONCE-THRIVING AUTOMAKERS SUFFERED SAGGING DEMANDS AND STAGNANT MARKETS ■ THE U.S. AND ALLIES LAUNCHED BOMBING RAIDS ON IRAQ ■ AND THE U.S FAMINE-RELIEF EFFORT IN SOMALIA BOGGED DOWN IN CLAN WARFARE . . .

1993

A mood of youthful optimism began to emerge in America as Bill Clinton, the first "baby boomer" President, took office.

SOMALIA

WARLORD COUNTRY

In a hostile land without government, the real problem is whether the rival clans can find a way to resolve their long-standing quarrels without reaching for rifles

THE BELEAGUERED RESIDENTS of Mogadishu had brief cause for rejoicing last week. Under the gaze of TV cameras, Somalia's leading warlords, Ali Mahdi Mohammed and General Mohammed Farrah Aidid, jointly announced that the so-called green line dividing their capital into separate sectors had been abolished. Thousands of men and women cheered as the two rivals promised that for the first time in more than a year, people were free to travel across the capital. "Today is a great day," declared Ali Mahdi, whose gangsters control the northern part of Mogadishu. "Starting from this minute, the green line is no more."

Alas for Somalis, that invisible line may yet prove to be as formidable and lasting as Beirut's infamous divide of the same name. Vandals and free-lance thugs celebrated the event in their own special way — with looting and shooting afterward. Several vehicles attempting to cross the green line were stolen by marauding gunmen. Journalists and relief workers who ventured near the line were robbed and threatened by teenage gangsters brandishing automatic weapons. "Whatever the two men say," observed an aide to Ali Mahdi, "the people of Mogadishu will not mix. There is too much hostility."

The attempt by the warlords to dismantle Mogadishu's green line was intended to show the world that they can resolve their differences without outside intervention. Western observers believe a gradual reconciliation among Somalia's warring clans would be an essential prelude to the restoration of some form of responsible central authority. The commanders of the U.S.-led military force insist that their mission is limited to ensuring the delivery of food to hundreds of thousands of starving

Somalis and that political reconciliation would be a serendipitous by-product. But the green line thuggery points up the difficulty of creating even a semblance of order. With no government to speak of, even the

Warlords Aidid and Ali Mahdi: "cheers, then looting and shooting"

most powerful warlords have limited influence over their satraps elsewhere and no hope at all of exercising control over free-lance bandits. As looting and extortion are reduced in areas under military protection, the warlords are losing their means of paying the gunmen — and that only causes their authority to erode further.

The rising tension is forcing American commanders to tighten the rules on confiscating Somali weapons. Until now, the troops have seized arms displayed openly and with hostile intent. Now the U.S. military is promising to take a more aggressive role in ridding Somalia of the heavier weapons and the "technicals" — gun-equipped pickup trucks — that have terrified the populace for the past two years. "Heavy weapons will be removed voluntarily or, if necessary, by force," a senior U.S. official told Reuters. "From now on, we're going to

be doing more enforcement." That will still leave untold numbers of small arms in the hands of Somalis, since the U.S. military has given no indication that it is about to order the wholesale disarmament of civilians or the warlords' armies.

It is the warlords' struggle for power that must be settled before peace can return to Somalia. Robert Oakley, the U.S. special envoy, believes Ali Mahdi and Aidid may actually turn out to be irrelevant to an eventual political solution. "Right now they are factors in the political landscape," he says. "But the Somalis don't like domination by a single political party. When people aren't fighting, they don't need military alliances." A former Somali journalist puts the issue in blunter terms: "The U.S. has to deal with these people to stabilize the environment in the short term. But when peace and democracy return to this country, they will be tried as war criminals. They are political bulldozers who killed thousands of people and destroyed national unity."

Ali Mahdi and Aidid, meanwhile, are trying to create new images of themselves as politicians and statesmen. Last week's green-line rally marked the first time since the two sides went to war more than a year ago that they have appeared together at a public gathering. Since the Marines landed, however, they have had several private meetings. Both grandly declared that the day of rule by rifle was over. "I believe only in democracy," said Ali Mahdi in an interview with TIME at his seaside villa in Mogadishu. "Every Somali has the right to be President. If left to myself, I would like to be a businessman once again. But if the Somali people wish me to continue, I will do my best to serve them."

THE WORLD'S "MEGACITIES"

ABUSED WOMEN WHO KILL

PRESIDENT CLINTON

TIME